Straight Writes and Jabs

BOOKS BY THOMAS HAUSER

GENERAL NON-FICTION
Missing
The Trial of Patrolman Thomas Shea
For Our Children (with Frank Macchiarola)
The Family Legal Companion
Final Warning: The Legacy of Chernobyl (with Dr. Robert Gale)
Arnold Palmer: A Personal Journey
Confronting America's Moral Crisis (with Frank Macchiarola)
Healing: A Journal of Tolerance and Understanding
With This Ring (with Frank Macchiarola)
A God To Hope For
Thomas Hauser on Sports

BOXING NON-FICTION
The Black Lights: Inside the World of Professional Boxing
Muhammad Ali: His Life and Times
Muhammad Ali: Memories
Muhammad Ali: In Perspective
Muhammad Ali & Company
A Beautiful Sickness
A Year At The Fights
Brutal Artistry
The View From Ringside
Chaos, Corruption, Courage, and Glory
The Lost Legacy of Muhammad Ali
I Don't Believe It, But It's True
Knockout (with Vikki LaMotta)
The Greatest Sport of All
The Boxing Scene
An Unforgiving Sport
Boxing Is . . .
Box: The Face of Boxing
The Legend of Muhammad Ali (with Bart Barry)
Winks and Daggers
And the New . . .
Straight Writes and Jabs

FICTION
Ashworth & Palmer
Agatha's Friends
The Beethoven Conspiracy
Hanneman's War
The Fantasy
Dear Hannah
The Hawthorne Group
Mark Twain Remembers
Finding The Princess
Waiting For Carver Boyd

FOR CHILDREN
Martin Bear & Friends

Straight Writes and Jabs

An Inside Look at Another Year in Boxing

Thomas Hauser

The University of Arkansas Press
Fayetteville
2013

ISBN-10: 1-55728-644-2
ISBN-13: 978-1-55728-644-4
e-ISBN: 978-1-61075-531-3

17   16   15   14   13   5   4   3   2   1

⊝ The paper used in this publication meets the minimum requirements of the American National Standard for Permanence of Paper for Printed Library Materials Z39.48-1984.

Library of Congress Control Number: 2013942079

For Anthony Catanzaro

Contents

Author's Note

Straight Writes and Jabs contains the articles about professional boxing that I authored in 2012 plus a more recent profile of Archie Moore. The articles I wrote about the sweet science prior to that date have been published in *Muhammad Ali & Company*; *A Beautiful Sickness*; *A Year at the Fights*; *The View From Ringside*; *Chaos, Corruption, Courage, and Glory*; *The Lost Legacy of Muhammad Ali*; *I Don't Believe It, But It's True*; *The Greatest Sport of All*, *The Boxing Scene*, *An Unforgiving Sport*, *Boxing Is*, *Winks and Daggers*, and *And the New . . .*

Fights and Fighters

In recent years, Sergio Martinez has become a writer's fighter.

Sergio Martinez vs. Matthew Macklin: Good Fighters, Good Fight

Sergio Martinez sat on a folding cushioned-metal chair, eating cashew nuts and sipping from a bottle of water. In two hours, he would enter a boxing ring to defend the middleweight championship of the world. Now, in a dressing room above The Theater at Madison Square Garden, he was engaged in quiet conversation.

Trainer Pablo Sarmiento, cornerman Russ Anber, cutman Dr. Roger Anderson, camp coordinator Marcello Crudelle, and manager Sampson Lewkowicz were with him.

The mood in Martinez's dressing room is constant from fight to fight. Organized, professional, relaxed until the final minutes of preparation when it changes to intense concentration.

Sergio held out his bag of cashew nuts to the others in the room. Anber took a handful.

Latin rap sounded in the background; the music of Rene Perez Joglar, who lives in Argentina and is friends with Martinez. Later, the sound would change to Calle 13, Sergio's favorite group.

At 9:30, Dr Anderson put cotton plugs soaked in adrenaline in Martinez's nostrils to constrict the blood vessels. Sergio's nose had been broken and bled profusely in his most recent fight. This was a precautionary measure. Five minutes later, Anderson removed the plugs.

Sergio's hands were wrapped. He gloved up, stretched, shadow-boxed, and hit the pads with Sarmiento.

New York State Athletic Commission inspectors Ernie Morales and Sue Etkin looked on.

Martinez is an athlete. He was about to engage in a high-stakes athletic competition. The difference between winning and losing could equate to millions of dollars in future earnings. The punishment he absorbed in the ensuing hours might damage him for life.

Yet one had the sense that, as a child growing up in Argentina, Martinez faced challenges on the streets that were as formidable as this one every day. Boxing enabled him to escape from a world of deprivation. It's a timeless tale with few happy endings.

"I rule my life by pleasure and necessity," Martinez said five years ago. "The pleasure of giving my life another life; the necessity of giving another life to my family."

And now . . .

"Martinez is one boxing story every aficionado should feel a sense of ownership about," Bart Barry has written. "He is not running for office in the Philippines. He does not have charges pending against him in Nevada. Martinez makes a match with a larger man every time he defends his belts. He gets hit plenty and finishes each defense with a knockout. If there is a downside to having as boxing's middleweight champion of the world a Latino who both looks and fights better than Oscar De La Hoya, it doesn't spring to mind."

Martinez has struggled and fought honorably for what he has achieved in his life. The same can't be said of the people who run boxing's world sanctioning organizations and demean the sport with their sale of tarnished indulgences.

On April 17, 2010, Martinez won a unanimous 12-round decision over Kelly Pavlik to claim the WBC, WBO, and linear middleweight crowns. The WBO soon stripped him of his belt on a technical ruling that appeared motivated by the desire to collect a quick sanctioning fee for a "championship" fight between Danny Jacobs and Dmitry Pirog. But that was of secondary concern to Martinez. His focus was on the WBC title, which had special meaning to him because it was once held by the great Argentinean middleweight, Carlos Monzon.

Martinez was loyal to the WBC, and the WBC betrayed him.

After Sergio defended his title with a dramatic one-punch knockout of Paul Williams on November 20, 2010, the WBC orchestrated a slight of hand that saw him relieved of his title and given the right to fight for an overpriced "diamond belt." That cleared the way for Julio Cesar Chavez Jr (a favorite of WBC president Jose Sulaiman) to fight Sebastian Zbik on June 4, 2011, for what was euphemistically called the WBC middleweight championship of the world.

Martinez wanted his title back. After Chavez beat Zbik, the WBC promised Sergio that, if Julio were allowed to fight an interim defense against Peter Manfredo Jr, the organization would order Chavez to fight Martinez next. On November 19, 2011, Chavez beat Manfredo. Even then, Martinez vs. Chavez remained a pipe dream.

Meanwhile, Sulaiman further angered Sergio with an ugly comment about the treatment of women. After Floyd Mayweather Jr (who pays substantial sanctioning fees to the WBC) was sentenced to ninety days imprisonment as a consequence of being found criminally guilty of beating up a woman for the third time, Sulaiman said that Mayweather should not be stripped of his WBC title.

"Beating a lady is highly critical," Sulaiman decreed. "[But] it is not a major sin or crime."

Martinez is a vocal advocate for the protection of battered women. On December 29, 2011, he declared, "Just a few days ago, Don Jose made some controversial statements in reference to Floyd Mayweather's sentence for domestic violence. I know that he sent an apology, but I have the right to ask from Don Jose a public apology about the insensitive comments that he has said about the violence against women."

Then, in the same press conference, Martinez went further, renouncing the WBC diamond belt "for my dignity, for my pride, and for my manhood."

"Don Jose Sulaiman spoke to me," Sergio explained. "He asked me to move aside and to let Chavez fight Rubio on February 4. I was shocked. From then on, I felt like there was a knife that had been stabbed in my back. Don Jose said that I had authorized his decision. That's an absolute lie. I have not authorized that fight. That fight is the end of a lie. I won't represent the WBC again until they make the fight that is obligatory, the fight which was voted on by unanimous decision to happen at the WBC's convention. I'm not planning on defending the WBC diamond belt anymore. I hate the cowardice that Chavez has taken on in avoiding every day the fight with me."

Six days later, for good measure, Martinez told Radio Belgrano AM 950 in Argentina, "Nobody will forget that Chavez was the biggest coward in the history of boxing."

In response, Sulaiman bellowed like a harpooned seal. In a January 24,

2012, column entitled "Hook to the Liver," the WBC president wailed, "One of the feelings of sadness that kept me low for a few days was the reaction of Sergio Martinez, who blasted the WBC and me with his uncontrollable mouth when I had always thought of him as a gentleman."

That same day, Sulaiman told FightNews.com, "As President of the WBC and a close friend of Julio Cesar Chavez Sr and his sons, I wish to emphasize that Julio Cesar Chavez Jr is in no way scared of Sergio Martinez. I know Chavez. He's a great boxer with power in his fists and he's a Mexican idol. The bout on February 4th between Julio Cesar and Marco Antonio Rubio will be a great bout full of courage and honor."

On February 4, 2012, Chavez defeated Rubio over the course of twelve lackluster rounds that Sulaiman called a candidate for "fight of the year."

"Sergio Martinez has class," says Lou DiBella (Sergio's promoter). "Jose Sulaiman doesn't know what 'class' is."

Meanwhile, Martinez needed an opponent for a March 17 date on HBO. Matthew Macklin stepped into the breach.

Macklin was born and lives in Birmingham, England. But he's of Irish heritage, which on St. Patrick's Day was a definite plus as far as selling tickets. He's articulate, gracious, easy to talk with, and a good story teller.

One of Matthew's tales involves Billy Graham, who rose to prominence as Ricky Hatton's trainer and worked with Macklin for four years. Just before Hatton turned pro, Graham wanted to buy a house and went to a bank to take out a mortgage. The bank manager reviewed Billy's financial records and told him that there simply wasn't enough there to qualify for a loan.

"You don't understand," Graham implored the bank manager. "I've got this kid from Manchester. He's eighteen years old. You have no idea how good he is. He's going to be a world champion."

Matthew also has a self-deprecating sense of humor.

"Why did you become a fighter?" he was asked.

"Because I was stupid. And by the time I got smart, I was hooked."

Macklin came into the fight against Martinez with a 28-and-3 record and 19 knockouts to his credit. His most impressive performance was a June 25, 2011, split-decision loss against WBA middleweight beltholder Felix Sturm. The bout was contested on Sturm's home turf in Cologne,

Germany. Virtually every observer (apart from two of the judges) thought that Matthew won.

"I beat Sturm," Macklin said afterward. "And I thought I won the fight clearly enough that I was beyond being robbed."

But one learns to be skeptical about a fighter whose best credential is a loss, regardless of how unfair the decision might have been. And Matthew's record was devoid of world-class scalps. As fight night approached, the odds favoring Martinez rose as high as 10 to 1.

Macklin did his best to put matters in perspective. "Sergio is the best middleweight in the world and the real middleweight champion," he acknowledged. "He's a good fighter. And over my years as a pro, I've had some up and down performances. But Sergio is beatable. The media has the habit of taking a guy with a few good wins and a few good knockouts and making him out to be invincible. I expect to win this fight."

Still, Macklin faced a daunting task. He had to get through the early rounds. He had to get through the middle rounds. He had to get through the late rounds. And he had to find a way to win more than half of them or knock Martinez out.

The Theater at Madison Square Garden was sold out for Martinez-Macklin with 4,671 fans in attendance. Matthew didn't just come to acquit himself well. He came to win. There were times when the action was fierce and the outcome of the fight very much in doubt.

Martinez's most effective weapon in the early going was a punishing jab that snapped out like a serpent's tongue and caught Macklin flush before Matthew could react. In round two, a straight left hand propelled Macklin back into the ropes, but it looked as though the champion was stepping on the challenger's foot at the moment the blow landed.

The drama built throughout the fight. Macklin waged a controlled measured battle and was a hard puzzle to solve. After a slow start, he swept the middle rounds and was credited with a knockdown near the end of round seven when a chopping overhand right coming out of a clinch caused Martinez to touch the canvas with his glove. It appeared as though the cause of the "knockdown" was Sergio stumbling over Matthew's left leg. Regardless, after seven rounds, Macklin was up by a point or two in the eyes of most observers.

He didn't win another round.

In the eighth stanza, Martinez picked up the pace, fighting more aggressively. Macklin responded in kind. But the champion's jab and straight lefthand were finding their mark with increasing frequency.

And Macklin was tiring. First in the final thirty seconds of each round; then in the final forty-five. He took Martinez's punches well, but he was taking too many of them. And he was beginning to lose form.

"I figured I was behind by a few points," Matthew said afterward. "If you lose, you lose. Whether you lose on points or get knocked out, you've still lost. I could have played it safe but I was trying to win, so I started taking chances."

Martinez keeps his punching power late. When he goes for the kill, his smile turns to a snarl.

With twenty seconds left in round eleven, Macklin threw an arcing left hook and was floored by a faster straight left hand . . . He rose, wobbly . . . was floored by another straight left . . . rose for the second time . . . and was saved by the bell.

He returned to his corner looking very much like a beaten fighter. At that point, trainer Buddy McGirt wisely stopped the contest.

"He was getting hit with clean shots," McGirt said later. "The only way he could win was by knocking Sergio out, and that wasn't going to happen. There was no reason to send him out for more."

The punch stats showed Martinez outlanding Macklin 183 to 135, with his biggest edge coming in rounds nine through eleven when he landed 56 power punches. The challenger was good enough to test the champion but not to beat him.

"I gave it one hundred percent," Matthew said afterward.

And so he did. Macklin did more than fight a courageous fight. He fought a good one. But Martinez had superior footwork and faster hands. His punches came from angles that were unfamiliar to Matthew. And Sergio hit harder.

The most pressing question now is who Martinez will fight next. One reason he's so entertaining to watch is that, at various times in each of his recent fights, he has looked vulnerable. He starts well and finishes strong, but has shown a tendency to lose the middle rounds. If two hundred years of boxing history is a reliable guide, there will come a time when he is unable to rally late.

Sergio is a small middleweight. He weighed in for the Macklin fight at 157.6 pounds after eating full meals all week. Fighting at super-middleweight would be a mistake. If Julio Cesar Chavez continues to avoid him, there are other opponents (such as Dmitry Pirog and Gennady Golovkin) who could test him at the middleweight level. Several "name" opponents in the 154-pound ranks would also make for an attractive match-up.

In sum, Martinez is beatable. All fighters are. But he won't go easily. Against Macklin, once again, he did what he had to do to win. For the fourth time in a row, after flirting with defeat, he closed the show with a dramatic knockout.

In the fighter's respective dressing rooms after the fight, their faces told the tale.

Martinez was largely unmarked as he summarized the battle just won. "Think . . . Relax . . ."

Sergio slapped his fist into the palm of his right hand . . .

"BOOM! . . . Over."

Macklin's face was a different matter. There were ugly bumps and bruises and a gash beneath his left eyebrow that needed five stitches to close. Sadness and disappointment were etched in his visage. So was pride.

"I got beat by a fighter who was better than I was tonight," Matthew acknowledged. "If you get beat, you get beat. It's better than being cheated. A month from now, the Sturm fight will bother me more than this one."

Bernard Hopkins has said, "If you don't know how to control your emotions, that's a signed death warrant in boxing." Chad Dawson controlled his emotions when it mattered most—in the ring against Hopkins.

Hopkins–Dawson II: The Champion

Drama is keyed to the personal lives of the participants. Regardless of what the rest of the world thought, the April 28, 2012, rematch between Chad Dawson and Bernard Hopkins at Boardwalk Hall in Atlantic City was high drama for Dawson and everyone who cares about him.

Dawson, age twenty-nine, was born in South Carolina and grew up in Connecticut. He's soft-spoken and laid-back with a gentle demeanor; a bit on the shy side with strangers, but talkative when he feels comfortable with someone.

"My father had seven children by the time he was twenty-one," Chad recounts. "I have four brothers and two sisters. None of us has ever been in jail. We might not be the smartest people you'll ever meet, but none of us has a criminal record. Our parents taught us to be good."

Chad and his wife, Crystal, have four sons ranging in age from eight to eight months.

"I enjoy being a father," he says. "I'm most happy when I'm in my house with my kids. When I was little, my father never took me to school. I take the three oldest to school every morning; pick them up after school too. Having kids made me grow up a lot. I'm a lot more responsible now than I was before. My brothers and sisters and I grew up poor. I don't want my kids not to have the things they need to live right, but there's a line you have to draw. I'm still learning how to say 'no' to them."

"It's hard to get me mad," Dawson continues. "I'm not an angry person. But some of the stuff that goes on in the world; I watch the news a lot and I hate it when I see people hurting other people, especially kids. I don't understand how a father and mother can hurt their own kids, but they do. I'm a boxer and a father, and I always separate Bad Chad Dawson from Daddy."

Dawson got into boxing at a young age. His father, Rick Dawson, fought professionally from 1982 through 1984 and compiled a 1-6-1 record. The guy he beat finished his career with 3 wins against 48 losses and 30 KOs by.

"My father took me to the gym when I was eight and put me in the ring with my older brother, Ricky," Chad remembers. "Ricky gave me a bloody nose, but it was no big thing. He did that at home all the time."

"This is just my opinion," Dawson says, choosing his words carefully. "But my father didn't have a good career and the truth is, I don't think he expected me to make it. He looks at me now, and I think he's saying, 'I was there; I could have done it.' All the things he wanted to do in boxing, I'm doing them now. And he says to himself, 'That should have been me.' He doesn't get as much joy out of what I've done in boxing as I'd like him to."

Prior to facing Hopkins, Dawson had beaten some good fighters; most notably Eric Harding, Tomasz Adamek, Glen Johnson (twice), and Antonio Tarver (twice). His one loss was a technical-decision defeat at the hands of Jean Pascal in a fight cut short by an ugly gash caused by a head butt above Chad's left eye. At various time, he has held the WBC and IBF 175-pound titles.

The knock against Dawson has been that he lacks the fire inside that makes a fighter great; that he fights like he'd rather be doing something else; and that he's as happy out-boxing opponents as he is blowing them away.

"I hear the criticism from the media," Chad says, "But most of it comes from guys who never put on a pair of gloves in their life, so I brush it off. You need the media. The media gives us publicity. The media pays our salaries. But except for that, why should I care what they say?"

Still, Dawson is prone to adding to the conventional perception of his approach to boxing with thoughts like, "When I'm waiting in the dressing room before a fight, I want it to be over . . . Training camp is hard for me. Most of the time, I'd rather not be there. One of the kids starts talking and I'm not with him to hear it; or there's something else I miss that's going on with my family . . . Right now, boxing is more of a job for me than anything else. I don't like stupid stuff, ugliness, greed, disrespect. And I've been in boxing a long time, so I've run into a lot of stupid. If I didn't have a wife and kids, I'd probably have given it up by now. But if I wasn't in boxing, I don't know what I'd do. Probably nine-to-five somewhere, go home at the end of the day, and not worry about getting hit. You don't want to get hit. It's a bad feeling."

"Boxing keeps you humble," Dawson adds. "As far as I'm concerned, it's not about becoming a big star or calling yourself a legend. It's about winning fights."

Bernard Hopkins is the antithesis of Chad Dawson. He loves fighting. As Robert Ecksel wrote recently, "Hopkins is monomaniacal. He's the sun around which all planets revolve. He's the black hole at the center of our galaxy whose gravitational pull sucks everything into its maw. Always referring to himself in the third person, it's Bernard Hopkins this and Bernard Hopkins that until one's head throbs from the intensity."

Hopkins turned pro in 1988 after a fifty-six-month stint in Graterford State Penitentiary. He lost his first fight and went on to craft a ring career of monumental proportions.

"I didn't plan what happened to me in boxing," Bernard says. "I planned to not get in trouble again. I never wanted to go back to prison. So I did things right and made myself the best that I could be, and great things happened."

Hopkins is very much into control in all aspects of his life.

"There's a lot of fighters that are as talented as me," he says. "There's some that have more natural gifts than me. But no one—no one, no one, no one—is more disciplined than me. Every fighter is hungry when he's poor. The great ones stay hungry when they're rich."

In the ring, Hopkins projects an aura of strength; both physical and mental. He talks like a street fighter. "I want to throw punches that hurt. When I hit someone, I want to be able to take some of your soul with me."

But he fights like a scientific one.

"Hopkins is precise," Bart Barry observes. "His motion is efficient. He does not take two steps if one suffices. He strikes more than he punches. His fists go to the place he wants them. He hits you where he desires."

"Bernard is not a football player," adds Hopkins's trainer, Naazim Richardson. "Bernard is not a basketball player. Bernard is a fighter. He's one of the few out there today who has truly learned the craft of boxing."

"I still love the fundamentals of boxing," Hopkins says. "I still love the art of boxing. I still love the hit and not get hit in boxing. I still love that you can be aggressive but you can be aggressive smartly. It keeps my fire always burning."

Hopkins is unique as a fighter in that he will be remembered more for what he accomplished in the ring when he was old than when he was young. His age was first weighed against him when he fought Felix Trinidad in 2001. Bernard was thirty-six; Felix was twenty-eight. Hopkins dominated from start to finish before knocking his undefeated foe out in the twelfth round.

There have been setbacks since then when Bernard's age showed; most notably in losses suffered at the hands of Jermain Taylor (twice) and Joe Calzaghe. But one could be forgiven for starting a Bernard Hopkins birther movement; that is, demanding to see his long-form birth certificate to determine if he was really born in 1965.

"There's nothing unique I'm doing other than what's supposed to be done by anybody that has discipline," Hopkins told Tom Gerbasi last year. "Yes, you're seeing talent. Yes, you're seeing genetics and a little bit of good fortune. But what you're really seeing are the benefits of planting my crops; taking care of my life, my body, and my mind. I've invested in eating the best foods, staying away from drinking and smoking and partying. I'm like a luxury antique car that's in the best condition you can find."

Jean Pascal (who Hopkins fought twice) had a different view of Bernard's success and asked that he be subjected to "Olympic-style testing" for performance-enhancing drugs prior to their second encounter. That led an enraged Hopkins to declaim, "When a guy says something about my legacy and my history; the things that were said were deeper than having a guy in my bedroom, in my house with my wife, butt naked. I can forgive that before I can forgive what he said. When a guy says something to me to discredit me and have people thinking, 'Oh, this thing that he's done all these years is now under question'; yes, the ambulance will be right by any fight that happens. There will be one there, and don't be surprised if he's in it. I'm coming for him and he better be ready. We're going to war. Emile Griffith and Benny 'Kid' Paret."

That said; Hopkins declined to submit to the testing. His promoter, Golden Boy (which has championed "Olympic-style testing" for several recent Floyd Mayweather Jr fights), was silent on the issue.

Bernard wants to be regarded as a superstar and legend on the order of Jim Brown, Bill Russell, and Satchel Paige. Hence, the Hopkins mantra: "The reason that a lot of great basketball players who are in the Hall of Fame never got a ring is Michael Jordan. The reason that a lot of great fighters never got a ring is Bernard Hopkins . . . Tell your granddaughter, your grandson, your kids, that you're watching a person in this era like when Ray Robinson was in his; Ali was in his; Ray Leonard was in his; because this is the legacy I leave . . . I'm motivated by history; what other people did in the past and what history will say about me when I'm gone. When you get a taste of history, it's like being a drug addict. You can't let go."

A handful of fighters have crossed over into the public consciousness in the United States since Muhammad Ali left center stage. Sugar Ray Leonard, Mike Tyson, George Foreman, and Oscar De La Hoya head the list. Manny Pacquiao and Floyd Mayweather Jr come close but aren't quite there. As for Hopkins; let's be honest. Bernard could walk through Times Square tomorrow and most people would have no idea who he is. He's a big fish in what has become the small pond of boxing.

Let it also be said that, while Hopkins purports to shake off criticism the way a duck shakes off water, he is, as Bart Barry notes, "fantastically preoccupied with others' opinions of him."

Still, Bernard is on solid ground when he says, "There's people who hate me, but they respect me. I didn't kiss ass; I didn't sell out; I didn't buck dance. Nobody gave me anything. I fought my way to the top. I took it. I'm cut from a different cloth than other fighters."

That brings us to Bernard Hopkins vs. Chad Dawson.

They met in the ring for the first time on October 15, 2011. Prior to that fight, Hopkins touted his experience.

"You take my resume," he said at the August 9, 2011, kick-off press conference in New York. "You take Chad Dawson's resume. Harvard. Community college. Who are you going to hire? Experience counts. I'll go with the professor over the guy who just got his degree every time."

But when the fight came, it was a non-event. With twenty-two seconds left in round two, Bernard missed with a right hand, leveraged himself onto Dawson's upper back, and appeared to deliberately push his right forearm down on the back of Chad's neck. At the same time, he wrapped his left arm around Dawson's torso to steady himself and apply additional pressure to Chad's neck. In response, Dawson rose up and, using his shoulder, shoved Hopkins up and off. Bernard fell backward to the canvas, landed hard on his left elbow and shoulder, and lay there. Asked by a ring physician and referee Pat Russell if he could continue, he said only if it was "with one hand."

Initially, Russell declared Dawson the winner on a second-round TKO. Ultimately, the California State Athletic Commission changed the verdict to "no contest." That ruling allowed Hopkins to retain his Ring Magazine and WBC belts.

Bernard's partisans are fond of saying that their man has aged like fine wine. But on the night of Hopkins-Dawson I, the wine tasted like vinegar.

Antonio Tarver, who fought and lost to both Hopkins and Dawson, told FightHype.com, "Bernard reminds me of an old slick con-artist. This man didn't even attempt to fight. Look at the tape. Chad Dawson knew that he was going to take that out. He was furious that Bernard was trying to cop-out to an injury like that. You want to prove that you're hurt; I need to see an MRI. Where was the shoulder deformed? If you pop something out, you gonna see the bone sticking out of the shoulder. Bernard should have got off of the canvas and attempted to fight and not just hold his arm like he couldn't use that arm and like the arm couldn't move. He should have attempted to fight. He never attempted because his mind was already made up. He made the decision to lay on the canvas and cop-out to whatever shoulder injury he claims he had. I don't know how Bernard can live with himself, robbing the public like he did. He put the mask on and stuck-up every pay-per-view buyer that night."

Dawson was equally skeptical, branding Hopkins a "quitter" who performed his own personalized version of "no mas."

"Courage isn't crying and complaining and pretending you got hit low or your shoulder is hurt when things aren't going your way," Chad said. "A real champion gets up off the canvas and tries to fight. Courage is [Gabriel] Campillo getting knocked down twice in the first round by [Tavoris] Cloud and getting up hurt and fighting his way back into the fight. Bernard Hopkins is the opposite of courage. What he did to me in that fight; that was going to be my night and he took it away from me by play-acting and crying. I lost all respect for him that fight. I don't like him, and I think he's a phony."

Give Hopkins credit in that he signed for a rematch. But Dawson's antipathy remained; fueled in part by the fact that, as a consequence of Bernard claiming injury in their first fight, Chad was forced to accept the short end of a 70-30 purse split in Hopkins-Dawson II.

"I really don't believe Bernard Hopkins was hurt," Dawson said during a teleconference call to promote the rematch. "He said he dislocated his shoulder, but we didn't see any weakness in his shoulder. We didn't see any doctor's notes or anything like that. I'm going to keep saying this; Bernard did not want to be in the ring with me that night. Maybe he undertrained and he didn't expect to see what he saw. Maybe he needed more time to get in better shape. I don't know; but I know what happened that night. I looked into Bernard's eyes, and Bernard did not want to be in the ring that night."

But nowhere was Dawson's disdain for Hopkins more clearly on display than at Planet Hollywood in New York when the February 22, 2012, kick-off press conference for the rematch was held.

"I want to make one thing clear," Chad told the assembled media. "I came to fight, and he pulled a stunt. Legends don't act the way this guy acts. Legends don't do the things this guy does. Legends don't punk out."

Then Dawson stepped away from the podium, stared directly at Hopkins, and challenged, "Don't be a punk this time."

As fight night approached, Dawson was a 7-to-2 betting favorite. The general feeling was that he was too fast and too strong for Hopkins to handle and that he was also a more confident fighter than in the past. One reason for his confidence was that he had reunited with trainer John Scully.

Scully fought professionally from 1988 through 2001 and was good enough to go the distance with the likes of Michael Nunn and Henry Maske. By the end of his career, he'd compiled a 38-and-11 record with 21 knockouts and one "KO by." If one throws out the last ten fights on his ledger, it improves to 35-and-4.

"I loved fighting," Scully says. "When you're in the ring, even if it's just a four-round preliminary fight, you're the star."

Dawson has made the rounds of trainers during his pro career. He started out with Brian Clark (who trained him in the amateurs). Clark was followed by Scully, Dan Birmingham, Floyd Mayweather Sr, Eddie

Mustafa Muhammad, and Emanuel Steward. After a lackluster May 2011 performance against Adrian Diaconu, Dawson returned to Scully.

"Chad is positive he's going to win this fight," Scully said in the days leading up to the rematch. "He was confident the last time, but this is something more. Now he's sure he's going to win."

"Chad has always had the ability to be a great fighter," Scully continued. "Now he's ready to put it all together and fight great for an entire fight. All this legends crap that Hopkins does gets in the head of the guys he's fighting. Jermain Taylor ignored it and beat him. Joe Calzaghe ignored it and beat him. Hopkins will try to get into Chad's head, but that won't happen."

Gary Shaw (Dawson's promoter) was in accord, adding, "I'm very confident. I never thought Hopkins was hurt last time. We never heard anything about his going through rehab or anything like that. My only fear is that, somewhere in this fight, Bernard will find a way out again."

But there was an alternative view. Too often, Dawson is a reactive fighter rather than a proactive one. His work rate can be slowed by an opponent's inactivity. And Hopkins has a master's degree in delay, frustration, and opportunistic counterpunching.

"Fighters fight to be able to say, 'I told you so,'" Bernard noted. "I was called old when I fought Felix Trinidad, and that was ten years ago. I was called old when I fought Antonio Tarver, and that was six ago. I was called old when I fought Kelly Pavlik, and that was almost four years ago. The well isn't dry yet."

★   ★   ★

Chad Dawson arrived in his dressing room at Boardwalk Hall on fight night at 8:20 PM. The core of Team Dawson was with him. Trainer John Scully, lawyer-advisor Walter Kane, cutman Rafael Garcia, strength-and-conditioning coach Axel Murrillo, Steve Geffrard (one of three sparring partners Chad worked with in training camp), Chad's father, his brother Jermaine, camp aide Charles Robinson, and "G" (a close friend).

Wearing a navy-blue warm-up suit with white stitching on the jacket, Dawson sat on a folding cushioned metal chair and put his feet up on another chair in front of him. He spent next the thirty-five minutes in that posture, listening to music through a pair of headphones with his eyes closed, nodding his head in rhythm to the sounds that were echoing in his brain.

At 8:55, referee Eddie Cotton entered the room to give Chad his pre-fight instructions.

"The referee will be important," Scully had said earlier in the day. "We need a referee who's smart enough to see what Bernard is doing and also has the mindset to stop it when Bernard goes over the line, which he'll do as long as he gets away with it. The worst thing would be if the referee lets Bernard do his thing and has a different set of rules for Chad. I've told Chad again and again; he can't go into this fight walking on pins and needles because of what happened last time. If Bernard pulls down on his neck again, Chad has to throw him off again. He cannot let Bernard manhandle him."

Dawson removed his headphones. Cotton went through the standard litany of instructions ending with, "Do you have any questions?"

Scully held out his hands, palms up. "You know," he began.

"I know," Cotton interrupted. "I saw the last fight."

Scully proceeded to list a series of tactics that Hopkins has employed throughout his ring career.

Cotton promised to keep a close eye on things.

The referee left. Dawson put his headphones back on and resumed listening to music. Scully and Garcia engaged in quiet conversation.

At 9:15, still listening to music, Chad put on his ring shoes, stood up to see how they felt, and sat down again.

Rick Dawson went down the hall to watch Hopkins's hands being taped. Naazim Richardson (Bernard's trainer) arrived moments later to watch Rafael Garcia tape Dawson's hands.

Garcia worked quickly. In twenty minutes, the job was done. Richardson nodded in Rafael's direction and told the state athletic commission inspector who had overseen the process, "I have the utmost respect for this man. I've been watching him for a long time." Then Naazim clasped Garcia's hand. "Thank you, sir. It's always a pleasure."

All the while, Chad's headphones had been on.

At 9:55, Dawson took off his track suit and put on his protective cup followed by steel-gray trucks with green trim. Then he began shadow-boxing in the center of the room, his first exercise of the evening.

Garcia gloved him up.

At 10:25, Chad and Scully went to work, hitting the pads in earnest.

Earlier in the day, the trainer had told his charge, "There will be times tonight when you wonder what Hopkins is doing." At that point, Scully had postured, wiggled his body, and moved his shoulders in exaggerated fashion. "He's resting, is what he's doing. Don't let him do it."

Now the instructions were more pointed.

"Jab . . . Jab . . . There you go. You got it . . . One jab . . . One jab . . . Double jab . . . When his hands go up, go to the body . . . Don't let him get comfortable . . . Push him back . . . One-two . . . Hook up top . . . There you go. Perfect . . . You've done all the hard work. It pays off now . . . If he gives you rounds, take them big . . . Nasty jab . . . Nasty jab . . . That's it. Stick him . . . If he comes inside, dig to the body . . . Jab . . . Long left . . . Attitude . . . You got the legs; he doesn't . . . One-two . . . That's it . . . Don't try to be perfect. Let your hands go and you'll hit what's there. Anything you can hit, hit it . . . Stay mentally strong . . . Close the show."

Fifteen minutes later, Dawson was sweating profusely. Garcia helped him into his robe and Scully offered some final words of motivation.

"You got too much for him, but you got to bring it. You know what you can do. Go out and do it. Be what you're supposed to be. Take what's yours."

★   ★   ★

The ethos of the fight was set early with Dawson seeking to engage and Hopkins fighting as though he wanted a twelve-round staredown. Bernard avoided exchanges to the greatest extent possible by means of lateral movement and retreat. When that didn't work, he clutched, grabbed, led with his head, mauled, went low, hit on the break, and did everything else he could to blunt Chad's assault.

There was a time when Hopkins debilitated opponents with vicious body blows. "When they knock down a building," he once said, "they don't start at the top. They break down the foundation." But against Dawson, Bernard largely eschewed the body, preferring to fight at a safer range.

Prior to the fight, Carlos Acevedo had suggested, "The bout might end with members of Human Rights Watch storming the ring to prevent further abuse of the crowd."

That didn't happen. But in truth, Hopkins–Dawson II was short on action.

Dan Rafael called it "a horrible, almost unwatchable fight filled with mauling, clinching, and feinting, mostly initiated by Hopkins."

David Greisman observed, "It was ugly, as everyone expected it to be. And that was Hopkins's fault, as everyone expected." Then Greisman added, "Do any of the people who were booing Saturday night in Boardwalk Hall want to tell me what they expected to happen?"

Indeed, after round four, HBO commentator Jim Lampley advised a national audience, "Somewhere, there are some great light-heavyweights rolling over in their graves at the dreadful action so far."

Lampley's comment came shortly after a key moment in the fight. Thirty seconds into the fourth stanza, a Hopkins head butt opened an ugly gash on the outside of Dawson's left eye.

"Keep your composure," Scully told his fighter between rounds. "Keep fighting. Let the cutman do his job."

Garcia did a masterful job of controlling the blood from that point on.

Near the end of round five, Dawson spun Hopkins around and Bernard made a beeline for the ropes, looking very much like a man who wanted to dive through them to end the fight. The crowd reacted accordingly.

"It looked to me like he was starting to jump out of the ring," Chad said in his dressing room after the fight. "And then he figured the fans wouldn't buy it."

As the bout progressed, Hopkins showed that he has one of the best chins in boxing. And he lets his right hand go pretty fast for an old man. When Dawson landed solid shots to the head, which he did on occasion, Bernard fired back. That said; by the late rounds, Chad was landing two-for-one in exchanges and scoring to the body well.

In round eleven, Hopkins was clearly tired and looking for a breather. Toward that end, he sank to the canvas in a clinch and, moments later, tackled Dawson in a move that sent both men to the canvas. Cotton had warned Bernard for infractions on several occasions earlier in the fight but had never taken a point away for cumulative fouling. This would have been an ideal time to do so.

Then came the decision of the judges. Luis Rivera's score was announced first: 114–114, a draw. When the fighters entered the ring, Hopkins had been cheered and Dawson booed by the crowd of 7,705. But the fans in attendance were fair minded enough to react derisively to Rivera's scorecard.

Steve Weisfeld and Richard Flaherty restored sanity to the proceedings with 117–111 ledgers in Dawson's favor. This observer also had Dawson on top by a 117–111 margin.

Hopkins left the ring after the fight, refusing to do a post-fight interview with HBO. "What did he do to win that fight?" he demanded in typically churlish fashion. "They [the two judges who scored the fight for Dawson] did what they wanted to do. The only way I knew I would win is if I knocked him out. The public can judge for themselves."

So let's answer Bernard's question: "What did Dawson do to win the fight?"

Hopkins has said in the past, "I have two rules for boxing. Number one; I hit you. Number two; you don't hit me."

According to CompuBox, Dawson outlanded Hopkins in ten of the twelve rounds and was even in the other two. He had a 126-to-82 edge in "power punches" landed, pressed the action throughout the fight, and was in better shape when the contest ended.

"He's a slick-ass fighter," Chad said in his dressing room when the battle was over. "Low blows, hitting on the break; you name it, he did it. He head-butted me seven, maybe eight times. It was obvious that the head-butt that caused the cut was on purpose. There were a couple of times when I almost lost my composure because of all the dirty things he was doing. But Scully kept telling me to stay disciplined, keep the heat on, keep my composure. Don't throw it all away on something dumb."

Chad shook his head and smiled.

"It's funny the way things work. Now that I beat him, there's a different feeling inside me about him than I had before. I don't feel sorry for him. But a lot of the bad feeling I had is gone."

The post-fight press conference was marked by mutual respect between the fighters. They shook hands and Hopkins went so far as to call Dawson "a worthy champion."

One observer noted that Bernard and Golden Boy CEO Richard

Schaefer had the look of corporate raiders who were planning to make a run at signing Dawson (whose promotional contract with Gary Shaw expires in August). There are people in boxing who like Shaw and people who don't. But virtually everyone agrees that Gary has done an exceptional job in getting Chad to where he is today.

Hopkins, in all likelihood, will continue to fight. In the past, he has acknowledged, "Father Time is nobody's friend. My body will tell me when it's time to go." But he has also declared, "I'll fight as long as I have the desire to continue to win and not embarrass myself and embarrass the sport. I'm not still fighting because I can't turn the lights off and leave the room. I'm still fighting because that's what I do. It's what I am."

Bernard can still beat a lot of fighters. Given the politics of the game, he can still win a phony belt. But the reality of the situation is that, over the past seven years, he has had twelve fights and won six of them. He hasn't knocked out anyone since Oscar De La Hoya in 2004.

Meanwhile, Chad Dawson isn't claiming greatness. He isn't telling everyone within earshot that he's a legend. But he's the best light-heavyweight in the world right now.

I saw Manny Pacquiao vs. Tim Bradley differently from most observers.

Pacquiao-Bradley in Perspective

A wave of outrage has swept over the boxing community with regard to the scoring of the June 9, 2012, fight between Manny Pacquiao and Tim Bradley. The overwhelming majority of fans, writers, and commentators who watched the fight thought that Pacquiao was a clear winner. Jerry Roth agreed that Pacquiao had won, although his 115–113 scorecard was closer than many observers thought appropriate. Duane Ford and C. J. Ross ignited a firestorm of protest, scoring the bout 115–113 in favor of Bradley.

I'm poor candidate to audition for the Greek chorus. On fight night, sitting in row E of the press section, I thought the decision could have gone either way. And I scored the fight 115–114 for Bradley.

Was I wrong? Later in this article, I'll recount the thoughts I had after watching a replay of the fight. For now, let's put Pacquiao-Bradley in perspective.

In recent years, Pacquiao has taken boxing on a glorious ride. Fans in the United States became aware of him when he knocked out Lehlohonolo Ledwaba in 2001 to claim the IBF super-bantamweight crown. A string of triumphs followed, highlighted by a 2008 demolition of Oscar De La Hoya and devastating knockouts of Ricky Hatton and Miguel Cotto.

Floyd Mayweather (Pacquiao's rival for boxing supremacy) has been packaged as a superstar. Pacquiao is viewed by millions of fans around the world as a superhero. There's a difference.

In his native Philippines, Pacquiao is thought of as the heart of his people. Two years ago, he was elected to Congress. It's likely that, next year, he'll run for governor of Sarangani province. The Philippine constitution requires that the country's president be at least forty years old. Pacquiao will turn forty on December 17, 2018. The first presidential election after that will be contested in 2022.

Fanciful?

Yes. But also possible.

Nor is Pacquiao's influence limited to his native land. Earlier this year, *Forbes* placed him fourth on its list of the "most influential" athletes in the United States.

Tim Bradley doesn't have to make his way through a mob of adoring fans each time he steps out onto the street or goes to the gym. But the more time that people spend with him, they more they like him.

Bradley grew up in the not-so-good part of Palm Springs, California, as a middle child with two sisters. His father was a hard taskmaster. Tim grew up with a lot of anger in him.

"I got into fights all the time," he recalls. "I'm talking about from the time I was seven or eight years old. Anytime anyone looked at me wrong, I'd get into it with them. It's different now. I like to be respected, but I've learned to treat other people with respect. Beyond that, what can I say? I'm a family guy. I love friends and family. I like to make people happy. I'm outgoing, stubborn, ambitious. I work hard and do whatever it takes to get what I want. I don't want anything given to me. I want to earn it. For me, happiness comes from the pursuit, from the journey. I live in the moment. Whatever life brings me, I deal with it."

Other tidbits of information include, "I used to wait tables. I liked doing that because I like talking to people. But I don't think I'd want to wait tables now. And I used to sing in the church choir. I can carry a tune."

Bradley excelled in multiple sports when he was young. "I was always the smallest but the strongest kid in my class," he recalls. "I was fast and ran a pretty good mile. In junior high school, I scored thirty touchdowns in flag football in ten games."

But his primary love was boxing.

"When I was in sixth grade," Bradley remembers, "I had a friend named Julio. He used to train at a gym. In school, we'd slap-box, just fooling around. Julio told me I should go to the gym with him. I begged my dad to let me do it. Finally, my dad got tired of me talking about it and brought me in. I met my first trainer that day. His name was O. J. Kutcher. O. J. looked me over and said, 'Someday, you'll be a champion.' I told him, 'You say that to everyone.' And he told me, 'No, I don't. I see something special in you.'"

That same day, Kutcher put Bradley in the ring with Julio to see what he could do.

"I was a street-fighter," Tim recalls. "I lived in a tough neighborhood and wouldn't let anyone bully me. Most of the fights I had, I won. When Julio and I fooled around slap-boxing in school, I always got the better of him. So now I'm in the ring with Julio. I say to myself, 'I'm going to dominate, doing what I always do.' I got tamed pretty quickly. Julio kept popping me in the face, snapping my head back with his jab. The madder I got, the more I got hit. My head hurt. My neck was sore. I had a bloody nose and my lip was split. I was mad, sad, angry, crying. Julio shut me down. He kicked my butt. He humiliated me. He killed my pride. I came out of the ring with tears running down my face, and my dad asked me, 'Is this what you want to do?' I said yes. And Julio was nice about it. He patted me on the back and told me, 'Don't worry; it's just the first day. You'll get better.' He was right. Three weeks later, we got in the ring again and I busted him up."

"I loved going to the gym," Bradley continues. "The people there were like family to me. I didn't want to miss a day. I always wanted to run more, spar more, work harder. It got to where my parents used it as leverage with me. If I did something wrong or if there was something right I didn't do, I couldn't go to the gym. And O.J. changed my life. He didn't sugarcoat anything. He told it the way it was, but he believed in me. He was like my dad away from home, the way he cared about me. He even went to school sometimes to check up on my grades. Then, when I was fourteen, O.J. had a stroke and never recovered. I watched him pass. I was there when they turned off the machine that he was hooked up to. That was very hard for me. I still miss him. If he was here, if I could see him again now; first thing, I'd tell him I was happy to see him. I'd ask if he wanted to grab a bite to eat and catch up on things. Then I'd tell him how grateful I am that he was in my life; that I did what he told me I could do and I hope he's proud of me."

Bradley turned pro in 2004 with Joel Diaz as his trainer and his father, Ray Bradley, as Joel's assistant. Diaz had his own checkered past to contend with. A professional fighter with a 17-and-3 record, he was forced out of the ring by a detached retina and found himself drinking heavily.

"I'd take my gun in the middle of the night and go up in the mountains and cry and shoot into the mountains," Diaz told writer Peter Nelson. He also found employment as a bodyguard for a childhood friend who was a drug dealer. Then the dealer was forced by circumstances to flee the country and Diaz had an epiphany that his life was going nowhere good, so he returned to boxing as a trainer.

Meanwhile, Bradley had few illusions about the trade he was about to enter.

"Al Mitchell [a trainer who worked with several U.S. Olympic teams] sat me down when I was an amateur," Tim recalls. "He told me straight out, the professional game is a ruthless game. It can eat you whole, swallow you up, and leave you with nothing. Only two percent of the guys who turn pro make enough money to change their life. That's one out of fifty. And even if you make the money, a lot of guys live beyond their means, blow all their money, and wind up where they started."

Bradley's career in the professional ranks has been fueled by a Spartan work ethic.

"I've been around a lot of fighters," says Cameron Dunkin, who has managed Bradley for the past three years. "And I have never—I mean never—been around a fighter who works harder and is more focused on doing what he has to do than Tim is. He takes his career more seriously than any fighter I've ever known."

That focus helped Bradley craft a 28-and-0 record and brought him the WBC and WBO junior-welterweight crowns. He won his belts the hard way. First, he traveled to England to face Junior Witter (a titlist that few fighters wanted to meet) in his own backyard. Then he decisioned Lamont Peterson and Devon Alexander. Those three opponents had a composite record of 84-1-2 at the time Tim fought them.

"Fighting makes me happy," Bradley says. "Boxing is a beautiful sport. You can tell a lot about a person's character by the way he fights. It lets you see what he's like inside. You can always find excuses, but either you perform in the ring or you don't. To be a great fighter, you need skills and basic talent. You need to be smart; you have to think in there. You need courage, heart, and determination. If you can dish it out but can't take it, you won't go anywhere in boxing. And it helps if you have a mean streak. For me, that comes from my childhood."

How competitive is Bradley?

"I would love to go back in time and fight Marvin Hagler," Tim says. "Ray Leonard would move on me; slap me around while I chased him.

Hagler would stand there and fight. Probably, I'd get my butt kicked, but it would be a great fight."

There were kick-off press conferences for Pacquiao-Bradley in California and New York. Both fighters were gracious with Tim cast in the role of a credible challenger.

"I'm grateful to Manny Pacquiao for giving me this opportunity," Bradley told the media. "There's no one in the world I'd rather fight. I hope he regrets it. I'm not just coming to look good. I'm not just coming to survive. I'm not just coming for a paycheck. I want the throne."

Bob Arum, who'd guaranteed minimum purses of $26,000,000 to Pacquiao and $5,000,000 to Bradley, declared, "People tell me I'm underestimating Bradley. No, I'm not. Bradley is a very good fighter. That's what the public wants."

Pacquiao, for his part, warned his challenger, "When someone hits me, I hit back."

There was a brief spat when Alex Ariza (Pacquiao's strength and conditioning coach) opined, "The guys we're sparring with in the gym are better than Bradley. If he's afraid of Amir [Bradley had turned down a fight against Amir Khan in 2011], I don't know what he's thinking, fighting Manny. He's obviously just there to get paid. He's not there to win, for sure."

That earned a sharp rejoinder from Joel Diaz, who noted, "Alex Ariza can say whatever he wants. He's never been in camp with Tim Bradley. He hasn't even stepped in the gym to see Tim Bradley train. If he has better fighters in his gym than Tim Bradley, how come nobody knows them? How come they're not world champions?"

When the media tour was over, Bradley observed, "I'd never met Manny before. Each time we came face to face, we were sizing each other up. He has big legs, but he's no bigger than me. My abs are as good as his. He was very friendly, but it was a kind of scary nice."

Then Tim added, "Before I fought Devon Alexander, people were saying how good he was. Then the fight started, and I was like, 'This is it? This is what everyone is raving about?' I've been studying Pacquiao for years. People say, 'He's blazing fast. He hits so hard.' I want to see for myself if he's as good as people say he is and if I can compete with that. Manny can fight. He's great at what he does. I want to prove that I'm better than he is."

Bradley trained for the fight at home, living with his wife and three children.

"I don't have a big entourage," he said. "There's not a lot of people riding on my coattails. I don't need a bunch of guys who are there for no reason except they're being paid. This is a chance for me to put some serious money away and secure my family's future. My team will be Joel Diaz, my father and mother, my wife, and Sam Jackson [a close friend]. What we're doing has worked so far, so why change?"

As he'd done prior to his eight most recent fights, Bradley went vegan for the full three months of training. His diet included kale, spinach, broccoli, brown rice, brown pasta, fruit, almonds, walnuts, grain, and supplements for extra protein. Everything was gluten-free.

"I never ate vegetables when I was a kid," Tim explained. "I used to hate vegetables. But if you prepare vegetables properly and put the right spices in, they taste good. There's no Big Macs or fried chicken on this diet. If it has eyes or a momma, I'm not eating it."

As for the fight itself, the assumption was that, once the bell rang, neither guy would have to look hard to find the other. The prevailing view was that two issues would define the outcome: "How much, if at all, had Pacquiao's skills diminished?" and "How good is Bradley?"

Bradley is in his prime and had beaten some very good fighters.

"He's tough," Freddie Roach (Pacquiao's trainer) acknowledged. "He comes forward and is very aggressive. He's very strong and muscular up top. He's a physical fighter. He uses his head and elbows a lot, and Manny sometimes has trouble with that. But Ricky Hatton fought that way too, and look what Manny did to him. Manny will win this fight," Roach concluded. "He's faster; he's more experienced; and he has a lot more power."

Punching power was Pacquiao's biggest edge. He has it. And Bradley doesn't. Tim had only twelve knockouts in twenty-eight pro fights. He stopped an aging Joel Casamayor in his last outing. But one had to go back to a fifth-round stoppage of Nasser Athumani in 2007 to find a knockout on his resume before that.

Also, three years ago, Bradley was knocked down and hurt badly in the first round by Kendall Holt. He survived and won a twelve-round decision. Pacquiao is faster than Holt and hits a lot harder. Tim likes to trade punches with opponents. There was doubt as to whether he could survive a firefight with Manny.

"All fights are different," Pacquiao said. "I don't take this fight lightly. Bradley is undefeated and he is a champion. I know what he's feeling. But I am confident that I will win."

As an added precaution, Roach brought a new crop of sparring partners into the gym to force a harder, less friendly pace than Manny had grown accustomed to in recent training camps.

On the other side of the ledger, the case for a Bradley victory began with the premise that Pacquiao is no longer the fighter he once was. Exhibit 1 in support of that theory was Manny's last fight against Juan Manuel Marquez. Most people had predicted a dominating win for Pacquiao. The judges gave him a majority-decision triumph. The consensus at ringside was that Marquez deserved the nod.

Pacquiao called his outing against Marquez "a not so happy fight" and added, "I was in one-hundred-percent physical condition, but I had some family issues that I had to deal with. I also underestimated him."

Roach noted, "It was the first bad night we had in ten years. We all predicted knockouts and so forth. It was a little embarrassing. But Marquez is always going to give Manny trouble. He's a very good boxer and very smart."

Freddie also echoed his fighter, saying, "We had a great training camp for Marquez. But on the week of the fight, everything fell apart. Manny had some personal problems and they affected the fight. All of the distractions around him caused him to fight poorly. I don't think Manny will let that happen again."

But the fact remained that Marquez had entered the ring to face Pacquiao with a significant power deficit. And Juan Manuel had found a way to neutralize Manny's power, not just once but each of the three times they'd fought over an eight-year span.

"I was surprised that Pacquiao couldn't get Marquez out of there," Bradley said. "Marquez is a great fighter, but he's thirty-eight years old and past his prime."

There was also a belief that Bradley's head-first style of fighting posed a particular danger for Pacquiao. More than most elite fighters, Manny seems to be bothered by the sight of his own blood. Head-clashes are more likely when an orthodox fighter faces a southpaw. Pacquiao is left-handed. And head clashes occur with remarkable frequency whenever Bradley fights.

"Bradley comes in head first," Roach said. "We've been working on how to nullify that. We have a lefty fighting against a righty. Their heads may clash. It's something I'm concerned about."

There was also an issue regarding what kind of shape Pacquiao was in. On April 21, 2012, Alex Ariza (Manny's strength and conditioning coach) left Pacquiao's training camp in the Philippines without Roach's foreknowledge to work with Julio Cesar Chavez Jr.

"I had Amir Khan and Manny Pacquiao, my two top fighters there," Roach complained. "Alex wanted to go work with Chavez Jr, and I told him, 'I think it's a bad move.' Alex is very good at what he does, but he overdid it. His head has gotten too big, and we need to calm him down a little bit."

Ariza's defended his decision, asserting that he'd spoken with Pacquiao, who "gave me the green light and said, 'Yeah, go help him. I'll see you in LA. It's okay.'"

Manny confirmed Ariza's version of events, saying, "They are making a big issue of that. But Alex asked permission of me, if I'm okay that he goes back to LA. If I don't agree, he's not going to leave."

Ariza leaving training camp for two weeks meant less torturous strength and conditioning sessions for Pacquiao in the gym. There were those who thought that this easing of his training regimen was part of Manny's thinking.

As expected, Bob Arum spoke glowingly of Bradley's chances, telling the media, "When you look at Manny's opponents, the freshest guy he has fought will be Bradley. The others he has fought have been great names like Cotto, Margarito, De La Hoya and Hatton. Bradley is not a great name, but he's a great fighter and young and fresh. The most important element with Bradley is his mind. He's a very very determined young man. He's confident in his abilities and determined, and that is a tremendous plus for any athlete."

Arum, of course, was hyping the fight to sell on-site tickets and pay-per-view buys. But he was correct in his appraisal of Bradley's self-belief. Again and again in the months leading up to the fight, Tim made the case for his impending success:

★ "People say, 'Bradley doesn't have power.' But dudes sure do like to hold when they get close to me. I'm not the biggest puncher in the world. I don't have one-punch knockout power. But I can back you off me and keep guys honest with my power. I have stinging power. Anyone who thinks I don't, come down and spar with me."

★ "Pacquiao is a great fighter. He's fast; he's explosive; he's well-schooled. I know all that. But I think I can make him pay for the things he does wrong. You've never seen anybody just walk through me with power, and it won't happen on June 9. I've been on the canvas before, so it's nothing new to me. The most hurt I ever was in the ring was in my twelfth pro fight against Eli Addison. In the second round, we both threw right hands and missed and our heads collided. I got whacked on the right side of my temple and didn't know where I was at. I lost control of my body. I thought I was walking fine, but I was staggering around like Zab Judah did against Kostya Tszyu. People were laughing. They thought I was kidding around. Then the referee said 'box' and Addison came at me. I was on autopilot. The next thing I remember, it was the seventh round. But I won the decision. That's the kind of fighter I am. I know that, sometime in the fight, Manny will hit me with a big shot. The question is, what happens when that happens. He doesn't scare me. His punches have sting. His punches hurt. But except for Ricky Hatton, he hasn't shown one-punch knockout power."

★ "I don't just rush in. I'm hard to hit. I have really good eyes and a good boxing sense. Pacquiao doesn't fight well inside. I do. Pacquiao sets up his punches with his feet. My footwork is as good as his. I'm as fast as he is. I know what he can do, what he likes to do, and what he doesn't like. I think he'll be surprised by how strong I am, how fast I am, and how good I am. Manny has more power than I do, but skill wins fights. I don't just have muscles. I know how to use them."

★ "Pacquiao has been fighting slower opposition lately. Ever since De La Hoya, the only guy he fought who had any speed was Marquez. Marquez was quick, and you saw what happened in that fight. My opponents have been young lions; Devon Alexander, Lamont Peterson, Junior Witter. Pacquiao has been fighting guys who are past their prime, guys that are slipping and sliding down the mountain. I'm on my way up."

★ "I can't come out too fast. I've got to be smart; go out for a few rounds, read him, and then start picking him apart. I have to find out what his best punches are and feel him out and get the timing down. I can't throw wide punches to get to him because, if I do, he'll come straight down the middle and BOOM. He likes to mix it up. You know how you slow down a fighter like that? You fight him. I'll be going at a fast pace for every minute of every round. Thirty-six minutes, twelve full rounds. And I won't fade the way the other guys he's fought lately faded. The longer it goes, the more dominant I'll be."

★ "Freddie thinks his fighter is more skillful than me. Maybe he is; maybe he isn't. I don't care what Freddie Roach thinks. He can say whatever he wants. He isn't in my training camp and he won't be in the ring fighting for Pacquiao. Junior Witter watched film. Lamont Peterson watched film. Devon Alexander watched film. Freddie Roach can watch all the film he wants and say anything he wants. Freddie Roach has never been in the ring with me."

★ "Nothing is guaranteed in boxing. You don't win fights with your record. You win fights with what you do on the night of the fight. In boxing, it's always about right now. I know when to box and I know when to brawl. I'm physically and mentally prepared. I can hang with anybody. I went through a lot of things in and out of the ring to get to this point in my life. Pacquiao's people don't know what they got themselves into. It's my time now."

Bradley believed in himself. There was no doubt about that. And there was another factor to be considered.

There are very few choirboys at the elite fighter level. Pacquiao's persona and all that he has accomplished outside the ring have been an important part of his rise to global superstar status. But in recent years, there have been rumblings that, behind the scenes, there was trouble in paradise. Now some not-so-wonderful details were surfacing and becoming part of the Pacquiao story.

Pacquiao and his wife Jinkee have four children. He professes to be a devout Catholic. But over the years, there has been a pattern of infidelity in his life.

In May 2009, GMA News in the Philippines reported, "In 2006, Pacquiao admitted engaging in a one-night stand with Joanna Rose Bacosa, who would later claim that the world's greatest southpaw fathered her son, Emmanuel John Pacquiao. Bacosa brought the matter to court, accusing Pacquiao of violating Republic Act No. 9262, and sought support for the boy. Making one of the biggest splashes was the boxer's rumored affair with sexy actress Ara Mina. The actress was rumored to be the reason why Pacquiao abandoned his training in the United States in 2007 and resumed it in the Philippines. The two starred in the 2007 Metro Manila Film Festival entry *Anak ni Kumander*, where they had to lock lips nine times to perfect a kissing scene. In early 2008, photos of Pacquiao dancing with an unknown young lady in green at the Embassy in Taguig City proliferated on the Internet."

Jinkee defended her husband at the time, saying, "I trust Manny. He loves us and our kids. Our relationship is strong."

That would change.

Meanwhile, Pacquiao had developed a serious gambling habit, suffering losses well in excess of a million dollars annually. Arum would later acknowledge, "He was addicted to it. Manny had one of the worst gambling habits of any athlete I've ever known."

And Philippine tax officials filed a criminal complaint against Pacquiao for failing to produce documents to investigators who were examining "discrepancies" in his tax returns.

"If Mr. Pacquiao is not hiding something, then he should submit all the documents required by the BIR," Bureau of Internal Revenue officer Rozel Lozares said. "He is a lawmaker and we expect him to respect the law."

Chris Mannix of *Sports Illustrated* would later reference what he called the fighter's "Charlie Sheen–like behavior."

Finally, Jinkee decided that she'd had enough. In the days leading up to Pacquiao's November 11, 2011, fight against Juan Manuel Marquez, she resolved that she would no longer tolerate her husband's promiscuity. Whether or not Manny was actually served with papers demanding a divorce on the night before the fight is open to debate. What is clear is that, not long after the fight, Pacquiao declared that he'd experienced a religious awakening and would change his lifestyle in numerous ways.

The new Manny Pacquiao pledged fidelity to his wife, sold his ownership in a Manila casino, divested himself of his one-thousand-rooster cockfighting operation, shuttered his sports bar, pledged that he would give up all other vices, and re-dedicated himself to his faith.

"The old has passed," Pacquiao proclaimed. "The new has come.

When I committed my life to the Lord, I gave up many things that were not in keeping with what the Bible teaches. The sins I committed over and over, I stopped doing. It's better for me now. I found a new way of life. It is the right way. I read the Bible before, but now I have learned to obey the word of God. The manual to my life is the Bible. I have peace of mind now. I am always happy every day because I am following the word of God. I know, if I die today, where I'm going. I'm not worried about what fits in this world. I'm worried about what happens to me in my eternal life."

"Manny had money and fame before," longtime adviser Michael Koncz explains. "But he always needed action. Gambling, cockfighting, women. All those things kept him from being bored. Even with politics; he loved the challenge of getting elected. But getting elected is one thing; achieving after you've been elected is another. I think Manny expected that he'd be faced with tough decisions every day in the political arena and have accomplishment after accomplishment. But politics doesn't work that way. It's not as immediately gratifying as a knockout. And what has happened is, now when Manny has time to fill, he reads the Bible and shares the Bible. When he wants to feel that he's making a difference in people's lives, he shares the Bible with them. He's more relaxed and more content than I've ever seen him."

Jinkee was pleased by the change in her husband. "Our lives were like a roller coaster ride," she said. "Now it's very different than before. It's full of trust. Now we have a happy life together."

Arum also hailed Pacquiao's transformation. "Manny's life was careening off the rails," the promoter declared. "It's different now for him. He goes to sleep on time, in bed with his wife, not guilt-ridden. He's at peace with himself. From somebody who has visited the training camp a few times, the difference in Manny's face is so apparent. He's not as tired as he was and he's not as worn as he was. There's a glow in his face. I think this religious awakening has been all good on his part. I'm a little prejudiced because I'm religious myself. But I believe when young athletes find religion it will greatly enhance their careers. When an athlete has a religious experience, it's a great thing."

Freddie Roach also took a positive view.

"He has more focus and more energy," the trainer noted. "In the past he'd come to the gym with rings under his eyes from getting so little sleep because he'd been out late all night. Now he shows up fresh and, when he's done, he does his Bible study and goes to sleep. I have no doubt it's going to make Manny a better fighter. He and God are very close right now, and he's just a better athlete with no distractions."

There were some bumps in the road. It was pointed out that, despite Pacquiao's recent religious reawakening, he was continuing a lucrative endorsement deal with Hennessy cognac. There was also a flap when Manny spoke publicly against gay marriage.

More significantly, Pacquiao told Filipino television personality Korina Sanchez that he was thinking seriously about retiring from boxing because the sport conflicted with his devotion to God. That was followed by an interview with Bob Velin of *USA Today* in which Manny said, "Hitting each other is not good. So I was thinking I'm not going to stay long in boxing."

That earned a riposte from veteran boxing writer Charles Jay, who observed, "Except that Pacquiao's not retiring. He's simply talking about leaving boxing in 2013, or after three, four or five more fights, which frankly, may be when he was going to leave the sport anyway. The contradictions are all over the place. Pacquiao revealed that he was seriously considering retirement after God appeared to him in a dream and told him to quit boxing. If you are going to push yourself as some sort of messenger of God, and God tells you to do something, you don't 'seriously consider' it. In other words, we are to believe that God told him to do something, and Pacquiao said something like, 'Okay, good idea. I'll think about it. But first let me sign for this fight against Timothy Bradley, and then have a couple more fights, and of course, there's the possibility of that fight with the evil Mayweather. Sometime next year, I'll get back to you.' I thought the idea was that God didn't want him to be a fighter anymore. I don't think He asked him to win a couple of additional championship belts first, then hang 'em up."

Bradley had his own take on it all.

"I'm a spiritual person," Tim said. "But I'm not religious. I believe in one God and I embrace Christ as my Lord and Savior, but I don't go to church every Sunday. To me, the way religions do things, too much of the time it's like a cult. I can't tell you that anyone else is wrong, but I can tell you what I believe. I believe that every person can be saved. I believe that murderers can go to heaven. God is in my heart. I live my life the best way

I can. Am I right? No one knows the whole truth of what is. Do I know? No, it's faith. I'm not perfect, but I'm the best person I can be. I don't throw my religion in anybody else's face. Manny has his way of doing things, and I have mine."

The media center at the MGM Grand in Las Vegas was less frenetic during fight week than had been the case for other recent Pacquiao events. Pay-per-view buys were tracking in desultory fashion, and the NBA conference championship series between the Miami Heat and Boston Celtics posed a problem. Ultimately, Miami-Boston went to a seventh game on Saturday night, which pulled an undetermined number of potential buyers away from the fight.

Equally important, the NBA playoffs deprived Pacquiao-Bradley of important media coverage. ESPN was televising the Heat-Celtics series, which meant that the sports entertainment colossus devoted its multiple platforms far more to basketball than to boxing. The fight also faced same-day competition from the Stanley Cup finals, French Open, and Belmont Stakes

Publicist Fred Sternburg (a fixture in Pacquiao's camp during big promotions) was asked if he saw any difference between Manny's demeanor in advance of the Bradley fight as opposed to previous events.

"Yes," Sternburg answered. "Manny has been on time all week."

But there were other differences. In recent years, Pacquiao has seemed to enjoy the rituals of fight week. Now he appeared to be tired of them. He was more subdued than in the past; more somber, possibly, than serene.

"His last few fights, he hasn't been the old Manny," Roach explained. "I think he has something to prove to the people."

But in the eyes of some, Pacquiao already had one foot out the door. "My family wants me to retire," he said. "My wife, my mom, my kids." And one had to ask whether the demands that come with the devotion of the Filipino people were transforming the idolatry of millions from an inspiration to a burden.

Sugar Ray Leonard, who has been there done that, wondered aloud, "Is it too much now?"

Bradley had no such internal conflicts. He was enjoying the spotlight and took to the big-fight atmosphere the way a duck takes to water. There were times when he seemed like a hero out of central casting. Smart, well-spoken, gracious, a family man with solid values and a megawatt smile that lights up a room when he enters. He has a compelling personality and seemed to believe in himself as much as a fighter can.

During an hour-long "satellite tour" two days before the fight, Bradley was in good spirits.

"I feel wonderful . . . I feel good . . . I'm great. How are you? . . . Thank you . . ."

Among the thoughts he offered were:

★ "When I was a kid and won a tournament, I'd be all excited and show everyone my trophy. This fight is about a lot more than a trophy. The money I'm making on Saturday night will change my life and my family's life. Winning will change things even more."

★ "I know that Manny is a great fighter. But he has to prove to me that he's better than me. We'll find out on Saturday if I'm great or not. One thing I know is that, when it's over, I'll be satisfied that I trained as hard as I could, fought as well as I could, and put it all on the line."

★ "Sure, I'm nervous. If I wasn't nervous, there'd be something wrong with me. But I'm sleeping fine. I love pressure. When I'm under pressure, I perform. The more pressure, the better I fight."

★ "The stage is ready. The lights are on. I believe with all my heart that this is my time."

Bradley's confidence was contagious. Pacquiao was a 4-to-1 favorite at the MGM Grand Sports Book. But there was an undercurrent of sentiment in the media center that an upset might be brewing.

Manny had catapulted to superstardom with scintillating victories over Oscar De La Hoya, Ricky Hatton, and Miguel Cotto. He was dominant in triumphs over Joshua Clottey and Antonio Margarito but slipped a bit against Shane Mosley. His most recent performance, against Juan Manuel Marquez, had been disappointing. It was a matter of conjecture whether his newly found religious fervor would spur him on in the ring against Bradley or blunt his aggressiveness.

Tim emphasized that latter point, noting, "Pacquiao's life is going in a lot of different directions. He's here; he's there. One day he's fornicating. Then he's not. But it seems like he's trying to get away from boxing."

Bradley, on the other hand, was a hungry fighter. More than simply saying all the right things, he seemed to believe them and gave every indication of being ready to translate his belief into reality. The presumption was that he would come as hard as he could for as long as he could on fight night; that he would dig as deep as possible, whereas Pacquiao might not. After all; against Marquez, Manny had shown a disinclination to walk through fire in the late rounds when it appeared as though Juan Manuel was in the lead.

In sum; Pacquiao's aura of invincibility was glowing less brightly than in the recent past. Alex Ariza acknowledged, "You can race your car in high gear for just so long before there are problems."

And trainer Don Turner, who was monitoring the proceedings from his home in North Carolina, opined, "I've been around boxing a long time. Let me tell you what I've learned from watching guys like Ali and Evander and Larry Holmes. When the bell rings, Pacquiao's belief in Jesus might help him. But Jesus won't."

There were comments that Bradley would be a good spokesman for boxing if he won; that he was about the future, whereas Manny might be about the past.

"Hell must be freezing over," Tim said when told that quite a few members of the media were picking him to win. "This is great."

The biggest concern voiced by members of Team Bradley was that, if the fight went to the scorecards, their man wouldn't get a fair shake from the judges.

★   ★   ★

"On the day of a fight," Bradley has said, "it's like there's this huge rock on my back and I want to get it off. Then, right before I leave the dressing room, things become sort of like an out-of-body experience. When I walk to the ring, some fans are cheering 'Go, Bradley!' Others are shouting, 'You're going to get knocked out.' None of that means anything to me. When I step between the ropes, the nervousness leaves me. I say to myself, 'I own this ring.' And I look across the ring at the other guy and say, 'You made a mistake, buddy.'"

The first two rounds of Pacquiao-Bradley were closely contested with all three judges splitting them evenly between the fighters. According to

CompuBox, Pacquiao outlanded Bradley 11 to 10 in the first stanza, but I gave that round to Bradley because I thought he fought more effectively.

Pacquiao dominated rounds three through six of what was then an exciting action fight. Bradley fired back when hit and pumped punches to the body when Manny tried to tie him up on the inside. But Pacquiao scored more effectively, particularly when punches were fired in bunches.

"He was fast," Bradley acknowledged afterward. "And he stunned me a couple of times in there."

In round five, I made two notes: "Bradley more respectful now of Pacquiao's power . . . Can Manny keep it up for twelve rounds? If so, he wins."

In round six, I wrote, "Pacquiao looks very good . . . Pacquiao unloading . . . Bradley walks to his corner at end of round with a weary discouraged look."

At that point, I had Pacquiao ahead 59–55 (the same score as Jerry Roth). Duane Ford and C. J. Ross had it 58–56.

Then, in my eyes (and also in the eyes of all three judges), the momentum of the fight changed.

Before the fight, Bradley had said, "I'm a rough fighter. I come in aggressively. There will be no time off. I'll be fighting sixty seconds of every minute, three minutes of every round." But he'd also acknowledged, "Pacquiao hits hard, so I'll feel him out and see what he really has. If he does have power, then I'll have to be smarter in there and outbox this guy."

In round seven, Bradley started boxing. From that point on, I thought he controlled the pace of the fight.

Round eight: "Bradley boxing more now. Not pushing the pace . . . Pacquiao taking the round off. Looks a bit tired."

Round nine: "Some good flurries both ways . . . Bradley looks stronger and digging deeper . . . Pacquiao may be losing his power."

Round ten: "Pacquiao moving forward, but Bradley countering well."

Round eleven: "Pacquiao throwing one punch at a time."

Round twelve: "After an impressive start, Manny has looked ordinary the second half of the fight."

When I tallied my score, I'd given Bradley five of the last six rounds with one round even for a 115–114 scorecard in Tim's favor. Beneath those numbers, I wrote, "Pacquiao outfought Bradley the first half of the fight. Bradley outboxed Pacquiao in the second half. Manny at his best always finished strong. This time, he didn't. Like the Marquez fight, he wasn't willing to walk through fire in the late rounds to win."

Duane Ford and C. J. Ross scored the fight 115–113 in Bradley's favor. Jerry Roth scored it 115–113 for Pacquiao.

Looking at the round-by-round punch-stats after the fight, I questioned my scoring of several rounds. When I watched the replay, I could see how a majority of observers scored the bout for Pacquiao. Duane Ford and C. J. Ross didn't have the benefit of hindsight. I think they're honest judges, and I don't think the decision was a "robbery."

Bob Arum thought otherwise. In the media center immediately after the fight, the promoter declared, "I have never been as ashamed to be associated with the sport of boxing as I am tonight. To hear scores like we heard tonight; it's unfathomable. These people don't know how to score. Two of the judges [Ford and Roth] are too damn old to score anymore. What were they looking at? How do you explain it to anybody? What fight were they watching? They're honest, but they need to correct their vision. What we saw tonight was ridiculous. It's bizarre. This isn't arguing about a close decision. This is an absurdity. Everyone who's associated with boxing should feel ashamed."

As Bart Barry (who also scored the fight for Bradley) wrote afterward, "Bradley and Pacquiao were examples of graciousness ignored by almost everyone else." Pacquiao told the media that he thought he'd won, but added, "The decision has been done already, so we have to respect it and give credit to him. It's part of the game. I'm still here. Next time."

Bradley attended the post-fight press conference in a wheel chair with strained ligaments in his left foot and a badly swollen right ankle. "I stepped on the referee's foot and felt something pop," he explained. The other injury came when he pivoted awkwardly.

The injuries highlighted Bradley's fortitude and gave rise to the question of whether they'd hampered his performance. But he refused to cite them as an explanation or excuse, giving credit to Pacquiao for being a great fighter.

Meanwhile, a perfect storm was brewing. An overwhelming majority of on-site media had scored the fight for Pacquiao. The most notable exception was Brian Kenny (who ironically, called the fight for Top

Rank's international television feed). Kenny saw Bradley as a 115–113 victor and held to that view after watching a replay.

Here, I should note that, on *The Fight Game* this past Saturday night, HBO made a point of showing round seven (which all three judges scored for Bradley) without blow-by-blow commentary. Jim Lampley referred to the round as "the smoking gun." The point was then made that, according to CompuBox, Pacquiao outlanded Bradley 27 to 11 in that round.

I think that Bradley outlanded Pacquiao in round seven by a 16-to-12 margin. Don't take my word for it. Watch the round again without sound and decide for yourself.

Still, conspiracy theories abounded. Depending on one's imagination, either Arum bought off the judges (because his contract with Pacquiao was expiring and this was a way to lock Manny in for another fight). Or Richard Schaefer did it. Or maybe it was Al Haymon, Floyd Mayweather's omnipotent manager.

On June 11, Arum formally requested that the Nevada attorney general's office conduct a full inquiry into the circumstances surrounding the scoring of the bout.

"I want to investigate whether there was any undue influence," the promoter said, explaining his action. "They have to investigate the commission, how these guys were appointed, what was told to them before the fight, if anything. We have to investigate the judges. We have to investigate the betting pattern. And we have to investigate the promoter; that's me. If this was a subjective view that each of the judges honestly held, okay. I would still disagree, but then we're off the hook in terms of there being no conspiracy. But there needs to be an independent investigation because it strains credulity that an event everybody saw as so one-sided one way, all three judges saw it as close. The public has a right to know. The fighters have a right to know. The only way to restore fans' confidence in boxing is by letting an independent body investigate every detail of the fight, no matter how big or small. Sunshine never hurt anyone."

The story line of Pacquiao-Bradley is now the judging. But there are other story lines buried beneath the controversy.

First, all the talk about the decision has deflected attention from the fact that, for the first time in years, Manny failed to sell out an arena in Las Vegas.

Floyd Mayweather, despite considerable self-promotion, hasn't sold out the MGM Grand since 2007. Pacquiao fought before capacity crowds in Sin City on seven occasions during that same period.

Not this time. Documents filed with the Nevada State Athletic Commission show that 13,229 tickets were sold for Pacquiao-Bradley; 925 complimentary tickets were given away; and 2,070 tickets went unsold.

Similarly, Pacquiao's previous seven fights averaged more than 1,100,000 pay-per-view buys. Early numbers suggest that Pacquiao-Bradley will fall in the 850,000 range. Some of that shortfall can be attributed to the fact that Bradley has yet to develop a following. But the bloom appears to be fading a bit from the Pacquiao rose.

The arena for the weigh-in at the MGM Grand was configured for 6,000 fans. In recent years, every seat has been filled for Pacquiao appearances. This time, the announced attendance was 4,000. That seemed like a generous estimate. Also, on-site merchandise for Pacquiao-Bradley sold less well than for previous Pacquiao fights.

It's too early to proclaim the end of the Pacquiao Era. Indeed, the loss to Bradley might re-energize Manny as a fighter. But there's a question as to how much he has left. Against Antonio Margarito and Shane Mosley, Pacquiao appeared to be compassionate late in the fight. But he wasn't compassionate in his third fight against Juan Manuel Marquez. Against Marquez, he couldn't pull the trigger. And against Bradley, he faded as the bout wore on. Manny was at his most devastating physically and mentally for his fights against De La Hoya, Hatton, and Cotto. He's unlikely to get to that level again.

There may, or may not, be a rematch between Pacquiao and Bradley. Arum has indicated that he questions the economics and aesthetics of such a fight. That might be part of an effort to drive down Tim's contractually mandated purse minimum before a contract is (or is not) signed.

The assumption all along had been that, if Bradley beat Pacquiao, Top Rank would know how to make the most of it. One of the sad things in the way Pacquiao-Bradley has played out is that Tim has emerged from the fight more tarnished in the public mind than if the decision had gone against him. That's not fair.

The furor surrounding Pacquiao-Bradley has also been unfair to the judges.

Bad judging isn't a new problem in boxing. Outrageous decisions in club fights and high-profile bouts are far too common. But it's rare that they go against the house fighter. What's unusual here is that a controversial decision went against the house fighter (who's also the most popular fighter in the world).

In the days before Pacquiao-Bradley, numerous scenarios as to how the bout might unfold were discussed. There were predictions of cuts caused by head butts leading to a technical decision. There were predictions of knockouts and biased judging in favor of Pacquiao. No one who suggested that the decision could bring howls of protest prophesied that the winner would be Bradley.

Bad decisions can result from poor judgment or bias on the part of officials. Poor judgment can result from incompetence or a bad night. Biased officiating exists at every level of the sport. Everyone knows that it exists, and virtually nothing is done to eradicate it. In fact, the presumption is that officials are sometimes appointed precisely because they're biased.

I don't know C. J. Ross. I've watched Duane Ford at work over the years and know him casually. I think he's honest and a good judge.

Ford has taken a beating in the media. "I've had better weeks," he told me when we spoke last Thursday. "It hurts. Having judged as many fights as I have, you take criticism as part of the game. I love fighters. I love the trust they've given me over the years. That's sacred to me. But this has been a bit overwhelming and it has been hard on my family. I'm asking myself if I want to stay in the game."

Ford has been quoted in the *Las Vegas Review-Journal* as saying, "I thought Bradley gave Pacquiao a boxing lesson. Pacquiao missed a lot of punches, and I thought he was throwing wildly." In response to questions from Kevin Iole of Yahoo.com, Duane declared, "If this were *American Idol*, without a doubt, Pacquiao would have won. But it was not. Remember, it's a boxing match, and Bradley demonstrated his ability to box expertly."

Ford elaborated on those themes in our own conversation, saying, "When you're a judge, you're at arms length from the action. You see things that other people don't see. When the bell rings, you concentrate and focus. Then the bell rings again and you turn in your score. It's twelve separate fights. When a round ends, that fight is over. Unless you're totally focused, it's impossible to do the job right."

"I had Pacquiao leading after six rounds," Ford continued. "There were several times when I thought he hurt Bradley. But in the second half of the fight, I thought that Bradley landed some hard body shots and did an excellent job of standing his ground when he had to. It was a close fight. There were rounds that could have gone either way, and I scored them the way I saw them. I walked out of the arena that night knowing in my heart that I'd done an honest job."

There will always be controversial decisions in boxing. That's the nature of the sport. But the controversies rarely come when judges call them as they see them. Almost always, they come when judges call them the way they're supposed to see them.

Whatever investigation follows Pacquiao-Bradley should focus on more than one fight. Any official can make a mistake. The key is to look for patterns of misconduct; to explore the issue of which referees and which judges and which administrators in which jurisdictions frequently rule in a questionable manner.

The investigation should be keyed to the overall state of officiating in boxing. It should explore the way that judges and referees are trained and appointed. And most important, it should lead to the end of the system whereby referees and judges favor house fighters. It would be devastating if the ongoing furor over Pacquiao-Bradley instilled fear in the minds of judges who might otherwise have the temerity to rule against a popular house fighter.

Rather than beat up on two officials, boxing should use Pacquiao-Bradley as a teaching moment to press for unbiased competent decision-making across the board.

For many boxing insiders, the September 15, 2012, match-up between Sergio Martinez and Julio Cesar Chavez Jr was the most-anticipated fight of the year.

Martinez–Chavez: Peaks and Valleys

An athlete's life is characterized by peaks and valleys.

When Sergio Martinez was seventeen years old, he played forward in the #7 slot for a team called Defensoris in a junior amateur football (soccer) league in the province of Buenos Aires. Two days before his September 15, 2012, middleweight championship fight against Julio Cesar Chavez Jr in Las Vegas, Martinez sat in his suite at The Wynn Resort and Casino and recalled those days.

"We were playing against a team called Sportman," Sergio said. "It was a tournament that was important for me to play well in. There were a lot of professional scouts in the stands. If I did well, it could take me places."

"I was very inspired that day," Martinez reminisced. "We won 4 to 0, and I scored three goals. On the first goal, there was a free throw from one of my teammates and I lifted it in an arc with my right foot over the goalie. That put us ahead in the score. The next goal was my best of the game. I stopped the ball with my chest, dribbled it past four defenders, and scored on a finesse kick with my right foot. The third goal was at the end of the game. Their goalie was at midfield. I got the ball, dribbled all the way in, and scored on an empty net. After each goal, everyone was celebrating and hugging. It was an incredible feeling."

"I wasn't born with the instincts that a great football player has," Sergio continued. "My technique wasn't good, but I was fast and strong. My emotions were my Achilles heel. I was very emotional when I played football. The next game was for the championship. There was a tie and the game went to penalty kicks. If I make my kick, we play on. If I miss it, we lose.

"I placed the ball down in front of the goal," Sergio recalled. "Then I got nervous. The goalie got bigger and bigger in my mind and the goal got smaller and smaller. I kicked the ball and it went slowly to the goalie, right to his hands. He didn't even have to move to field it. I was humiliated and embarrassed. It was one of the worst moments of my life. Because of my failure, we lost the championship game. I was so devastated that I quit the team."

Martinez has come a long way in the world of sports since then. Three years later, at age twenty, he walked into a boxing gym for the first time. He's now thirty-seven years old with a record of 50 wins, 2 losses, and 2 draws. For the past two years, regardless of the games that sanctioning bodies play, he has been widely recognized as THE middleweight champion of the world. He won the crown on April 17, 2010, with a twelve-round decision over Kelly Pavlik and successfully defended it with knockout victories over Paul Williams, Sergeiy Dzinziruk, Darren Barker, and Matthew Macklin. With roots in Buenos Aires, Madrid, and California, he gives special meaning to the phrase "world" champion.

Martinez has been hardened by his journey through life, but there's a warmth about him. He's comfortable in the spotlight but doesn't seek it out. He's an advocate for women who have been subjected to domestic violence and for children who've been the target of bullying in school.

"A world-class fighter doesn't have to act like a thug," Sergio says. "As a professional athlete who is in the public eye, I have a duty to speak out on behalf of people who need help and are not heard. When I was a boy, I had a pale face and was small. I always tried to do the right thing and stay out of trouble, so I was picked on a lot."

Martinez also has a sense of humor. Recounting the many jobs he held as his ring career moved slowly forward, he notes, "Working on roofs helped a lot with my footwork. You have to be very careful not to fall off."

Julio Cesar Chavez Jr has traveled a road very different from the one traveled by Martinez. He was born in Culican, Mexico, on February 16, 1986. His father, is widely regarded as Mexico's greatest fighter. Julio Cesar Chavez Sr finished his career with championships in three weight divisions and 107 victories to his credit.

Julio Jr grew up wealthy, a child of privilege. As the "son of a legend," he wasn't held accountable for his actions to the same extent as his peers. But if life was a bed of roses, there were a lot of thorns. His parents divorced when he was young, which is difficult for any child. And his father, in addition to being a Mexican ring icon, became an alcoholic and a drug addict.

"I thought he was going to die," Julio Jr said recently of his father's substance abuse problems. "I was getting used to the idea. I was expecting that call any time."

The development of a fighter is a marathon, not a sprint. Top Rank (which promotes Chavez in conjunction with Fernando Beltran) does it better than anyone. Julio Jr turned pro in 2003 with no amateur experience on his ledger. His ring career was nurtured on weak opponents who were only marginally trained in the art of hurting.

Sean Gibbons, who was hired by Beltran to facilitate matters in the Chavez camp, observes, "Julio's real growth as a fighter began when he started working with Freddie Roach for the John Duddy fight [in 2010]. That was the turning point. Julio wasn't sure if he could fight or not because so many people said he couldn't. That's when he got serious about training and conditioning. And at the same time, his father began dealing constructively with some of his own demons."

By mid-2011, Chavez's record stood at 42 victories and 1 draw in 43 fights. Then the powers that be engaged in an ugly sleight of hand.

Martinez was the WBC middleweight champion by virtue of his victory over Kelly Pavlik and a brutal one-punch knockout of Paul Williams. But Chavez is the godson of WBC president Jose Sulaiman, whose ego and love of sanctioning fees knows no bounds. In undue course, Martinez was stripped of his title and a WBC "world championship" bout was arranged between Chavez and Sebastian Zbik with the understanding that the winner would fight Martinez.

Except after Chavez beat Zbik, he refused to fight Martinez. Instead, he defended his belt in succession against Peter Manfredo Jr, Marco Antonio Rubio, and Andy Lee.

"Of course, Chavez was being protected," Top Rank CEO Bob Arum acknowledges. "He didn't know how to fight. I had an obligation to the young man. We weren't going to make the fight until we knew he was capable of beating Martinez. If we had, it would have been like leading him to slaughter, and that's not how we do things at Top Rank."

By the time Martinez vs. Chavez was signed, the fight made far more sense economically than it would have a year earlier. In the preceding fifteen months, Julio had earned respect as a fighter and exceeded the expectations that many knowledgeable boxing people had for him. Martinez was the true middleweight champion, but Chavez had come to be viewed as a credible challenger.

That said; a lot of things stuck in Sergio's craw. He was deeply resentful of the fact that his championship was unfairly taken from him and handed to Chavez. Then there were the economics of the promotion. Instead of worrying that Martinez doesn't speak English, the powers that be might have pushed harder in the past to market him to boxing's huge Spanish-speaking fan base. As it was, Chavez had averaged more than 1,600,000 viewers for his three previous fights on HBO, while Sergio had averaged slightly under 1,100,000. Chavez-Martinez was a pay-per-view promotion. That put Top Rank and Julio in the driver's seat.

Chavez got top billing in the promotion. Worse; Martinez and his promoter, Lou DiBella, were on the short end of a 60–40 purse split.

Martinez is not a trash-talker. Over the years, he had steadfastly avoided demeaning opponents. The build-up to Chavez-Martinez was something different.

"I've known Sergio for a long time," Sampson Lewkowicz (Sergio's manager) said. "I've never seen him this motivated or this angry. He has always treated his opponents with respect. But he feels that something was stolen from him and given to Chavez and that Chavez let it happen."

The trash-talking began on the kick-off media tour. It continued on HBO's *Face Off* and tele-conference calls to promote the fight. Among the thoughts that Martinez offered were:

★ "Chavez has been hiding in the hen house. Now it's time for the chicken to come out. The chicken will go out on its plate. I will take all the feathers off the skin of Chavez Jr."

★ "I do not respect Chavez as a champion. The only reason he is called a champion is because of his last name and who his father is. You have certain duties as a champion. You must defend your title against the best and never take the easy road. Chavez was supposed to fight me for two years, but he kept avoiding the fight. A victory for me would be justice because Chavez is a lie."

★ "Take a picture of him now because, after the fight, you will not recognize him. I will really beat him up. He won't be eating solid food with the few teeth remaining after I get through with him. The judges can be present, but I won't give them too much work to do."

★ "Some ask me why I antagonize Chavez Jr. I'm not insulting him. I'm just saying what will happen. I'm telling the truth."

Then there were the direct verbal exchanges between the two men. Chavez was expected to enter the ring on fight night with a significant weight advantage:

Martinez: "If he weighs twenty pounds more than me, I'll have a bigger target to hit."

Chavez: "My size will be important. But I am not relying on my weight to win the fight. It will be my boxing and my intelligence."

Martinez: "So you are lost, then. How are you going to catch me, Julio?"

Chavez: "The ring is a square like this [pointing to the table.] You can't get out."

Martinez: "Neither can you. I hope your corner protects you. I hope the referee protects you. I hope the doctor protects you. Because I am going to hurt you. I will probably make you retire from boxing because I'm going to beat you up. You're living in a delusion based on your father. When will you start being your own person, not just the son of so and so?"

Chavez: "I will never stop being my father's son."

Martinez: "Of course not. But once you're in the ring, it will be just you alone, and not with your father."

Shortly before the July 12 kick-off press conference in New York, the fighters posed on the second floor of the Edison Ballroom for photographer David Drebin in conjunction with the pay-per-view promotional campaign. For almost an hour, they stood under bright lights, wearing only their shoes, socks, and boxing trunks. A championship belt was their sole prop. From time to time, a photographer's assistant sprayed water on them to simulate perspiration and give them a glow. There were staredowns, fistic poses, smiles, and glares on command.

It's natural time at a time like this for a fighter to measure his foe.

"What are you learning about Chavez?" Martinez was asked.

"I'm not learning anything," Sergio answered. "I'm just having fun."

Chavez was having less fun.

"He has been talking a lot of bullshit," Julio told the media after the press conference began. "His ego is too big. On September 15, all that bullshit he's been talking, he's going to have to eat it."

Later, in a more pensive mood, Chavez added, "It's always the same story. They don't give me credit. I will always be criticized for being seen as riding on my father's coattails and I have learned to live with it. I will let my record speak for itself on whether I should be taken seriously or not. I've been sitting them down with the facts, one by one. He's just the next one."

There was a buzz in the media center at The Wynn in Las Vegas during fight week. Chavez-Martinez was a fight that fans wanted to see; not one that was being force-fed to them. There was no opponent that boxing aficionados preferred either man to fight. Stylistically, the match-up all but guaranteed excitement.

By Tuesday of fight week, the Thomas and Mack Center (where the bout would take place) was sold out, guaranteeing a live gate of $3,052,475. Each fighter seemed confident as the week progressed. Julio sat through the obligatory media interviews and appeared to be on an even keel; concerned with the level of the challenge in front of him but ready to face it. Chavez-Martinez would be the first time in his career that he'd entered the ring as an underdog. But Freddie Roach (Julio's trainer) said that the issue hadn't come up in conversation between them.

Meanwhile, Martinez continued to be openly disdainful of his foe. Part of that was sincerely felt scorn and anger. Part of it was designed to get into Julio's head and raise self-doubts by sending the message, "Don't enter the ring with the confidence of a champion because you are not a champion."

"I want to fight the best, not like Junior," Martinez said. "He hasn't fought anyone who ranks in the top one hundred pound-for-pound. He has shown progress in his fights since he won the belt. That will make our fight better, but I will still knock him out."

Three days before the fight, at the final pre-fight press conference, Sergio threatened to "break Julio's face in a thousand times."

That brought an angry response from Chavez. Earlier in the week, Julio had declared, "Sergio says a lot of things about me that are not true.

He is an ignorant person and a snob. He is underestimating me, both as a person and as a boxer. He will pay for it in the ring."

Now, looking directly at his tormentor, Chavez declared, "I'm going to send you into retirement on a stretcher."

The following day, Martinez was in a reflective mood. He receives several hundred text messages a day. Sitting in his suite at The Wynn, he was answering them as he spoke.

"Chavez seems like a nice guy," Sergio said. "I don't hate him. Maybe, after the fight, we can be friends. But now there is animosity between us because he stood back and allowed a shameful thing to happen. I respect every fighter. It takes courage to enter a boxing ring. But I cannot respect Chavez as a champion because he didn't earn his title. The belt was taken away from me and given to him outside the ring. I will take it back inside the ring. That is where a true champion gets his title."

The odds favored Martinez by a 7-to-4 margin. The assumption was that his southpaw stance and feints would give Chavez trouble; that Julio had never been hit as hard as Sergio would hit him; that Chavez would be unable to adjust during the course of the fight from Plan A to Plan B; that Martinez was the hungrier fighter.

"Chavez is very strong and durable." Sergio said as he texted. "He has become more mature as a fighter and learned how to control distances. But nothing about him as a fighter worries me. He has a good body shot, a good chin, and a lot of bad habits. He is taller than me, but that was true also of Kelly Pavlik, Paul Williams, and Sergeiy Dzinziruk. He can weigh whatever he wants on the night of the fight. Kelly Pavlik was much bigger than me. My speed, movement, and intelligence in the ring will be my advantage. I'm very patient. I will wait to do what I have to do, find the right distance, feel the tempo of the fight, and control him."

Chavez's training regimen was also a factor for those who thought that Martinez would win the fight.

Rather than train at Freddie Roach's Wild Card Gym in Hollywood, Julio had insisted that he and Roach relocate to the Top Rank gym in Las Vegas. Freddie agreed. Then Julio upped the ante, demanding that they train at the hours he wanted and, after that, missing a half-dozen training sessions. There were also times when Roach was called upon to make "house calls" and train Chavez in the living room of the mansion that Top Rank had rented for him.

"We've had an unusual training camp," Freddie conceded. "Julio works when he wants to. As long as we get the work done, I'm happy. Put me wherever and I'll do my job. But it does bother me a bit."

Two days before the fight, Roach elaborated on that "bit." He was exhausted, having worked with Chavez from one until four o'clock that morning.

"The worst thing in the world for me is to wait, not knowing," Freddie said. "Julio doesn't want to train during the day, so we plan to do it at night. Eight o'clock . . . Nine o'clock . . . I'm waiting and he's sleeping. And of course, the guys in camp won't wake him up because they're afraid he'll fire them if they do. Then I get a call. Julio is on his way. Once I get the call, I'm fine. Until then, it drives me crazy. I sit there, thinking of the best way to kill myself."

"Maybe he needs the sleep," Roach continued. "I get more out of him in the gym when he's rested. But we're in the gym half the time, and half the time we're in the living room of the house he's staying in. We move the couches and we have imaginary ropes. There's a reason fighters train in the gym and not in someone's living room. For strategy, we have to be in the gym. It was different with Julio before he won a championship. Until then, he did everything I asked him to."

"What would Eddie Futch [Roach's mentor] do in this situation?" Freddie was asked.

"He'd quit. He wouldn't put up with it."

"Why do you stay?"

"The father and Top Rank asked me to," Roach answered. "It's partly out of respect for them. And it's a different world today from the way things used to be. I can get Julio ready this way, but it's harder for me to get him there. I don't know. When this fight is over, I'll have some thinking to do."

It's axiomatic that, if a fighter doesn't give one hundred percent in training, he won't be at one hundred percent during a fight. Still, Roach was optimistic regarding his fighter's chances on Saturday night.

"Sergio is a great athlete and his speed will be hard to deal with," the trainer acknowledged. "He has faster feet and faster hands than Julio and will dictate whether it's a war or a boxing match. But we're just starting to see how good Julio can be. He fought the best fight of his life in his last fight [against Andy Lee] and he's getting better all the time. The time is right now for him to fight Martinez. We'll deal with whatever Sergio brings."

Chavez echoed those thoughts, saying, "I've been working while Martinez has been talking. He said I wasn't at his level. But I've worked very hard to get to his level."

And Bob Arum put his two cents in, declaring, "Martinez is going to take body shots like he never felt before."

The biggest worry some Martinez partisans had was that Sergio's disdain for Chavez was such that he wouldn't fight smart and might take unnecessary chances in the ring.

Gene Tunney once posited, "There is nothing more dangerous for a boxer than to underestimate his opponent." Lou DiBella sounded a comparable theme, referencing Sergio's trashtalking and noting, "Whenever you see a guy act differently than he usually does, you worry a bit."

More significantly, Martinez is thirty-seven years old with a lot of wear and tear on his body. There had been no "easy" fights for a long time. Throw out his perfect one-punch knockout of Paul Williams, and he has looked like a gifted but vulnerable fighter.

Chavez, clearly, had room for improvement over past performances. Moreover, despite his unconventional training schedule, he appeared to be in excellent condition. After struggling to make weight for recent fights, Julio weighed-in for his confrontation with Martinez at 158 pounds; two pounds under the middleweight limit and one pound less than Sergio.

A prizefight is about two men trying to beat each other up. Neutralize an opponent's offensive arsenal; penetrate his defense to do damage; and protect yourself at all times. The greatest practitioners of the art of boxing are known as "champions."

Chavez wanted recognition as a true champion. But wouldn't get it unless and until he beat Martinez. Both men knew that.

★   ★   ★

Sergio Martinez arrived at his dressing room at the Thomas and Mack Center on September 15 at 5:30 PM. Red-cushioned folding metal chairs ringed the room. The walls were cream-colored cinderblock. The three men and one woman who would be in Martinez's corner during the fight were with him: trainer and chief second Pablo Sarmiento, Naazim Richardson, Dr. Roger Anderson (Sergio's cutman), and physical therapist Raquel Bordons.

Bordons is a doctor who teaches and practices physical therapy in Spain. She had been in Martinez's camp for the final few days prior to his two most recent victories. This time, she'd been summoned ten days before the fight to deal with a slight muscle tear on the upper-left side of Sergio's ribcage. The injury was painful and interfered with his breathing.

Sebastian Martinez (Sergio's brother), Miguel Depablos (a friend), and Nathan Lewkowicz (Sampson Lewkowicz's son) rounded out the group.

At HBO's request, Martinez went next-door to be weighed on "the unofficial HBO scale." Chavez refused a similar request. Sergio had gained eight pounds since the weigh-in. The assumption was that Julio would enter the ring at close to 180.

Returning to his dressing room, Martinez took a smart phone from his pocket and began texting. Normally, he listens to music in the hours before a fight. But the speakers he'd brought with him weren't working. The next few hours were spent talking quietly with members of his team, communicating electronically with well wishers, and tending to the rituals of boxing. For much of the time, Bordons massaged his upper body.

Nathan Lewkowicz went next-door to wish Matthew Macklin (Sergio's most recent opponent) well in an undercard bout that he'd be fighting against Joachim Alcine. He returned with a prize. Matthew had offered his speakers to Team Martinez.

Soon, Latin rap sounded in Sergio's dressing room.

Macklin and Alcine appeared on a large flat-screen television mounted on the wall at one end of the room. Their encounter was brief. Macklin stopped Alcine in the first round.

"I am happy for him," Sergio said. "I like Matthew. Tonight he is my friend."

Referee Tony Weeks came into the room to give Sergio his pre-fight instructions. The Martinez camp was comfortable with Weeks, who has a reputation for being even-handed and competent. That was particularly important here, since Chavez was perceived as "the house fighter."

Macklin entered the dressing room, fresh from his ring triumph.

Sergio's face lit up. "Matthew!" he exclaimed.

The two men embraced.

Macklin offered a quick "good luck" and left.

Martinez began moving slowly around the room in rhythm with the music. Then he lay down on the industrial gray carpet. Bordons stretched his legs and massaged his upper body. When she was done, Sergio rose and moved around the room again; this time, jabbing and shadow-boxing.

At eight o'clock, Sarmiento gloved Martinez up.

Sergio hit the pads with Pablo for the equivalent of three rounds with a minute between each segment.

Dr. Anderson greased Martinez down.

Bordons massaged Sergio's upper body one last time.

Sarmiento helped the fighter into his ring jacket.

One consideration to be factored into determining whether a fighter will win or lose is whether he really wants to be in the ring that night.

Sergio had the fight he wanted for the largest payday of his career. There was no place on earth that he would rather be.

The atmosphere was electric inside the arena. It was a pro-Chavez crowd, but Martinez had his followers.

Prior to the bout, Roach had cautioned, "I've told Julio again and again, 'You can't just follow Martinez around the ring. If you do, you'll walk into a left hand. You have to cut the ring off.' Julio doesn't miss a beat in the gym. In the gym, he has the strategy down perfectly based on the way Martinez moves. But the gym and the fight are two different places."

"And another thing," Roach continued, "We've watched the tape of Sergio's fight against Pavlik a lot. He took some of the middle rounds off. Julio can't let him rest. When Sergio tries to rest, Julio has to make him fight."

Chavez had echoed that theme, saying, "I have to stay on top of him all night long; don't give him room to move or time to think."

But on fight night, those plans didn't come to fruition.

Chavez fought cautiously in the early going, allowing Martinez to circle, dart in and out, and control the distance between them. Also, Sergio threw punches—a lot of punches, mostly jabs and straight lefthands—that landed consistently. His jab, in particular, discouraged Julio from coming forward aggressively. When Chavez did manage to work his way inside, rather than tie him up. Martinez drove him off with punches or pushed him back with the superior strength of his legs and upper body.

In round three, a left uppercut opened a cut inside Chavez's mouth. By round five, the skin around his left eye was discolored and swollen. Round six saw him bleeding from the nose.

Round after round, Martinez pot-shotted his opponent and rested when he wanted to. The only difference between one round and the next was that Chavez got beaten up more badly in some rounds than others. The fight had the look of a matador versus an overmatched bull.

There were times when Sergio chose to trade punches. Almost always on those occasions, he got the better of the action. Chavez showed a good chin but not much more. He might have made a greater effort to take the play away from Martinez. But that's easier said than done when an adversary is getting off first and throwing seventy-five punches a round. Julio simply couldn't solve the puzzle in front of him.

In the late going, Martinez was standing in the center of the ring at the start of each round, while Chavez was slow to get off his stool. After round nine, Roach threatened to stop the fight if his charge didn't show him something in the next three minutes that indicated he could win.

But the boxing lesson continued with Martinez circling, jabbing, getting off first.

A clash of heads in round ten opened a gash on Sergio's scalp to go with a cut above his left eye. But Chavez looked far worse for wear than Martinez.

In round eleven, Julio managed to corner his foe on several occasions. But each time, Sergio's punches drove him off.

Going into the final round, Martinez had outlanded Chavez by a 314-to-141 margin. The fight was a shutout on two of the judges' scorecards with Julio winning a solitary round on the third. Chavez could have won the last stanza 10–0 and it wouldn't have mattered.

Then the matador got gored.

Chavez started slowly in round twelve, moving forward with his hands held high. His left eye was swollen shut. His right eye was ringed by abrasions and his lips were puffy.

Martinez kept circling, jabbing. Twenty-eight seconds elapsed before Julio threw his first punch of the round, a tentative stay-away-from-me right hand. Ten seconds later, he offered a meaningless jab. Both punches missed.

One minute into round twelve, Chavez had thrown three punches and landed none. Then he stepped up the pace and forced Martinez against the ropes. With 1:28 left, Julio scored with a sharp left hook up top that hurt Sergio. Two more hooks landed flush.

Suddenly, with 1:23 left in the fight, Martinez was on the canvas and in trouble.

There was pandemonium in the arena. For Martinez, that "pandemonium," translated in classic Greek, was "the region of all demons."

Getting up off the floor comes from pride and a fighter not wanting to go back to that place in his life where he came from.

Sergio crawled to the ropes and lifted himself up at the count of six.

Referee Tony Weeks beckoned Chavez in. Julio had seventy seconds to finish the job. Those seventy seconds showed why many people (this writer included) feel that boxing at its best is the greatest sport of all.

Chavez now loomed very large in front of Martinez, and the ring seemed very small.

Julio went for broke. Sergio, too dazed and weak to tie Chavez up and with his legs too unsteady to move out of danger, hurled punches back at his foe.

With one minute left in the fight, Martinez tried to clinch and Julio dismissively threw him to the canvas. Sergio staggered to his feet. Weeks, appropriately, chose not to give him extra time to recover and ordered that the action resume immediately without wiping Sergio's gloves.

Fifty two seconds remained. But now, Chavez too was exhausted.

At the final bell, both fighters knew that Martinez had won.

In the dressing room after the fight, Martinez and Raquel Bordons embraced; then broke down in tears. During the fight, she had worked on him in the corner after round four and again after round seven.

"Without you, this wouldn't have been possible," Sergio told her.

Martinez had bruises beneath each eye. Two staples would be needed to close the gash on his scalp. Five stitches were necessitated by the cut above his left eye. He'd also suffered a hairline fracture of his left hand (most likely in round four) and torn ligaments in his right knee (when knocked down in the final round).

Naazim Richardson stood in a corner of the dressing room, observing the scene.

"The thing that made Sergio win is the thing that made him almost lose," Richardson offered. "When Chavez got in close, Sergio drove him off with punches instead of tying him up. That slowed Chavez down, but it also meant that Sergio was more likely to get hit if Chavez punched with him."

Naazim paused for a moment, then noted, "Probably, in the gym they aren't allowed to hit Chavez too hard. So when Sergio hit him hard, it played with his mind and slowed him down."

As for Chavez, regardless of what his critics said, he'd salvaged his honor in the final round.

"It is an important experience for my life," Julio told the media at the post-fight press conference. "In life, you lose and you win. But I lost with dignity and I tried my best."

The unanswered question, of course, is, "Would Julio have won if he'd trained more diligently and fought more aggressively in the early rounds?"

A rematch to answer that question is in order. Chavez-Martinez caught fire as a promotion in the final two weeks. When the fight was signed, there was a projection of 300,000 pay-per-view buys. Based on early reports, that number is now 475,000.

Boxing has a new rivalry.

It should also be noted that Tony Weeks did an exemplary job of refereeing Chavez-Martinez. He let the fighters fight, cautioned them when appropriate, and most importantly, handled the situation correctly when Sergio went down.

During round twelve, a lot of people had flashbacks to March 17, 1990, when Julio Cesar Chavez Sr, trailing badly on the judges' scorecards, scored an improbable twelfth-round stoppage over Meldrick Taylor. On that night in Las Vegas, referee Richard Steele halted the action after the first knockdown of the fight with the fighters on opposite sides of the ring and only two seconds left on the clock. A lot of people felt that Steele had a pro-Chavez agenda.

The only agenda that Weeks evinced in Chavez-Martinez was to do his job as fairly and competently as possible.

One might also reference Chavez Sr's February 20, 1993, victory over

Greg Haugen in front of a record 132,247 fans in Mexico City. Prior to that bout, Haugen derided Chavez's 84-0 record as having been built against "Tijuana taxi drivers that my mom could whip." After being knocked out in the fifth round, Haugen acknowledged, "They must have been very tough taxi drivers."

At the July 12 kick-off press conference in New York, Chavez derided Martinez for appearing on the Argentinean version of *Dancing with the Stars* and proclaimed, "I think he has found his real profession as a ballerina."

Martinez is one tough ballerina.

I met Paulie Malignaggi several days before his first professional fight and have covered him ever since.

Paulie Malignaggi Won't Go Away

On July 7, 2001, Paulie Malignaggi made his pro debut at Keyspan Park in Brooklyn. Even then, he had a mouth. Two days before the fight, he told Tom Gerbasi, "I'm boxing's next superstar. Paulie Malignaggi is going to make it up the ladder quickly. I'm going to win multiple titles. I'm going to explode on the scene. I'm looking to make a big splash. And once you see me, I'm going to be here for a while."

Paulie's opponent that night was Thadeus Parker. It was Parker's first and last fight as a pro.

"I was real nervous before the fight," Malignaggi remembers. "Then, in the ring when the referee was giving us instructions, I looked into Parker's eyes and saw that he didn't want to be there either. I stopped him in the first round, which, let's be honest, hasn't happened for me too many times. After that, I showered and walked around the stadium feeling like a celebrity."

That feeling lasted until Paulie arrived at the post-fight party and wasn't allowed in because he was underage.

"Two guys stopped me at the door," he recalls. "They were nice about it but they were like, 'Sorry; you're not twenty-one.' Finally, Dave Itskowitch [who worked for promoter Lou DiBella at the time] got there and convinced them to let me in."

"I've got so many memories of that weekend," Paulie continues. "I remember checking in at the Embassy Suites Hotel in Battery Park the day before the fight. In my whole life, I'd never had anything more than a single room in a hotel. At Embassy Suites, I had a bedroom and small living room, which I thought was the coolest thing in the world. Petey [longtime friend Pete Sferazza] and I picked up two roundcard girls who were checking in at the same time. We saw them a few times afterward, but nothing came of it. On the day of the fight, I went for a walk after lunch and passed the World Trade Center. I thought about going up to the top to see the view. Then I said to myself, 'No; I'm fighting tonight. I should go back to the hotel and get some rest. I'll come back another time. The Twin Towers will always be here.' And you know what happened. Two months later, the Twin Towers were gone."

The preceding paragraphs could serve as a metaphor for Paulie Malignaggi's journey through boxing: Win . . . Get barred at the door . . . Keep fighting . . . Win some more . . . Dreams crumble . . . Don't give up . . . Time moves on.

Paulie isn't one of the kids anymore. He has been fighting professionally for eleven years and will be thirty-two years old in November.

Malignaggi has style. What he doesn't have is a one-punch equalizer. His record shows seven knockouts in 36 pro fights. That means he builds his victories by avoiding firefights and adding up the points round-by-round-by-round.

Steve Kim writes, "It can be argued very easily that Malignaggi's personality is more entertaining than most of his prizefights. Not only does he have the gift of jab but the gift of gab."

Other observers have been less kind.

"It's frustrating to give so much of myself in so many ways," Paulie says. "And then people who have never boxed a round in their life sit there and criticize me, like they're giving me a grade in school. Boxing isn't a report card. Boxing is life and death."

On June 10, 2006, after winning his first twenty-one fights, Malignaggi went into the lion's den to face a prime Miguel Cotto at Madison Square Garden on the eve of New York's annual Puerto Rican Day Parade.

Anthony Catanzaro (Paulie's business advisor and friend), recalls, "In the dressing room before the fight, we could hear the roars. And we knew it was not our crowd. Those people didn't just want Cotto to win. They wanted Paulie's blood."

They got it.

Malignaggi fought valiantly, winning four out of twelve rounds on two of the judges' scorecards and five on the third. But he suffered a brutal beating in the process.

"I was in the hospital afterward with a fractured orbital bone," Paulie says of that fight. "I had surgery on my face. People watch a fight and, when it's over, they turn off the TV and go to bed. The next day, they're out doing whatever they want to do. My whole life changed after that fight. I spent the whole summer recuperating."

A lot of people wrote Malignaggi off after he lost to Cotto. Not many fighters come back from a beating like that and are as good as they were before.

"Sometimes you get humbled and come back stronger," Paulie says.

One year later, on June 16, 2007, Malignaggi crafted a twelve-round shutout against Lovemore Ndou to capture the IBF 140-pound crown. It was his shining moment in boxing. Thereafter, he had two successful title defenses before being stopped by Ricky Hatton in the eleventh round. His record now shows four losses, each of them to a world champion (Cotto, Hatton, Juan Diaz, and Amir Khan).

On three occasions, Paulie's career has been sidetracked by a broken hand. He has permanent nerve damage in his face, a residue of the Cotto fight.

"Pain is temporary," he says. "Pride is forever."

Through it all, Malignaggi has kept fighting.

"Boxing is like a drug or a bad girlfriend," he told Tom Gerbasi. "Sometimes you get hooked and you realize that maybe it's a problem. But at the same time, the high you get off it is so good that you just keep coming back. There's nothing like the roar of the crowd in the middle of that violent atmosphere and being in a fight. It's a getaway from reality and there's nothing like the rush of adrenalin."

On April 29, 2012, Paulie traveled to Ukraine and dethroned WBA 147-pound title holder Vyacheslav Senchenko in the ninth-round. Anyone who thinks that boxing's belts don't matter should think again. Beating Senchenko didn't make Malignaggi more marketable. But beating Senchenko for the WBA welterweight title did.

On October 20, 2012, Paulie's journey through the sweet science brought him back to Brooklyn. The site was Barclay's Center, the recently opened state-of-the-art arena that's home to the NBA Brooklyn Nets. His opponent was Pablo Cesar Cano of Mexico (26-1-1 with 20 KOs).

On August 5, 1931, "Slapsie" Maxie Rosenbloom (nicknamed for his lack of punching power—nineteen knockouts in 298 pro fights) defended his light-heavyweight title by outpointing Jimmy Slattery at Ebbetts Field.

Until the October 20 card at Barclays, Rosenbloom-Slattery held the distinction of being the last world championship fight in Brooklyn.

That said; Brooklyn has a rich boxing tradition.

Barclays, Golden Boy (which promoted the October 20 show), and Showtime (which televised it) were quick to point out that there had been thirty-seven previous world title fights in Brooklyn. Heavyweight champions Floyd Patterson, Michael Moorer, Mike Tyson, Shannon Briggs, and Riddick Bowe were born in the borough. James J. Jeffries knocked out Bob Fitzsimmons at the Coney Island Athletic Club in 1899 to seize the heavyweight crown. John L. Sullivan, Joe Gans, Sugar Ray Robinson, Benny Leonard, Harry Greb, Tony Canzoneri, Sandy Saddler, Jake LaMotta, Abe Attell, Terry McGovern, Battling Nelson, and Tommy Loughran all fought in Brooklyn.

The October 20 card was advertised as featuring four "world championship" fights, which enabled each of the four major sanctioning bodies to collect a sanctioning fee. In addition to Malignaggi-Cano, there was Danny Garcia vs. Erik Morales (WBC-WBA, 140 pounds), Hassan N'Dam vs. Peter Quillin (WBO, 160 pounds), and Randall Bailey vs. Devon Alexander (IBF, 147, pounds).

Also, the "A" side of the undercard was heavy with Brooklyn fighters. That included Danny Jacobs (now making a heroic comeback from cancer); Luis Collazo (a former world champion who'd been plagued by lifestyle issues while compiling a 5-and-4 record over the previous seven years); Dmitriy Salita (a nice man, who has been marketed largely on the basis of his being an Orthodox Jew); Eddie Gomez (a talented but untested prospect from the Bronx); and Boyd Melson (a thirty-one-year-old West Point graduate who's as good as he's going to get).

Malignaggi-Cano shaped up as the most competitive championship bout of the night. Ultimately, it became a non-title contest, when Pablo failed to make weight, tipping the scales at 147.8 pounds. There was talk of cancellation. But Cano agreed to give $50,000 of his $150,000 purse to Malignaggi (raising Paulie's stake to $400,000) and was required to weigh in again at 9:30 on Saturday morning at not more than 157 pounds.

The main event, Garcia vs. Morales, should have been cancelled.

There was a time when Morales could beat the best. No more. He has now had eleven fights in the past seven-and-a-half years and lost seven of them. At the August 30 kick-off press conference at the Marriott Hotel in Brooklyn, El Terrible looked terrible. His face was puffy and he was clearly overweight. Not just overweight for a fighter. Overweight. At the final pre-fight press conference, he looked old, tired, and beaten up. The betting odds ran as high as 10 to 1 against him.

Worse, two days before the fight, word leaked out that Morales had tested positive for clenbuterol. Twice.

The powers that be tried to put a good face on things. The fact that this was the first fight card at Barclays Center gave it a certain buzz. At the final pre-fight press conference, Oscar De La Hoya told the assembled media that tickets were selling like hotcakes and people had to act fast to get them while supplies lasted. Earlier in the day, Barclays had posted an announcement on its website stating that the first 250 Brooklyn residents with valid IDs who went to the box office between 10:00 AM and 6:00 PM on Thursday or Friday would be given four complimentary tickets.

Giving away tickets for a fight is a pretty good indication that demand is lukewarm. Giving away four tickets per person is a pretty good indication that demand is frigid.

With regard to the fight itself, Paulie voiced confidence throughout the proceedings.

"I know what it's like to be young and motivated and have your whole future ahead of you," he said of his opponent. "I was twenty-three years old one time too. When you're young and the dream is in front of you, you can taste it every time you get in the ring. But Cano's future on Saturday night won't be what he wants it to be."

As for fighting in Brooklyn, Paulie declared, "Every fighter wants to have a big fight in his home town. All this talk about Brooklyn is good marketing, but it's also heartfelt. When I was a kid, I used to dream about fighting at Madison Square Garden. But that's because there wasn't a showcase arena in Brooklyn. Now that they've got Barclays Center, this is where I want to be."

Still, the experience was bittersweet. The October 20 fight posters featured photos of Garcia and Morales, not Malignaggi. In Paulie's fights against Cotto, Hatton, and Khan (his biggest previous outings), he'd been the "B" side of the promotion. This time, he wasn't even in the main event.

★　★　★

Malignaggi arrived at his dressing room on fight night at 7:10 PM. Trainer Eric Brown, Anthony Catanzaro, Umberto Malignaggi (Paulie's brother), and Pete Sferazza were with him. Over the next few hours, Steve Bash (Paulie's attorney), Zach Wohlman (a sparring partner and friend), and Victor Perrone (another friend) would join him.

The room was twelve-feet-square with a mirrored wall and Formica counter that extended the full length of the enclosure. There were a half-dozen chairs and no lockers.

Paulie put on his boxing shoes and began shadow-boxing in front of the mirror. An earpiece ran from an iPod in his warm-up jacket to his ear. Hip-hop, Lloyd Banks, "Shock the World." After shadow-boxing for several minutes, he sat on the floor with his back to the wall and did some stretching exercises.

Golden Boy publicist Monica Sears entered and checked out Paulie's hair.

"I thought you said you were going to have a red streak."

"Next time," he told her. "If they cut down the interviews and all the other promotional stuff I have to do, I'll have time to do my hair."

At 7:55, Eric Brown began wrapping Paulie's hands. Normally, that would come later in the evening. But Brown also trains Peter Quillin, who'd be fighting Hassan N'Dam in the second Showtime fight of the night. Paulie was in the third. The meant adjusting normal routines and, for Eric, moving back and forth between dressing rooms.

"I know how much pressure there is when you fight for the title for the first time," Malignaggi had told the trainer earlier in the week. "Do what you have to do with Peter. I've been here before. I know what I have to do. Peter needs all the support he can get."

At 8:15, the first *Showtime* bout began; Randall Bailey vs. Devon Alexander. Bailey, the beltholder, was so disrespected that his name had been listed after Alexander's in pre-fight promotional material. He was a 6-to-1 underdog.

Paulie watched the action on a large flat-screen television mounted on the wall.

"Randall doesn't want to jab," Paulie told Umberto. "Randall doesn't want to throw combinations. All Randall wants to do is to land that one big righthand. But Randall doesn't have legs. Devon will box him smart."

The fight was painfully slow, with Alexander avoiding exchanges whenever possible en route to a unanimous decision triumph. Bailey set a CompuBox record for futility, landing only forty-five punches in twelve rounds.

At 9:15, Eddie Claudio (who would be refereeing N'Dam vs. Quillin appeared on the screen.

"Eddie refereed my first amateur fight in the Golden Gloves," Paulie noted. "That was a long time ago."

N'Dam-Quillin began. It was styled as a "championship" fight, although each man has found it hard to crack the top-ten in some middleweight rankings.

Paulie shadow-boxed on and off. When he sat, it was in relative isolation with the iPod running to his ear.

N'Dam had more heart than skill. Quillin knocked him down six times to prevail on each judge's scorecard.

In back-to-back fights, two belts had changed hands.

Eric Brown returned. At 10:15, he and Paulie began working the pads.

"You're the champ," the trainer exhorted. "Make him understand that. Make him swallow that jab. Make him gag on that jab. It's your night, baby. You're at home now. Go out and show Brooklyn what they've been missing."

When Paulie entered the ring, he conjured up images of the season's first Christmas tree. A red-white-and-green robe; red-and-white shoes with green laces; red-white-and-green tassels; and red-white-and-green trunks with red-white-and-green fringe (a lot of it).

Round one was a strategic feeling-out stanza. In round two, Malignaggi opened up a cut on Cano's left eyebrow and appeared to be where he wanted to be.

But at age thirty-two, Paulie isn't as slick as he once was. When he was young, he had fast hands, quick reflexes, good legs, a great boxing brain, and heart. Now he has slower hands, diminished reflexes, aging legs, a great boxing brain, and heart.

For most of the fight, Cano was the aggressor. He landed his share of low blows. But he also did damage with legitimate body shots and solid right hands up top. Paulie failed to jab effectively at times, particularly in the second half of the bout. He also got hit more often and with cleaner punches than a fighter of Pablo's caliber would have hit him with several years ago. And he didn't make Cano pay when Pablo missed.

By the middle rounds, Malignaggi looked tired. From that point on, he was often in strategic retreat. By round nine, Cano's body work was taking a toll. In round eleven, Pablo threw a righthand. It was the type of punch that a young Malignaggi would have seen coming and slipped. This one landed. For only the second time in his career, Paulie went down. He was on his feet quickly. But for many observers, the knockdown sealed the deal.

When it was over, Glenn Feldman scored the contest 118–109 for Cano. Judges Tom Miller and Nelson Vazquez gave Malignaggi the nod by a 114–113 margin.

Bobby Hunter of Fight Score Collector compiled the cards of twenty-nine members of the media who watched the bout. They favored Cano by a 19-to-8 margin with 2 draws. Of the eight media personnel who thought Malignaggi won, none gave him the nod by more than a single point.

According to CompuBox, Pablo outlanded Paulie 262 to 217 with a 165-to-57 edge in power punches. This writer scored the fight for Cano.

In the dressing room after the fight, Team Malignaggi was unanimous in voicing the view that the decision in Paulie's favor was well-deserved. But the evening's happenings had left their mark. There were ugly welts on Paulie's upper body. His face was bruised with purple blotches beneath each eye. Dried blood trickled down from a cut beneath his left eye.

Paulie took off his trunks and lay down on his back in a corner of the room. Several minutes later, he sat up and leaned against the wall. Pete Sferazza put a makeshift ice-pack on top of Paulie's head and another behind his neck.

"I was tired," Paulie said. "The body punches fucking hurt me. He didn't land the hook much. But he went low a lot and his right hand to the body got through somehow."

"He caught me on the knockdown," Paulie continued. "In the Cotto fight, as I was going down, I said to myself, 'Oh, shit. I'm going down.' It was like that here too. The difference is, this time, I felt I was winning the fight. All I had to do was get up and not get knocked out."

Paulie lay down again

"I need ice on my head but I've got the chills."

Umberto Malignaggi sat beside his brother. The final fight of the evening, Danny Garcia vs. Erik Morales came on the television screen. Paulie sat up and watched the action.

Morales looked lethargic. There was a roll of flesh around his waist. The outcome of the bout was a foregone conclusion from the first seconds of the opening round. Garcia ended matters with a left hook up top in the fourth stanza.

"Yes!" Paulie shouted as Morales hit the canvas. "Fuck that cheater."

So what's next for Malignaggi?

He needs a belt now to be marketable at the level he wants to be at. Fortunately, he still has one. His dream fight is a rematch against Ricky Hatton. It wouldn't be for revenge. Paulie has nothing against Hatton personally. But he wants to set the record straight on a fight that he acknowledges losing but thinks he could and should have won. And the money would be big.

"I could have looked better," Paulie says of his performance against Cano. "I know that. Maybe the way I fought will give Ricky confidence and he'll fight me."

And then?

"I don't plan on fighting much longer," Paulie acknowledges. "The reason I'm still fighting is because I have a lot to prove to myself. I feel like I underachieved during my prime years. I'm a two-time world champion, but I had so many more goals that I set out for myself. When I turned pro, I told myself that I should reach for the stars. I wanted to accomplish things that are almost impossible to accomplish. With goals like that, you're bound to be disappointed. But those goals are what motivate me."

"There are certain things I'll always wish I'd done differently," Paulie continues. "Most people feel that way about their life. But whatever I've done is history, and I can't change it now. I have a lot of goals and not enough time to achieve them. But I'm still hungry and I want to achieve as much as I can before my career is over. When I've retired, maybe I'll appreciate what I've accomplished more than I do now."

Most fighters fall short of their dreams. Then again, so does almost everyone else.

Fighters get old young.

Miguel Cotto Grows Old
at Thirty-Two

Years ago, Patrick Kehoe wrote, "We must be ever vigilant to record the truths and meanings that take place in the boxing ring."

With that in mind, let's take a look at Miguel Cotto's December 1, 2012, outing against Austin Trout at Madison Square Garden.

Cotto has fought with honor as a professional boxer for twelve years. At his best, he could choose between outboxing opponents and mauling them in the trenches. He was always willing to go in tough.

Miguel followed Felix Trinidad as the standard bearer for Puerto Rican boxing. He's soft-spoken with aura of dignity about him. An awareness of the gravity of what he does for a living is etched on his face. The desire for self-improvement through hard work has been a constant in his life. Late in his ring career, Cotto decided to learn English. To have learned it as well as he has at an advanced age is a significant accomplishment.

Cotto-Trout was Miguel's eighth fight at Madison Square Garden, where he has been a profitable franchise for seven years. Team Cotto and Golden Boy (the lead promoter for the fight) were priming Miguel for a big-money outing against Canelo Alvarez in Las Vegas on May 4, 2013. Viewed in that light, the choice of Trout as an opponent was a high-risk low-reward gamble. Austin is the kind of fighter who would always have given Miguel trouble. His 25-and-0 record had been built against limited opposition. But he's a tall elusive southpaw with skills.

Also, Cotto's power hasn't carried well to 154 pounds. Opponents at 140 said that his hook to the body felt like an iron wrecking ball. Opponents at 154 take his punches and return fire.

Fighters rarely say that they aren't as good as they used to be. But at the final pre-fight press conference for Cotto-Trout, Miguel acknowledged, "I'm getting older. Everybody knows it. I just want to be the best myself that I can be."

British promoter Frank Warren once observed, "The knockout punch is about perfect timing. So is matchmaking; picking the right guy at the right time."

Many boxing people believed prior to Cotto-Trout that the selection of Austin as Miguel's opponent was the product of careless matchmaking.

There's a special feel to a night at the fights at Madison Square Garden. But Cotto-Trout never caught on as a must-see promotion. There were 21,239 fans in the arena when Miguel exacted revenge against Antonio Margarito in December 2011. This time, the announced attendance was 13,096 and the atmosphere was far less torrid.

Despite being the fighter with a belt, Trout entered the ring first and was introduced first as well. Then the action began.

During fight week, Miguel had looked older than his thirty-two years. When he got in the ring, he still looked older.

Cotto was the aggressor early in the fight. He knows how to cut off a boxing ring, and he worked the body nicely when he got inside. But for the most part, Trout kept him at bay with good footwork and a stiff jab. By round six, Miguel was visibly tiring. Then he stopped pushing the pace, which allowed Austin equal say in the flow of the fight.

In the second half of the bout, Cotto gave it all he had. He seemed to dig deeper than Trout. But as the Gospel According to St. Matthew recounted in a somewhat different context, Miguel's spirit was willing but his flesh was weak. The reserves of strength simply weren't there.

The scoring of the judges was a lopsided 119–109, 117–111, 117–111 in Trout's favor. Most ringside observers (including this one) thought the fight was closer than that. But one was hard-pressed to find an impartial observer who thought that Miguel had won.

After the fight, Cotto told the media, "I still have boxing in my mind. I just want to rest with my family the rest of the year. I never make excuses. I accept my defeats and I learn from them and I just move forward."

What Miguel should learn from this fight is that it might be time to retire. He's still a capable fighter. There will always be a sanctioning body eager to designate a Miguel Cotto fight as a "world championship" bout (for a sanctioning fee, of course). But he isn't Miguel Cotto in the ring anymore and never will be again.

Cotto is an "old" thirty-two. Twelve years of professional boxing on top of a high-profile amateur career have put considerable wear and tear on his body. The beatings he suffered at the hands of Antonio Margarito and Manny Pacquiao took something out of him, physically and psychologically, that will never be restored. He can fight on as a name opponent in the manner of Shane Mosley, winning some and losing some while taking debilitating blows to the brain. Or he can retire with dignity and look back on his career as a job well done.

Billy Graham, who trained Ricky Hatton from his first pro fight through the glory years of Hatton's career, once said, "The last thing I want for my fighters is longevity. Longevity takes a fighter into dangerous waters."

Miguel Cotto should ask himself, "How much money is enough? How many more blows to the head in the gym and in fights should I take before I say, 'It's over.'"

"If you hang around boxing long enough," Marvelous Marvin Hagler said, "you get what's coming to you."

The End of the Pacquiao Era

Manny Pacquiao and Juan Manuel Marquez have waged one of boxing's great rivalries. Their first three fights, contested over the course of eight-and-a-half years, showcased two elite warriors with speed, intelligence, power, and skill. Neither man was able to dominate the other. They were equal in the ring, both champions.

Pacquiao-Marquez IV is now part of that history. It began with a dramatic ebb and flow. Pacquiao went down hard in round three when Marquez landed an overhand right as Manny was pulling straight back with his hands down. Two rounds later, Juan Manuel's gloves touched the canvas when a straight left caught him flush. That was followed by toe-to-toe action with Pacquiao getting the better of it. After five rounds, all three judges had the Filipino icon ahead by a 47–46 margin.

By round six, Marquez's face was a bloody mess and his nose appeared to be broken. The scene brought back memories of Chuck Wepner walking back to his corner after a particularly hard round against Sonny Liston.

"I can't breathe," Wepner told his manager, Al Braverman. "My nose is broken."

"You got a mouth, don't you?" Braverman responded.

Marquez could breathe through his mouth. And Pacquiao, more than most fighters, is willing to gamble in the ring. Often, that has been his edge. But sooner or later, most gamblers who come to Las Vegas go home losers.

With seconds left in the sixth round, Pacquiao made a fatal mistake. He overcommitted on a careless jab with his head high and his left hand out of position to block a return counter. Marquez smacked him with a vicious righthand. Manny went down face-first, unconscious.

The punch joins other classic blows that the recipient never saw coming.

Gene Fullmer was dominating every facet of his 1957 rematch against Sugar Ray Robinson. Then, in round five, a counter left hook stretched him out on the canvas.

"Up to then, I got to thinking I couldn't be knocked out," Fullmer said afterward. "And all at once, I realized anybody can. It's just got to be at the right place at the right time and you're gone."

Pacquiao was on the giving end of a similar blow when he knocked out Ricky Hatton three years ago. "That's what happens when you don't see a punch coming," Lennox Lewis (who got whacked by Hasim Rahman in South Africa) said of Hatton's demise. "Believe me; I know."

"I got careless," Manny said after regaining consciousness at the close of Pacquiao–Marquez IV. "I never expected that punch."

After the bout, Pacquiao made a precautionary visit to University Medical Center for a CT scan that was negative. Then he returned to his hotel suite and watched a DVD of the fight. According to publicist Fred Sternburg, as the bout unfolded, Manny told those in the room, "Spoiler alert. I don't think you're going to like how this ends."

As for what comes next; the assumption is that Pacquiao will keep fighting. He fought at a world-class level against Marquez. The one-punch knockout was shocking and dramatic, but also an aberration. Manny won't want his career to end on that note. And if the past is prologue, he'll soon need more money.

"Boxing is not a romance. It's a business," Bob Arum (Pacquiao's promoter) has said.

Marquez–Pacquiao V is one of many options for the future. But whatever comes next, The Pacquiao Era appears to be over. Commercially, a touch of "Pacquiao fatigue" has set in. Manny can still sell out the MGM Grand Garden Arena. But this time, he sold it out later than he usually does. Also, Pacquiao has now cobbled together a string of less-than-stellar performances capped by losses to Marquez and Tim Bradley.

Manny isn't a shot fighter. He's still capable of performing at a high level. But in recent outings, he has seemed diminished as a consequence of the natural aging process and, possibly, a loss of commitment and focus in training. One now has to wonder what this brutal one-punch knockout will do to his ability to take a punch?

Some fighters come back from a lights-out experience as good as they were before. Others (like Roy Jones and Jermain Taylor) are never the same again.

Also, in closing, it should be noted that the issue of PED usage hangs over boxing like a black cloud. In the past, there have been allegations with regard to Pacquiao. Marquez's associations and the recent dramatic change in Juan Manuel's physical condition have the appearance of impropriety. If boxing doesn't address this issue seriously now, the black cloud will turn into a deluge.

I interviewed Archie Moore at length in 1989, when I was writing Muhammad Ali: His Life and Times. *As time passes, I'm ever more grateful that I met him.*

Archie Moore Revisited

I

Archie Moore was a self-educated man who brought a philosophical veneer to a hard brutal sport. He's revered today, not for a handful of signature fights but as a symbol of skill, craftsmanship, and boxing genius who persevered in the face of adversity and overwhelming odds.

Moore represents the greatest of boxing's great and also the thousands of faceless fighters who toiled in his time. Late in life, he reminisced, "In the beginning, I fought for ten dollars a fight. Sometimes I was given a promise, nothing more. Guys like me, we were always marching, fighting, marching, fighting. Most of the time, it wasn't much fun."

Moore fought professionally from the 1930s into the 1960s. For years, the *Ring Record Book* listed his first pro fight as a knockout on an undetermined date in 1935 over an opponent named Piano Man Jones (possibly a misnomer for Piano Mover Jones). Boxrec.com and Moore's autobiography (*The Archie Moore Story*) reference his first opponent as one Billy Simms and say that the bout occurred on September 3, 1935.

The Ring Record Book credits Moore with 199 wins (145 KOs), 26 losses (7 KOs by), and 8 draws. Boxrec.com (now a more reliable source) lists 185 wins (131 KOs), 23 losses (7 KOs by), 10 draws, and 1,474 rounds boxed. Those are staggering numbers.

Facts blur when discussing Moore. He was a teller of tales, and even his date of birth is subject to conjecture. His mother said he was born on December 13, 1913. Moore claimed it was three years later. Information in a 1920 census report supports the 1916 date but is not fully dispositive of the matter.

What's known with certainty is that Moore was born in Benoit, Mississippi; the son of Thomas and Lenora Wright. His mother had previously given birth at age fifteen to a daughter named Rachel. Two years later, Archibald Lee Wright was born.

Archie parents separated when was eighteen months old, and he was sent with his sister to St. Louis to live with his aunt and uncle, Cleveland and Willie Pearl Moore. At that time, he later explained, "I became Archie Lee Moore, for it saved many questions put to my aunt when we moved from house to house. Moore is my name, and it is the name my children have."

"I idolized my uncle and wanted to be like him," Moore continued. "And I adore my auntie. Although she never had children of her own, she was a great mother in every sense. She gave us love and affection and taught us all the things a good mother should teach her children."

Moore went to Dumas and Jefferson grade schools and the Lincoln School, an all-black junior and senior high school in St. Louis. He learned the rudiments of boxing on the streets from friends and enemies alike. Then tragedy struck.

Cleveland Moore died as a consequence of injuries suffered during an initiation rite into a fraternal organization. Soon after, Moore's sister, who had married a man named Elihu Williams, died while giving birth to twins. One of the twins, a boy, died four months later. Auntie Willie took the other infant, a girl named June, in and raised her as her own.

Meanwhile, Moore's life was taking a downward turn.

"Moral character is a very pliable thing," he later noted. "It bends to circumstances. After my uncle's death, I began to run wild. I turned to petty thievery for personal monetary reasons. Stealing was such an every-day way of life that it was accepted by all of us. We reasoned that it was a matter of survival, a way of life in tough Depression times. I knew that eventually I would be caught. But the desire to have a little spending money forced me to overlook this."

Moore began by stealing lead pipes and copper wiring out of empty houses and selling the material for scrap. Then he graduated to bolder crimes. He was arrested three times. On the third occasion, a friend named Arthur Knox disconnected the pole from which a streetcar drew electrical power from an overhead power line. The streetcar came to a halt; the motorman got out to put the pole back in place; and Moore ran onto the car to steal the change from the cashbox. Given his previous arrest record, he was sentenced to three years at the Missouri Training School in Booneville. He was fifteen years old.

The reform school was largely self-sustaining. It had a stone quarry, brickyard, orchard, dairy, butcher shop, bake shop, and laundry. In Booneville, Moore later said, he reached a "personal crossroads."

"I had burned the bridge of formal education behind me," he wrote in his autobiography. "I now had a choice of which way to go and what to do. Either I could continue stealing, in which case I knew that I would eventually be caught and sent back to reform school, or prison when I was older; or I could try to get out of the ghetto by pursuit of an honest living."

Moore boxed while in reform school. By his own count, he registered sixteen knockouts in his first year, which gave him a reputation that the other boys respected.

"During my thinking hours, and I had plenty of them," he later reminisced, "I decided to make fighting my career. I determined to learn as much as I could, strengthen myself, and turn pro as soon as I was of age. I was paroled after twenty-two months and made a vow that I would never again do anything that would cause me to be sent back to reform school or jail."

Moore left the Missouri Training School at age seventeen. But as he later recalled, "My boxing aspirations, unfortunately, were all my own. No one shared them. I was seventeen, muscled, and totally without experience in the eyes of the men who made matches or managed fighters."

It was a condition of his parole that Moore get a job. His first employment was as a delivery man for an ice and coal dealer. But he quit after the first day when the dealer shortchanged him for his work. Next he found part-time employment as a household domestic. Then he joined the Civilian Conservation Corps.

The CCC was a federal program that was part of Franklin Roosevelt's "New Deal." Workers (mostly young men at risk) were paid thirty dollars a month, twenty-five of which was sent home to their families. They also received Army-barracks-style room and board.

Moore was assigned to Camp 3760 in Poplar Bluff, Missouri, and worked in the forestry division, cutting down and removing trees so roads could be carved out of the wilderness. He also helped organize a camp boxing team and further developed his own skills.

On September 3, 1935, some CCC workers including Moore attended a professional fight card in Poplar Bluff. In one of the preliminary bouts, a local fighter named Billy Simms fought an opponent who Moore later described as looking "like he had just jumped off a freight train."

"The boy quit in the first round," Moore recalled. "The crowd booed the fight, and Simms made a plea from the ring saying it wasn't his fault. My pals hollered back, 'We got someone to fight you,'"

Moore borrowed a pair of gloves, sneakers, and trunks from the promoter, stepped into the ring, and knocked Simms out. No weights are listed for the bout. What's known is that Moore was five-feet-eleven inches tall and fought his next two bouts the following year at 148 and 145 pounds.

Moore was honorably discharged from the CCC in early 1936 and returned to St. Louis, where worked briefly for the federal Works Progress Administration. Then he began to pursue his ring career in earnest.

The world was different then. Boxing and baseball were America's two national sports. A fighter's trunks were black or white. There were no roundcard girls or ring-walk music. Boxers didn't need a TV date to fight. In fact, there was no television. There were eight weight divisions with one champion in each division. Unlike today, a loss wasn't seen as removing a fighter from title contention. Winning a world championship was akin to becoming a made man.

For years, Moore was forced by circumstances to campaign as a vagabond boxer. Between 1935 and 1937, he compiled a 20-1-2 record, fighting in Missouri, Arkansas, Illinois, Iowa, Oklahoma, Indiana, and Ohio. Then he moved to San Diego, where he won nine fights in a row before returning to St. Louis at the end of 1938. He won five fights in a row in his hometown to bring his record to 33-2-2 before losing a ten-round decision to veteran Teddy Yarosz. After that fight, Ray Arcel (Yarosz's trainer) said of Moore, "He'll be a great fighter a year from now. All he needs is experience."

Moore moved from manager to manager and trainer to trainer during that time, as he would for much of his career. He hustled pool to make ends meet and studied boxing history, reading whatever he could find. After losing to Yarosz, he went west again for eight fights. Then, on January 4, 1940 (three days after marrying Mattie Chapman), he journeyed to Australia on what he later called "my solo honeymoon."

Moore was in Australia for eight months. His marriage failed to survive the separation. Three later marriages also ended in divorce. But he was undefeated in seven fights down under, winning six of them by knockout. There were four more fights in San Diego. Then near-disaster struck.

In February 1941, Moore suffered a perforated ulcer, underwent surgery, and (by his account) was "in a coma for five days, hovering between life and death." Peritonitis set in, extending his hospital stay to thirty-eight days. He later claimed that, during his time in the hospital, his weight dropped from 163 to 108 pounds. Midway though his recovery, he suffered an acute appendicitis. He was out of the ring for eleven months before returning to action on January 28, 1942, with a third-round knockout of Bobby Britt. It was the only recorded bout of Britt's career.

Twenty-two more fights on the west coast followed. Then Moore journeyed east, winning a ten-round decision over Nate Bolden at St. Nicholas Arena in New York. Massachusetts, Maryland, Michigan, New Jersey, Pennsylvania, Connecticut, Oregon, Wisconsin, Colorado, Washington, Washington, DC, Utah, and Florida were added to his itinerary. He also fought in Panama, Argentina, and Uruguay.

One can only begin to imagine what went through Moore's mind as he moved from town to town and fight to fight, winning most, losing some, for over a decade. Late in life, he looked back on what he called "the sad lonely days when hardly anybody knew who Archie Moore was. I was just another name in small print on a fight card; just another black kid spilling his blood to make a few bucks to stay alive in the hope that there were better days ahead. I would fight for short money in little towns. Then, my body still clammy with sweat because the little arena had no showers and I couldn't afford a hotel room, I would ride a dusty dirty bus or freight train to the next town, still hurting and bruised from my last fight. I thought of the filthy rat-and-bug-infested two-bit flophouses I had stayed in; and the cheap starchy foods eaten in crummy restaurants; and I thought of even leaner days when I didn't have a cent in my pocket and

I was so hungry and cold and tired that even the cheap food and dirty flophouses would have been welcome."

The heart of Moore's problem, legendary trainer Eddie Futch noted, was that "Archie was too good for his own good. He was victimized by his talent. No manager wanted to risk the title against him."

Veteran promoter and matchmaker Don Chargin puts Moore's dilemma in further perspective. "If you were a black fighter in those days," Chargin recalls, "the people in charge would tell you that you had to lie down or you didn't work. One reason that Archie fought so many tough black fighters early in his career was that neither guy would have to lie down for the other."

Thus it was that Moore fought twenty fights against Charlie Burley, Eddie Booker, Jack Chase, Lloyd Marshall, Jimmy Bivins, and Ezzard Charles; men he branded along with himself as "the killing row of Negro middleweights." His composite record against them was ten wins, seven losses, and three draws.

In 1945, ten years after Moore's pro debut, he moved up to the light-heavyweight division. "I was eaten with ambition and bitter because I never seemed to get my due as a fighter," he said. But he kept winning, following a simple battle plan.

"When I went into the ring," Moore later recalled, "I kept my thinking calm. I would plan a fight according to my opponent, his abilities, and his style. Every move I made was carefully calculated and planned. Even during the heat of battle, I usually managed to keep my thinking organized and follow my plan."

That plan had a simple foundation.

"A good jab is an absolute must if you want to be a good fighter," Moore explained. "If you can't master a good jab, you might as well give it up. A hard body shot will do more damage than one to the jaw. Try to hit your opponent high on the rib cage. When you do, you will hamper his movements on whichever side you hit him, and then you can work on that side more freely. I know it looks sensational to keep hitting a guy in the face. But believe me; it's body punching that wins fights."

And there was another essential ingredient.

"I've seen many excellent fighters, but the only ones I would bank on would be finishers," Moore declared. "Without that ability, you just aren't cut out to be a fighter. In Dempsey's day, they used to call it the killer instinct."

How good was Moore?

"He was great," Emanuel Steward said shortly before his own untimely death. "Some fighters intimidate opponents with a big punch. Moore intimidated fighters with his skills. He was a thinking fighter, very intelligent and analytical. He was patient. He took his time. There was very little wasted energy or movement. As a fight went on, he'd analyze his opponent, find his weaknesses, and figure out what he had to do to break him down. He was very strong physically, crafty, not particularly fast. He'd slip, parry, throw a stiff up jab, get in close. He was always in range where he could make a move and punch. Then, at just the right moment, he'd let that sneaky hard righthand go and knock his opponent out. He knew how to fight. And he had a lot of heart."

"Moore didn't have the sheer natural ability of guys like Sugar Ray Robinson or Ezzard Charles," trainer Don Turner adds. "And he didn't have the greatest chin in the world. But his defense was so good that he didn't get hit on the chin that much. He was crafty; he was cunning; he was elusive. He could punch and hurt you in a lot of different ways. The physical conditioning for elite fighters today is better than it was when Moore fought. But the technique that fighters had in those days was much better than it is now. Moore knew what he was doing in the ring. He could set you up, tie you up, do whatever he wanted to do. He had more ways to survive than anyone in the business. He could outthink anyone. He had endless determination. And he used everything he had."

Moore added victories over light-heavyweight contenders Holman Williams, Bob Satterfield, and Harold Johnson to his resume. But his championship quest remained unfulfilled.

"I fought many years longer than I should have had to before I got a shot at the title," he later wrote. "I felt like a guy trying to climb a glass mountain. I would climb two steps up and then slide four steps back. I scratched and clawed my way up that glass mountain until I could almost touch the peak with my outstretched fingertips. It was like a bad dream where you're trying to reach something but never can."

On July 24, 1950, Joey Maxim won the world light-heavyweight championship with a tenth round stoppage of Freddie Mills.

"We ducked Moore just like everybody else was doing," Doc Kearns (Maxim's manager) later acknowledged in his autobiography. "He was too smart, too skillful, too experienced, and carried too many blockbusters in his arsenal to take him on before we were forced into it."

Instead, Maxim fought a series of non-title fights, challenged Ezzard Charles unsuccessfully for the heavyweight crown, and prevailed over Sugar Ray Robinson, when Robinson wilted in the 104-degree heat at Yankee Stadium and was unable to come out for the fourteenth round.

Meanwhile, Moore had come to understand that, to force a championship fight, he had to create a public persona and get public opinion on his side.

"When Maxim won the title," Moore later recalled, "I really began to campaign in earnest. Eddie Egan was commissioner of boxing in New York State. I ran into him in the lobby of Madison Square Garden. He had been a great amateur light-heavyweight, and I thought he would be in sympathy with my plea. I approached him and told him who I was and what I wanted. He almost snapped my head off with a surly reply, saying he was a commissioner and not a matchmaker. He swept me aside like a bread crumb on a waiter's tip."

Undeterred, Moore mounted an extensive letter-writing campaign to sportswriters around the country, penning as many as thirty letters a day. Typical of these missives was one sent to Dan Parker of the *New York Mirror*.

Dear Mr. Parker,

Knowing of your unbiased reputation as a top sports writer, I felt I could appeal to you. As the number one contender for the light-heavyweight title held by Joey Maxim, I am avoided by him. He steadfastly refuses to fight me, choosing instead men who are in the second division. In addition to being unfair, this casts a negative light on boxing. Please use your column to tell your readers of the state of affairs in professional boxing.

Sincerely,
Archie Moore.

It was also around this time that Moore began referring to himself as The Mongoose, explaining, "The mongoose is a cagey and fierce animal; so fierce that he will fight the dreaded cobra, depending on technique to combat the cobra's swift and deadly blows. The mongoose is faster and he can feint the cobra out of position by waiting until the very last moment to move, making the cobra miss and miss and miss until he fails to retract effectively. The mongoose then moves in for the kill, seizes the cobra under the throat, and crushes his skull."

In 1951, Robert Christenberry succeeded Egan as chairman of the New York State Athletic Commission. Christenberry was more receptive than Egan had been to Moore's pleas. The National Boxing Association also supported Moore's cause.

More significantly. Moore agreed to retain Doc Kearns as an advisor and pay him a portion of his future earnings in exchange for a title opportunity.

"Doc Kearns is a sentimentalist about money," Archie noted.

And Moore agreed to a bout contract that guaranteed Maxim a $100,000 purse. Given the economics of the situation, that meant Moore would receive virtually nothing. Ultimately, his purse for the fight was eight hundred dollars.

On December 17, 1952, at age thirty-six (or thirty-nine) in his 160th professional fight, Moore finally got the opportunity to fight for a world title.

"It's hard to describe my feelings when I fought Maxim for the championship," he wrote in his autobiography. "In a way, it was almost anti-climactic because, when I received the word that I was to fight him, that was really the climax. I was sure I would win, and yet I wasn't sure. It's like a student who is about to take an important examination. He is confident that he will pass, but he isn't sure because he's not certain what questions will be thrown at him. That was the way I felt about Maxim. I knew I could beat him if I didn't get careless. Any fighter can be knocked out if hit hard enough in the right place, and there was always that possibility against a first-class opponent like Maxim. So while I was sure I would win, I wasn't sure. Anything could happen in a fight."

Maxim-Moore took place in St. Louis. Moore dominated throughout the bout and won a lopsided unanimous decision.

In his dressing room after the fight, Maxim told reporters, "These guys don't grow old. They just get better as they go. Moore is a better fighter than Ray Robinson. That sneaky right hand that he throws is murder. I knew he was good. I thought he would weaken in the late rounds, but he got stronger as the fight went on. Boy, is he tough."

As for the new champion—

"I was happy and proud after beating Maxim," Moore later recalled. "The morning after the fight, I bought the newspapers and sat there grinning like an idiot as I read that Archie Moore was the light-heavyweight champion of the world."

II

"Becoming champion created a new world for me," Archie Moore wrote in his autobiography. "It was tangible proof that I was doing a good job in my chosen profession. It fulfilled a need everybody has—the need to feel important. Winning the championship was also the fulfillment of a dream. And it's nice to have dreams come true."

As champion, Moore married for the fifth time. His new bride was a model named Joan Hardy, whose sister was married to actor Sidney Poitier. The Moore-Hardy union lasted until his death. Together, they had two daughters and three sons.

Meanwhile, Moore's ring career went on. In the fifteen weeks after beating Maxim, he won six over-the-weight non-title fights, including a unanimous decision over heavyweight contender Nino Valdes. On June 24, 1954, he decisioned Maxim in a contractually mandated rematch. That was followed by two over-the-weight non-title bouts in Argentina and a third fight against Maxim.

"For years," Moore later observed, "I couldn't get near Maxim. And now I couldn't get away from him."

That was because Doc Kearns still managed Maxim in addition to having a piece of Moore.

"If it weren't for fight managers," Moore grumbled, "a lot more fighters would have been millionaires."

During this time frame, Moore also began to have trouble making the 175-pound weight limit. That led to some unusual practices.

Moore claimed that he had learned invaluable nutritional secrets from an Aborigine while fighting in Australia in 1940. Being a teller of tales, Archie confided, "I was given a secret recipe by a dying Aborigine under a gum tree in a desert near Wootawoorwoorowwoora. At least, I figured he was dying. He looked mighty sick. And he made me promise I would never tell the secret of this semi-vanishing oil until he died. Well, how do I know he's dead? I ain't taking no chances."

Speaking of the Aborigines on another occasion, Moore maintained, "They were all quite lean and possessed tremendous stamina. They attributed this to the fact that they would chew on strips of meat, chewing until the last bit of juice had been extracted. This would nourish them and keep up their strength without adding any weight. They never swallowed the bulk of the meat from which they had extracted the juice. Of course, this chewing meat without swallowing it is not an easy thing to do. It takes great control to keep from swallowing a delicious piece of meat instead of just chewing on it and swallowing the juices before spitting out the bulk."

Publicist Bill Caplan, who spent time with Moore, says simply, "It wasn't pleasant eating with Archie when he was trying to make weight. He'd chew the meat for the juice and spit the rest out on his plate. No napkin or anything like that. Just chew, spit, chew, spit."

Following his third triumph over Maxim, Moore won three more over-the-weight non-title bouts and successfully defended his championship against Harold Johnson and Bobo Olson. Then he reached for the stars.

For much of the twentieth century, the heavyweight championship was the most coveted prize in sports. Three months prior to Moore beating Maxim to claim the light-heavyweight title, Rocky Marciano had knocked out Jersey Joe Walcott to annex the heavyweight throne.

Reprising a tactic that he'd used to get his title opportunity against Maxim, Moore sent hundreds of handwritten letters to sports writers around the country urging them to support a Marciano-Moore fight. That was followed by press releases, classified ads, and a "wanted" poster offering a reward for the capture and delivery of Marciano to "sheriff" Archie Moore.

"I got Marciano in a corner," Moore later reminisced. "People would ask him when he was going to fight me, and he could no longer say, 'I don't want to hurt that old man.' He had to either fight me or face the embarrassment of refusal the rest of his fighting career."

Marciano-Moore was contracted for and scheduled for Yankee Stadium. The challenger carried the brunt of the pre-fight promotion. Jerry Izenberg (then a cub reporter) recalls, "Archie was a blessing to the writers. He always gave us something we could write."

In the weeks leading up to the bout, Moore was often seen wearing a blue yachting cap. "It lends an impression that you own a yacht," he explained.

He also got maximum publicity out of his dietary habits by putting a lock on the training camp refrigerator and claiming that his nutritional secrets were "too valuable to be left lying around." A screen was erected around his table during meals to protect against prying eyes. In a similar vein, Moore carried a flask that he sipped from occasionally and told reporters that it was a secret brew prepared from a recipe given to him by a tribe of Aborigines in Australia.

"If the outcome of the fight was dependent on conversation," Arthur Daly of the *New York Times* noted, "Marciano wouldn't have a chance."

On September 21, 1955, a crowd of 61,574 filled Yankee Stadium for Marciano-Moore. Former heavyweight champions Jack Dempsey, Gene Tunney, Max Baer, James Braddock, and Joe Louis were at ringside. Another 400,000 fans watched the fight on closed-circuit television in 133 theaters across the country.

Moore's purse was $270,000; the largest of his career (equivalent to $2,250,000 in today's dollars). Marciano received $471,000. Moore weighed in at 188 pounds; Marciano, a quarter-pound heavier. The most youthful estimate dated Moore as three months shy of thirty-nine years old. Whatever his age, he was well past his prime. Marciano, an 18-to-5 favorite, was thirty-two.

Moore was a showman. After beating Maxim, he'd ordered custom-made robes for many of his fights. In his title defense against Harold Johnson, he'd entered the ring wearing a black satin robe with a gold satin lining, mandarin collar, and ten-karat gold edging. For Bobo Olson, he unveiled a white English flannel model with a gold satin lining, gold braids, and ten-karat gold epaulets.

Against Marciano, Budd Schulberg reported, "Moore entered the ring in a flowing regal robe of black brocade trimmed in gold with Louis XIV cuffs and a brilliant gold lining, under which he affected another silken robe of saintly white. Aeneas himself could not have born himself more proudly. Whether the venerable pugilist is truly a god or merely a fine play actor who has a way with Homeric material, I know that the gods of ancient Greece and Rome would have been delighted with him."

The fight itself was high drama.

"At the opening bell," Moore later recounted, "I came out of my corner to meet Marciano, and strangely enough he started backing away. I jabbed several times, but they went over Marciano's head as he was boxing pretty low. I thought I would change tactics and make him straighten up because he was pretty hard to hit while in the crouch. So in the second round, I feinted Marciano and took a half-step back. As he followed me in with a short overhand right, I took another short step backward so that he missed me by three inches and I came through with an uppercut that hit him right on the chin and he went down heavily on one knee and both elbows."

For only the second time in his career, Marciano was on the canvas. "I was dazed," he admitted afterward. "But my head cleared quickly."

Marciano rose at the count of two. Two minutes and thirty seconds were left in the round. Moore later contended that referee Harry Kessler erroneously began a mandatory eight-count, forgetting that the eight-count rule was not in effect for title fights.

"Rocky was a wide-open target at that point," Moore claimed. "Dazed, confused, and with absolutely no defense and no mobility. It would have been like hitting a punching bag. If I could have gotten him when he got up after the two count, I could have become heavyweight champion."

But film footage of the fight is at odds with Moore's version of events. It shows that the action resumed within three seconds of the time that Marciano rose from the canvas. Kessler didn't even wipe off his gloves.

Marciano survived the second round. Then, inexorably, he wore Moore down with brute force, battering his arms, upper body, and every other part of his anatomy that could be hit with heavy sledgehammer blows.

"Rocky didn't know enough boxing to know what a feint was," Moore mused years later. "He never tried to outguess you. He just kept trying to knock your brains out. If he missed you with one punch, he just threw another. Of all the guys I fought, Marciano hit me harder than everybody else combined. I felt like someone was beating all over my body with a blackjack or hitting me with rocks."

"I don't think I ever threw more punches in a fight than I did tonight," Marciano told reporters when it was over. "I just couldn't seem to get a clean shot at him. He'd hide beneath those arms and bob and weave and roll with the punches, so the only thing I could do was keep pitching them."

Marciano put Moore on the canvas twice in the sixth round. In round eight, Moore was knocked down for the third time but was saved by the bell. In round nine, he was counted out. "I had the braggadocio and the skill and the guts," he acknowledged. "But that wasn't enough. Marciano beat me down."

Of the final rounds, Budd Schulberg wrote, "The golden-robed god of the fistic wars was getting the hell beat out of him. The cestus-like fists of Marciano were punishing the old man terribly. The Greeks would have wept for Moore. In the end, he sat there in great sadness as the referee administered the fight game's numeric version of the last rites. There was tragedy in the way he sprawled there with the fight and the will beaten out of him; a very old man of forty-two who, some thirty minutes earlier, had been such an astonishing young man of forty-two."

Years later, Moore would look back on his conqueror and that night with a mixture of sadness and pride.

"The Marciano fight was like a dream come true," he wrote. "This was the one fight that I had always wanted—a fight for the heavyweight championship of the world. It is a bout I will always cherish. The cheer that went up when I decked Marciano was the most thrilling and inspiring sound I have ever heard. You cannot imagine what the roar of sixty thousand people can do to your spine. You stand under the lights with a fallen champion at your feet and, as one voice, the crowd salutes you. It is a thrill that cannot be measured. It is a memory I can conjure up by just closing my eyes. When I was knocked out, the same crowd saluted Rocky, and that is as it should be."

After losing to Marciano, Moore, in essence, told the boxing establishment, "You wouldn't let me fight for the light-heavyweight championship when I was in my prime. Why should I give it back to you now that I'm old?"

Over the next year, he engaged in a well-orchestrated sleight of hand that saw ten over-the-weight non-title fights against mediocre opponents and one championship defense in London against the non-threatening Yolande Pompey. Then opportunity knocked once more.

Seven months after beating Moore, Rocky Marciano retired from boxing without fighting again. The powers that be then decreed that Moore should be matched against Floyd Patterson for the vacant heavy-weight throne.

Moore-Patterson was contested in Chicago on November 30, 1956. Had Moore won, he would have been the oldest man as of that time to claim the heavyweight crown. As it was, Patterson, age twenty-one, became the youngest. He knocked Moore out in the fifth round.

Moore was simply too slow.

"I trained hard for the Patterson fight," he said afterward. "Too hard; I overtrained. I was stale. Patterson didn't surprise me when we fought. I knew what type of fight to expect and I got it. I planned to bring the fight to him and I wasn't able to. My reflexes were off and my timing was terrible. I was beaten as badly as I have ever been beaten in my whole ring career."

Moore had two more over-the-weight non-title fights after his loss to Patterson. Finally, on September 20, 1957, he entered the ring to defend his championship against a credible challenger for the first time in more than three years.

Twenty-two-year-old Tony Anthony was the opponent. Four months earlier, Moore had weighed 206 pounds for a fight against Hans Kalbfell in Germany. On the day of the Anthony fight, the Old Mongoose (as he was now known) had to get on the scales six times before making the 175-pound weight limit. Then he knocked Anthony out in the seventh round.

"He's the Einstein of boxing," the vanquished challenger said afterward.

"It's my candy," Moore said of his title. "And the only way you're going to get any of it is to take it away from me."

Twelve more over-the-weight non-title fights followed. Moore jour-neyed to Canada, Germany, and Brazil, and added Nevada and Kentucky to his itinerary.

"Do you know why I can continue on while others fade away?" he asked before answering his own question. "I am a man who has more faith in himself than others. Every day, I do something to improve my skill of the game, whether it is refining an old move or mastering a new one. I never stop learning. I realize age is just a number."

But the most fabled episode in Moore's ring career lay ahead. By late 1958, according to the *Ring Record Book* (which was considered the final authority on boxing records at that time), he had accumulated 126 career knockouts. That placed him in a tie with Young Stribling, a light-heavy-weight from Georgia, who was credited with 126 career knockouts before his death in a 1933 motorcycle accident.

Then Moore signed to defend his championship in Montreal on December 10, 1958, against a French-Canadian fisherman named Yvon Durelle.

"I'm aware that many observers tend to regard Durelle as just a rough club fighter with no style or class," Moore said of the impending contest. "I fought another fellow who fit this description—Rocky Marciano. Durelle is like one of those pit bulldogs that are bred to fight to the death. He never steps back. A fighter like Yvon is out only when the referee counts him out. You can't knock him out with a typewriter or a verbal opinion. December 10th could be the roughest night of my seven-year reign as 175-pound king."

In truth, Moore thought that Durelle was an easy mark. Archie appeared at the weigh-in attired in a tuxedo, camel's hair coat, and Homburg hat accessorized by a silver-headed cane. Durelle wore work pants, an old sweater, and rubber boots. Always the showman, Moore approached his opponent and asked, "Who is your tailor?" He then told reporters, "I am counting on Monsieur Durelle showing proper respect for a man old enough to be his father."

Durelle entered the ring on fight night knowing that he had a tough task ahead of him. Moore had no such foreknowledge. The eleven rounds that followed are now part of boxing lore.

Fifty-five seconds into round one, Durelle landed a perfectly lever-aged short right hand flush on Moore's jaw. Moore dropped to the canvas like he'd been shot. Through an act of Herculean will, he rose to his feet a fraction of a second before the count of ten."

Lester Bromberg, who was at ringside for the *New York World-Telegram and Sun*, recounted the impact of the blow that knocked Moore down for the first time: "The punch landed with the impact of a Marine battalion hitting a beach. Moore's legs instantly sagged. The shock running through his body appeared to disjoint it and he came down backwards like children's miniature blocks, his head rapping the floor loudly. If the punch hadn't stunned him, the smash of the back of his head would have. This clearly was a punch-paralyzed man, his right arm stretched limp, his left balanced strangely on his elbow, his torso flat to the thighs, and his right leg crooked in an inverted V. The French-Canadian fans were on their feet, screaming wildly. The gauche fisherman had nailed the defensive master. At five, Moore was still on his back . . . Six, seven, eight . . . Archie hauled himself to a knee. Nine . . . He managed to beat ten, but his feet could not have been heavier if he were mired in sand."

Dazed, Moore lurched around the ring, unable to defend himself. Durelle pounded him from post to post and felled him with a glancing left; then decked him for the third time with a brutal right hand. A minute and ten seconds remained in the round. Moore barely made it to his feet at nine. Boxing's ageless warrior looked ageless no more.

In later years, Moore would recount that first round as follows:

⋆ "The fight was about a minute old when he caught me with a right hand. I didn't see the right hand, but I felt it. It seemed like a bomb exploded in my head. The first thing that struck the floor was the back of my head. I felt a trickle of blood inside my mouth. I knew I had a concussion. I thought, 'Well, this is the way they happen.' I guess if I hit my head that hard on the street, I would have been killed."

⋆ "The first thing I heard was number five. I knew I had to get to my feet, but it felt as if the top of my head was blown off. I rolled to one knee. I think I was up at nine. Then he hit me again, and I thought he'd broken my head. I said to myself, 'Well, I guess this is the end for me, but I'm going to fight this son of a bitch. I'll die fighting him if it comes to that.'"

⋆ "The noise that Canadian crowd made was deafening. It sounded like the drone of a million bees in a small room. Over the roar of the fans, I could hear the referee shouting the count in my ear. And I could hear my corner man begging me to get up. I pushed myself to my feet. Then I was flat on my back again. Once again, I staggered to my feet. I came in with a left hook, and he split me with a right hand and I went down again. I thought, 'Oh, my goodness; this guy really can hit. And I began to pray softly to myself, "Oh, God; if I can just last this round and get to my corner."' Somehow, I managed to get to my feet. Finally, the bell rang and I stumbled to my corner."

In round four, Moore took the initiative. But less than a minute into round five, Durelle backed him into the ropes and landed a hard right high on the cheek that put the champion on the canvas again. Moore rose on wobbly legs. Once again, the end seemed near. Amazingly, he survived the round.

Then, remarkably, the fight turned.

In round seven, Moore knocked Durelle down. Ten seconds before the end of round ten, a barrage of punches put the challenger on the canvas for the second time. He rose on unsteady legs at the count of eight and was saved by the bell. At the start of round eleven, a six-punch barrage punctuated by a left hook to the jaw put Durelle on the canvas for the third time. Now the tables were turned. He struggled valiantly to his feet at the count of nine and Moore ended matters with a straight right hand that matched the blow Durelle had begun the carnage with in round one.

"The title is all I've got," Moore told reporters when the fight was over. "I just couldn't give it up.

"A champion," Jack Dempsey once said, "is someone who gets up when he can't."

Anyone who wants to learn about the heart of a champion should watch round one of Moore-Durelle on YouTube. Years later, Moore would reflect back on that night and observe, "The fight with Durelle was the fight that every fighter hopes to have. This is the fight that a fighter dreams about; getting knocked down and then being able to get up and conquer his opponent. I had always known that I would come to the end of the road someday. No fighter lasts forever. And I was in my forties, so losing after all these years was excusable. But there is no excuse for a champion not putting up the best fight he possibly can."

III

Moore's 1958 fight against Yvon Durelle was the star atop the Christmas tree of the Archie Moore legend. The bout was the first title fight held outside the United States to be televised live in America. And it captured the imagination of the nation.

The following weekend, Moore flew to New York and was introduced from the audience on *The Ed Sullivan Show*. At year's end, the Boxing Writers Association of America honored him as its "Fighter of the Year."

Jack Murphy of the *San Diego Union-Tribune* summed up the accolades, writing, "After nearly a quarter-century of fighting in tank towns and eating in greasy spoons, Archie Moore is finally getting the recognition and popularity he so richly deserves. In the aftermath of his spectacular brawl with Yvon Durelle, a lot of people have suddenly discovered that Moore isn't just a swaggering old con man engaged in a shell game with the public. There is a new appreciation for his exceptional fighting skills and an admiration bordering on awe for his courage. This was a fight that revealed what some of us have been saying for quite a spell. Moore is a fighter for the ages."

It has been said that Moore was more than a fighter. But that's true of all boxers. What separated him from many other fighters (and athletes) was that, in addition to his skills, he fervently wanted to be recognized as a thoughtful multifaceted man. And he was.

Moore had a way with words. Recounting how his half-brother, Louis, was arrested, Archie explained, "Louis was light-fingered by nature. Somehow, a man's watch got tangled up in his hand, and the man sent the police to ask Louis what time it was."

Very few writers can craft phrases like that.

"I liked him very much," Jerry Izenberg says. "His demeanor always matched the occasion. He was a terrific fighter and a fascinating guy. And I'll tell you something else. He was better than Ali at conning someone. With Ali, you laughed and you knew he was conning you. With Archie, you didn't always know that you'd been had."

"I met him several times," Emanuel Steward reminisced. "He was a wonderful man. Talking to him was like talking with a college professor."

Following his victory over Durelle, Moore's cachet was such that Samuel Goldwyn cast him as Jim, the runaway slave, in a 1960 film version of *The Adventures of Huckleberry Finn*.

"I was intrigued at the idea of making myself into another person," Moore said of his film role. "I wasn't put in the picture as a freak attraction to sell tickets. I honestly think I turned in a performance and not an appearance."

Hollywood agreed. In the ensuing years, Moore would have roles in *The Carpetbaggers* (starring George Peppard, Carroll Baker, and Alan Ladd), *The Fortune Cookie* (with Jack Lemmon and Walter Matthau), and television shows ranging from *Perry Mason* to *Batman*.

Meanwhile, Moore's ring career went on. On August 12, 1959, he fought a rematch against Durelle in Montreal. This time, he was properly prepared and knocked the Canadian out in the third round.

There were more over-the-weight non-title bouts. Moore discovered Texas and fought there three times in addition to doing battle in Italy and the Philippines. On October 25, 1960, the National Boxing Association stripped him of his championship for refusing to defend the title against a credible challenger. That left New York, Massachusetts, and California as the only jurisdictions to recognize the legitimacy of his championship claim. He had one final title defense; a fifteen-round decision over Giulio Rinaldi at Madison Square Garden on June 10, 1961. Then those three states also withdrew recognition of his crown.

Moore's last six fights were fought as a heavyweight. He scored knockout victories over Pete Rademacher, Alejandro Lavorante, and Howard King. Then, weighing 201 pounds, he battled to a ten-round draw against future light-heavyweight champion Willie Pastrano.

Pastrano later recounted that, at the pre-fight physical, Moore couldn't read the eye chart: "He was saying 'A . . . B . . . C . . . D.' The doctor says, 'For Chrissakes, Archie; that's not right.' Archie says, 'Well, Willie ain't gonna be that far away from me.'"

By then, Moore had bought 120 acres of land near San Diego and built a training camp called "The Salt Mine." In addition to preparing for his own fights, he'd begun working with other boxers. One of the young men he trained briefly was an eighteen-year-old heavyweight with a 1-and-0 record—a former Olympian named Cassius Marcellus Clay Jr. Their union lasted about a month in late 1960 before Clay rebelled against the discipline and housekeeping chores that Moore imposed on trainees and returned home to Louisville.

Two years later, on November 15, 1962, Clay and Moore met in the ring. Their confrontation was typical of boxing; a young up-and-coming fighter against an over-the-hill "name" opponent. Moore was being paid for his marquee value. Yet elements of the match-up were intriguing. Clay had been in fifteen professional fights. Moore was a veteran of more than two hundred. And more important from a promotional point of view, they were boxing's greatest outside-the-ring showmen

As expected, Moore-Clay was preceded by verbal pyrotechnics. Cassius predicted that "the old man" would fall in four. Moore responded, "I don't enjoy being struck by children," and added, "I view this young man with mixed emotions. Sometimes he sounds humorous, but some-times he sounds like a man that can write beautifully but doesn't know how to punctuate. Clay can go with speed in all directions, including straight down if hit properly. I have a good solid right hand that will fit nicely on his chops. The only way I'll fall in four is by toppling over Clay's prostrate form."

Clay was a 3-to-1 favorite. The fight was contested in Los Angeles, where 16,200 fans paid a California indoor record of $182,600 to see the bout.

"My plan when I went into the fight," Moore later explained, "was to move around and catch him with hooks to the body because no one had hit him to the body much. Slow him down and then maybe get him with a sneaky right hand. But his speed was too much for me, and I was made for him in that I used a wrap-around defense to cover up. I would leave the top of my head exposed, and that's what he wanted. You see, he had a style; he would hit a man a lot of times around the top of the head. And if you hit the top of a man's head, you disturb his thoughts. A fighter has to think. But if someone is plunking you on top of the head, you cannot think correctly. And this is what he did. He made me dizzy and he knocked me out."

Four months after losing to Clay, Moore entered the ring for the last time. On March 15, 1963, he fought a thirty-nine-year-old professional wrestler named Mike DeBiase, who had issued a challenge to Moore after Archie refereed one of his matches.

Only eight hundred fans attended Moore-DiBiase. The gate was under two thousand dollars. It was DiBiase's first pro fight and it wasn't pretty. Moore ended matters at twenty seconds of the third round.

After retiring as an active fighter. Moore faced new challenges.

"Twenty-nine years of a man's life aren't dumped that easily," he wrote. "I had so many memories that, when I thought of having left the ring forever, it gave me a kind of empty feeling."

But he soon found other horizons, becoming actively involved with a number of youth programs. It was more than a hobby or public-relations gesture. He took the work seriously and invested an enormous amount of time and energy in helping to mold young men and women. There were various business ventures. And he continued training other fighters; most notably, George Foreman.

Moore was with the Foreman team when George upset Joe Frazier in Jamaica in 1973 to claim the heavyweight crown, and also one year later when he lost to Muhammad Ali in Zaire. When Foreman began his comeback in 1987 after ten years away from boxing, he again sought Moore's counsel. Given the need to slim down from three hundred pounds, Big George considered the merits of Moore's "Aborigine diet."

"I would try some of the things, chew the meat and not swallow it, things of that nature," Foreman said afterward. "But when Archie wasn't looking, I'd eat it."

Moore had aged well as a fighter and that continued to be the case long after his ring career was over. He remained mentally sharp in his old age; no mean achievement for a man who'd had more than two hundred professional fights.

Late in life, reflecting on his ring accomplishments, Moore saw himself in the arc of history. "A Negro champion feels he stands for more than just a title," he observed. "He is a symbol of achievement and dignity."

And he expressed pride in what he'd accomplished as a boxer.

"It makes me proud when someone mentions that they would sit by the radio and listen to my fights or when someone is excited just to shake my hand," Moore declared. "I'm proud that I beat fighters who were young enough to be my sons. I am very proud of being able to say that I dropped Rocky Marciano when I fought him. Life's road is not always smooth. But if you haven't had any bad times, how can you appreciate the good ones? My rugged road was very interesting and rewarding at the end."

He often travelled with a sixteen-millimeter film of his first fight against Yvon Durelle and showed it to anyone who was interested if a film projector was available.

In 1994, Moore underwent triple heart-bypass surgery. He died in San Diego on December 9, 1998.

Archie Moore knew the craft of boxing as well as anyone. He had remarkable skills. But what sets him apart from other fighters is his longevity.

Fighters got old younger in those days. Joe Louis won his last championship fight at age thirty-four. Rocky Marciano fought for the last time twenty days after his thirty-second birthday. There were no modern conditioning techniques, no miracle surgery, and no performance enhancing drugs to prolong an athlete's career.

Three fights stand out in Moore's legacy: his winning the title from Joey Maxim at age thirty-six (or thirty-nine); his unsuccessful challenge against Rocky Marciano three years later; and his first fight against Yvon Durelle, when, by any count, Moore was well into his forties. The victory over Maxim was vindication for past wrongs. His efforts against Marciano and Durelle were flawed but heroic performances.

"I always went into the ring feeling that I could beat my opponent," Moore said of his ring career. "It didn't always happen that way, but I have a gift for understatement when talking of my losses. I recall the determined feeling I had to do better the next time when I lost, and the wonderful feeling I had when I won."

Offering thoughts with regard to his place in boxing history, Moore declared, "I must admit that I feel Archie Moore ranked up there with the best. Joe Louis was the best heavyweight I've ever seen. John Henry Lewis was the best light-heavyweight. But if anyone wants to dispute this and throw my name in, I'll listen to the discussion with rapt attention."

Hall of Fame matchmaker Bruce Trampler, a student of boxing history, observes, "You look at films of fighters and you make allowances for different conditioning and how technique has evolved and you project in your mind what someone like Jack Johnson would be a hundred years later. But at the end of the day, either a fighter has it or he doesn't have it. Archie Moore had it. He could fight."

Emanuel Steward proclaimed, "Archie Moore was incredible, one of the all-time greats. They don't even teach what he could do anymore. To be as good as he was for as long as he was; he might have been the greatest light-heavyweight of all time."

As for Moore the person; Archie could be irascible, stubborn, prickly. But he was also capable of great kindness. After Floyd Patterson was knocked out by Ingemar Johansson in 1959, Moore sent the following letter to the man who had crushed his own heavyweight championship dreams three years before:

Dear Floyd,

The first bout is over. I know how you must feel. I hope you don't continue to feel bad. The same thing has happened to many great fighters. I hated to lose to you, and fate decreed it that way. Fate does strange-seeming things. If you are a believer [that] things happen for the best, listen to this and you can find your way out of a seeming tunnel.

Johansson was not so great. You fought a stupid battle. Look at the film. Evaluate it. Never once did you lead with a jab. All you did was move your feet and try to leap toward him. Now this man could bang a little. You gave absolutely no respect to your opposition. If you concentrate on your jab and move around this guy, you will be the first one to regain the crown. You can do it.

Your friend
Archie Moore

Working off his jab, Patterson knocked Johansson out in the fifth round of their rematch the following year.

"Moore was someone you wanted to be around," promoter Don Elbaum remembers. "He was a very classy guy who treated everyone with respect. I sent him a telegram wishing him a happy birthday one year. People did that in those days. And he sent me a telegram back, thanking me."

Writer W.C. Heinz called Moore "the most scientific fighter of my time and, outside the ropes, the most inventive."

Al Bernstein recalls, "Archie Moore was the most interesting athlete I've ever met. In fact, he was as interesting to sit and talk with in casual conversation as any person I've ever known. He had a lot of respect for boxing history and the people who made boxing what it is. He told me once about meeting Jack Johnson in a gym in Los Angeles. He said it was like God walking in. He was a good story teller but never tried to dominate the conversation. He was self-educated, very well-read. It wasn't a put-on. He didn't pretend to be something he wasn't by throwing out the names of a few writers he'd heard about. There was some double-talk from time to time, but you could discuss anything with him. If he didn't know about a subject and you did, he'd ask the right questions to learn about it for himself."

And Larry Merchant, who first encountered Moore as a young sportswriter at the *Philadelphia Daily News*, reminisces, "I received several long letters from him; letters that went beyond the entreaties for a fight against Marciano or whoever it was he wanted to fight that year. Those letters were one of the things that created a context within which I covered boxing and, to a certain degree, all other sports. He was a man of dignity. He had great pride and grace. Over time, he evolved into a philosopher and, in some respects, an intellectual. Despite all the injustices that were heaped upon him as a black man and as a fighter, he always seemed to be smiling at the world rather than snarling at it. He influenced my life, and I don't say that lightly. He showed me that writing about sports could be deep and he showed me that writing about sports could be fun."

"When Archie Moore came around," John Schulian wrote, "the fight racket never seemed like the sewer it was."

After Moore died, there were myriad tributes. One of the finest came from George Foreman, who wrote in *Time Magazine*, "In all the years we talked while Archie was teaching me, he never complained about the years of being the number one contender [when he couldn't get a title shot]. When he talked of the night he won the light-heavyweight championship but no money, there was that gleam in his eye. When he uttered the word 'champion,' that made me too want to be a champion. Archie stands as a tower for all athletes, saying, 'If you want it, leave your excuses behind and come get it.'"

Curiosities

Lou DiBella has a frenetic way of doing things. It's never boring.

Lou DiBella on Epix

The first fight televised on Epix was Vitali Klitschko vs. Odlanier Solis on March 19, 2011. The network now hosts boxing on a regular basis. Fights are shown live approximately once a month on a Saturday afternoon (usually around 4:30 PM East Coast time). That's a throwback to the era when the sweet science was an anchor for Saturday afternoon sports programming.

"Our budget is a small fraction of what HBO and Showtime spend on fights," Epix acquisitions consultant Roy Langbord says. "But by focusing on the Klitschkos and Europe, we've been able to buy good fights that have been overlooked in the US market."

Epix takes the European feed for its telecasts. Fights are called from a three-man studio desk in New York. For the past year, Bruce Beck has handled blow-by-blow duties. The number-two seat has been filled by Dan Rafael. The industry-insider role has fallen at various times to Lennox Lewis, Sugar Ray Leonard, and Freddie Roach.

On November 10, 2012, Epix embarked on a grand experiment. It brought in promoter Lou DiBella to do commentary as the industry insider for its telecast of Wladimir Klitschko vs. Mariusz Wach and Robert Helenius vs. Sherman Williams.

In the past, DiBella has done spot commentary on telecasts of his own *Broadway Boxing* shows. Earlier this year, he sent a video of his work to Travis Pomposello (executive producer of Epix Sports). Travis took it from there. Before long, DiBella was slated for his Epix debut.

Inquiring minds wanted to know: "Could Lou sit still through two fights? Could Lou cope with turning his cell phone off for the two hours that he would be on the air? Could Lou control his emotions without stifling his emotional appeal?"

Seth Abraham (former president of Time Warner Sports) was the architect of HBO's boxing program. He and DiBella presided over the network's sports department during its glory years.

"Wow!" Abraham exclaimed when apprised of DiBella's pending engagement. "I'm rarely speechless, but this is one of those times. Lou obviously knows boxing as a sport and a business. I think his biggest challenge will be to impose moderation and control on himself. People in boxing know Lou, and they'll be looking for one set of things from him for entertainment. But the average viewer will be looking for something else. For the average viewer, this will be about the fights, not about Lou. Will he know when to shut up? Will he explain and complement the visual or overwhelm it? It will be interesting; that's for sure. It's a fascinating choice."

The commentating team that DiBella coordinated with at HBO was similarly intrigued.

"This should be fun," Larry Merchant said enthusiastically.

"Lou always has something to say," Harold Lederman offered. "I can't wait to hear what it is."

Jim Lampley was effusive in his praise.

"If anything can double Epix's subscription rate in one night, this is it," Lampley posited. "Lou has common-man appeal. He's in psychological harmony with the sport. He looks and feels like a boxing guy the same way that John Madden looks and feels like football. He's one of my favorite conversationalists, whether he's ranting or philosophizing. He knows the sport and he knows the business. I can't imagine that he won't be great on the air. I think it's fantastic."

Steve Farhood was behind the microphone when DiBella commentated on a handful of *Broadway Boxing* fights.

"When one of Lou's fighters scores a knockout," Farhood noted, "Lou forgets that he's an analyst on a TV show. He jumps up and down and his headset falls off. So it's an interesting situation with Epix. On *Broadway Boxing*, Lou can be Lou. But the higher a commentator goes, the more filters there are and the more he's expected to be politically correct within the context of boxing. I think it will work out. I do know that it's enervating when Lou joins us on *Broadway Boxing* because his energy is contagious."

Steve Albert (who called fights on Showtime for two decades) looked to the past and recalled, "This brings back memories of when I was announcing hockey for the Cleveland Crusaders in the old World Hockey

Association. My color commentator was the coach's wife. Every time Cleveland scored, she got so excited that she punched me in the arm. By the end of the season, I needed a sling. So knowing Lou, my advice to Bruce Beck and Dan Rafael would be to wear some sort of protective device."

"But seriously," Albert added. "Lou is charismatic and colorful. He knows the sport inside and out. Be honest, respect the viewer, and he'll do a great job."

Showtime boxing analyst Al Bernstein proclaimed, "I'm certainly more curious about this telecast than I was before. The one piece of advice I'd offer Lou is that he give serious thought to avoiding the 'F' word on the air. I know it's an organic part of his speech. But it wouldn't be appropriate under these circumstances."

Craig Hamilton spoke for boxing fans everywhere when he observed, "There's a school of thought that the last thing Lou DiBella needs is a microphone. And let's face it; putting Lou behind a microphone is a gamble because, as smart as Lou is, he's all emotion. But I'm sure that Lou isn't doing this to be part of a circus. He'll try to do the job right. John McEnroe on the tennis court behaved one way. But behind the microphone, McEnroe is very analytical and controlled. Lou could be very good at this. I'm glad they hired him."

Meanwhile, Lou declared, "I'm taking this very seriously. I won't just mail it in. I've watched videos of eleven Mariusz Wach fights. Obviously, I'm familiar with Klitschko. I've done my homework on Helenius and Williams and read the Epix briefing book. I'll be going to the preproduction meetings. I assume I won't fuck up. And whatever happens, I can't be as bad as some of the guys who are commentating on fights today."

At 4:30 PM, after a final rehearsal, DiBella and company were on the air. Because of European television commitments, Klitschko-Wach was the first fight on tap.

Klitschko, age thirty-six, was written off as an elite heavyweight in 2004 after being knocked out twice within the span of thirteen months. Corrie Sanders stopped him in two rounds. Lamon Brewster did the deed in five. But Wladimir prevailed in sixteen consecutive fights after that en route to a 58-and-3 record with fifty knockouts

As David Greisman wrote, "Long gone is the deer-in-the-headlights look that took over Klitschko's face as Sanders sent him down again and again. Now Klitschko looks like a lion presiding over his jungle, swatting powerfully at whomever dares enter his kingdom. Much of that has to do with the teachings of trainer Emanuel Steward. Much of that has to do with the way Klitschko has put those lessons into practice. He's gone from heavyweight scrap heap to heavyweight champion. He has learned to use distance and height; learned to work behind a powerful jab and not to lower himself by over-extending with his right cross. He has incorporated simple but deft footwork to take himself out of range of his opponent's attacks. He has learned how to avoid trouble. It isn't flashy. But it works."

Wladimir is now widely accepted as boxing's heavyweight king. Brother Vitali is the sport's crown prince.

Wach, age thirty-two, was born in Poland, lives in New Jersey, and (for unexplained reasons) is nicknamed "The Viking." His 27-and-0 record was devoid of quality opponents. Kevin McBride (who weighed in at a blubbery 296 pounds), Jason Gavern (a career opponent on a four-fight losing streak), and Tye Fields (a three-time first-round knockout victim) were the most recognizable names on Wach's ledger. Against Klitschko, Mariusz was a 20-to-1 underdog.

Most of the pre-fight talk on the Epix telecast was devoted the fact that this would be Wladimir's first fight in more than eight years without trainer Emanuel Steward (who died last month) in his corner.

When the moment of reckoning came, Klitschko and DiBella both started fast.

At the opening bell, Lou declared, "The first jab that hits Wach will probably be the best jab that hit him in his life." Seconds later, DiBella observed, "You can see the difference in their jabs. Klitschko's jab snaps. Wach's jab pushes."

Wladimir outlanded Mariusz 19 to 3 in the first stanza, which was a harbinger of things to come. As the fight progressed, Wach's game plan seemed to be to stand directly in front of Klitschko without applying pressure or moving his head. He showed an incredible chin (DiBella called it "the chin of God"), great heart, and not much more. Round after round, he absorbed hellacious right hands without going down.

The most brutal moments in the fight came in round eight, when Klitschko landed crushing blow after crushing blow (a 44-to-3 edge in punches landed in those three minutes alone). That led DiBella to opine, "I'd like to see the corner jump in here."

That would have been the sensible thing to do, but it didn't happen. Wach continued to take as much punishment as any fighter in recent memory. His courage gave the fight drama. The 120–107, 120–107, 119–109 decision in Klitschko's favor was a formality.

Then the scene shifted from Germany to Finland, where Robert Helenius faced off against Sherman Williams.

Helenius, age twenty-eight, entered the ring with a 17-and-0 record and a handful of victories over badly faded heavyweights like Sergei Liakhovich and Samuel Peter.

Williams has won once since 2008. He's forty years old, 5 feet, 11 inches tall (seven inches shorter than Helenius), and weighed in at a career-high 266 pounds.

Helenius and Williams both looked awful. Williams fought to survive, and Helenius turned in a drab dull plodding performance.

In round five, DiBella took stock of the situation, turned fan, and said of Helenius, "Right now, he's boring the hell out of me." Later, referencing Helenius's nickname ("The Nordic Nightmare"), Lou opined, "He might be The Nightmare; but right now, he's NyQuil."

It was a long ten rounds, with the fighters landing an average of seven punches per fighter per stanza. Helenius won a unanimous decision.

"It's harder to call a bad fight than a good one," DiBella said when the telecast was over. "But I'm satisfied with the job I did."

The feedback so far has been complimentary. It's hard to assess a commentator's performance on the basis of one telecast. But Lou is off to a promising start.

Meanwhile, it should be noted that one of the problems the Klitschkos have had in gaining worldwide acceptance is that their whole is less than the sum of their parts. If there were just one of them, people would be more inclined to say, "He's a great heavyweight champion."

There's something special about "one." Two of anything tends to devalue its worth.

There's only one Lou DiBella.

Sixteen years after the fact, this one rewrote history for me.

Evander Holyfield on the Night Before Fighting Mike Tyson

It's part of boxing lore. On November 9, 1996, Evander Holyfield shocked the world by knocking out Mike Tyson. Holyfield, it was said, went into the fight with absolute confidence and total belief in himself. "Tyson might frighten you guys," he told the media. "But he doesn't scare me. I've been everywhere he has except prison."

Except it turns out that things weren't that simple.

On June 8, 2012, I was sitting with Evander when Manny Pacquiao and Tim Bradley weighed in for their welterweight championship fight at the MGM Grand in Las Vegas. Pacquiao tipped the scales at 147 pounds, Bradley at 146. When it was time for the ritual staredown, Tim moved into Manny's space and postured aggressively.

Throughout fight week, Bradley had carried himself with an aura of confidence. Pacquiao, on the other hand, had seemed a bit somber. Thus, I was surprised when Evander said to me, "I think Pacquiao is more confident."

"Why do you say that?"

"Tim feels good right now," Holyfield answered. "But the night before a fight, when you're lying in bed and can't sleep, things change."

"Did you have trouble sleeping before a fight?"

Evander smiled.

"The night before I fought Tyson the first time was the worst."

Jack Dempsey famously said, "Fighters know fear. It's like a lump in your chest. You learn how to live with it. You don't talk about it and you try not to show it. But it's there."

This is what Evander told me about his state of mind before he fought Mike Tyson.

★   ★   ★

No matter how much you believe in yourself, there's always some doubt. The night before Tyson, with all the talk I'd heard about how great he was and how there was no way I could possibly beat him, I must have got out of bed a hundred times.

I shadow-boxed. I read the Bible. I went back to bed. I couldn't sleep. I got up again. Read the Bible some more. Shadow-boxed again. A lot of thoughts were going through my mind. The hardest fight I'd ever had was against Dwight Qawi. Fifteen rounds. I remember Qawi telling me during the fight, "They sent a baby to do a man's job." There was a time in that fight when all I wanted was to not get knocked out and make it to the end. I won but it took everything out of me.

Tyson was bigger than Qawi. Tyson was stronger than Qawi. He hit harder than Qawi. At the Olympic trials, I was a light-heavyweight and Tyson was a heavyweight. He was the only guy there who worked harder than me.

All I got was two, maybe three, hours of sleep, the night before I fought Tyson. The second time we fought, it was better. The whole day of the first fight, I was tired. I had a headache. I felt nauseous. Anybody can win if they don't get hit, but I knew I was gonna get hit. I said to myself that day, "This will tell me who I am. Winners make it happen. Losers let it happen. I can't hope Tyson gets tired. I have to make him get tired. I have to show him, If you hit me, I'm gonna hit you back harder."

Fear stops you from doing what you have to do to win. Confidence is the key to being the best. It's how you feel about yourself that matters. The worst mistake I ever made in boxing was telling Lennox Lewis that I was going to knock him out in the third round the first time we fought. Because when he got through the third round, his confidence level went up to the sky.

Walking to the ring for Tyson, I told myself, "It's time to perform." When I got in the ring, my legs felt weak. Like they were Jell-O. I was smiling, but it was an act. You can't stand there with your head down. You've got to make it look like, "Hey; no problem." I believed in myself. But I still had to make it happen, and I knew that Tyson wanted to make it happen differently.

Then the bell rang; my legs came back; and I did my job.

A tradition continues.

My 86-Year-Old Mother Meets . . .

In the 1980s and 1990s, my mother met Muhammad Ali several times. In 2007, I brought her to a press conference to meet Don King. Now, once a year, Anthony Catanzaro hosts a pizza party at Portobello's (83 Murray Street in Manhattan) in her honor.

Anthony is a popular figure in the Hauser family. My great-nephew (who turns four in October) thinks that Anthony is Thomas the Tank Engine in disguise. That's because, when we visited Portobello's late last year, Anthony sang, "He's a really useful engine, you know" a half dozen times.

This year, again, Anthony was a gracious host at the annual "My Mother Meets" pizza party. The idea behind these gatherings is to introduce her to an interesting mix of boxing people.

"Sitting between Seth Abraham and Lou DiBella is an interesting experience," my mother acknowledged after last year's lunch.

And I have to think that eating pizza with Paulie Malignaggi and Vinny Maddalone on either side (2010) is a life-affirming experience.

This year's gathering was on September 24. Teddy Atlas couldn't make it because of a previous commitment to speak at a local high school. But he sent chocolate and flowers.

Tom Gerbasi was also waylaid by a school commitment. He had to meet with his daughter's college-application counselor. But Tom telephoned to share a recollection about his mother.

"She got pissed off at me when I dedicated my first book to my father," Tom recalled. "She asked, 'Where's my dedication.' I told her, 'Hey; when you die, I'll dedicate a book to you too.'"

The official guest list (in addition to my mother, Anthony, and yours truly) was:

Brian Kenny—The former studio host for *ESPN2 Friday Night Fights*, Brian is currently a studio host for the Major League Baseball Network. He also does play-by-play for MLB Network and was recently hired as the desk host for *Showtime Championship Boxing*.

David Diamante—The ring announcer with the stentorian voice and dreadlocks. David's career has blossomed in recent years. In addition to ring announcing, he's now the in-arena voice of the NBA Brooklyn Nets and narrator of the new NBC Sports offering, *The Lights*.

Harold Lederman—HBO's "unofficial ringside judge," boxing's greatest fan, and possibly the nicest man in boxing.

That's heavy on people who make their living behind a microphone. So we added Michael Woods, esteemed editor of The Sweet Science (who's also a contributing writer for *ESPN: The Magazine* and crafts a boxing blog for the ESPN NY website).

Michael (inquisitive reporter that he is) began the conversation by asking my mother, "Can you tell us some embarrassing stories about Tom?"

I shut down that line of inquiry in a hurry and countered with, "Do you have a story you can tell us about your mother?"

"That would be a therapy session," Michael responded.

Brian asked my mother the same question she's always asked at these gatherings: "Have you ever been to a fight?"

"No; and I don't want to go. I don't want to be there when people are hitting each other."

"I can understand," Brian told her. "My wife watches fights on TV all the time. But the first time I took her to a fight, she was aghast. It's different when it's happening right in front of you."

For a while, we talked about the craft of television commentating.

"I was impressed with Paulie Malignaggi last week on Showtime," Brian noted. "Before the fight, I told him, 'You don't have to talk all the time. If you say one insightful thing each round, you're doing your job.' And he did."

Then the conversation segued to Don King.

"I enjoyed meeting him," my mother said.

"Don will make you feel like a million dollars," Brian explained. "But you're not getting a million dollars."

We ate pizza for two hours. In between bites, David Diamante talked about finding it hard to believe that he's where he is professionally. "I love my life," he told us. "I went through some dark times when I was younger. And to be where I am today; I wouldn't say I'm lucky, but I'm fortunate."

Harold and my mother referenced their various aches and pains.

"At a certain age, if you're not feeling bad, that's good," Harold said.

Eventually, the conversation turned to baseball.

"Yankee Stadium was hallowed ground," David proclaimed. "Once they tore down the old Yankee Stadium, nothing was sacred anymore."

"The best ballpark right now is AT&T Park in San Francisco," Brian posited. "It's intimate. They pack the place for every game. I love being at a ballpark; there's a feel to being there that's special to me. But my heart races a little more when I'm at ringside. I remember being in Memphis when Mike Tyson fought Lennox Lewis. Tyson was coming down the aisle. I turned to Al Bernstein and said, "Let's remember what we're feeling now. After the fight, we'll sit around and say, 'Oh, we knew all along what would happen.' But right now, it's 'Here comes Mike.'"

Then I learned something about my mother that I hadn't known before. Brian asked if she'd ever been to a baseball game.

"I went to a few games at Shea Stadium in the early 1990s."

I'd known that.

"And when I was seventeen, I went to a World Series game at Yankee Stadium. My boyfriend and I got up at four-thirty in the morning and stood on line for hours to sit in the bleachers."

That I hadn't known.

"I don't remember much about the game," my mother continued. "I went because my boyfriend—his name was Buddy—wanted to go. But it was exciting to be there. You knew the names of the players back then because they didn't change teams every year."

For the record; the Yankees played the Cardinals in the 1942 World Series. Stan Musial had just finished his first full season in left field for St. Louis. Joe DiMaggio patrolled centerfield for New York. The Cardinals won all three games at Yankee Stadium and emerged triumphant in the series four games to one.

As a remembrance of this year's "My Mother Meets" luncheon, Brian gave her a gift bag with a "Gertrude Stein" notepad and several other goodies. Harold drove her home afterward.

As for next year—

"Bring your mother to my restaurant in Easton," Larry Holmes told me recently. "I'll give her a champburger."

*Continuing a tradition from years past, the memories of fighters and oth-
ers in the sweet science who spoke fondly of their greatest moment in a
sport other than boxing follow.*

Boxing Personalities Remember "My Greatest Moment in Another Sport"

ARTIE PELULLO

It wasn't just my greatest moments in sports. Outside of getting married and my children being born, it was the greatest moment of my life.

I went to Cheltenham High School, which is a public high school in
Pennsylvania. Cheltenham's biggest rival is Abington High School. The
Cheltenham-Abington rivalry is one of the oldest football rivalries in
Pennsylvania.

In 1973, my senior year of high school, I played both ways. Guard on
defense and tackle on offense. I was a bull. I weighed 240 pounds and
could bench press 260. I made first team all-area and second team all-
state.

The game was at Abington. Each team had a 7-and-2 record, but
what really mattered was beating Abington. For anyone who went to
either school, it was like the Army-Navy game.

There were nine thousand people in the stands. With forty-five seconds left to play, we were winning 15–14. Abington had the ball on our
twenty-yard-line and lined up for a field goal. I was in the gap and took
off at the exact moment of the snap. The holder put the ball down. I'm
barreling toward the kicker and something in my head says, "Put your
hands up, idiot." So I put my arms up in the air. The ball hits my right
forearm. And the crowd goes crazy.

My teammates mobbed me on the sideline. I felt so good, and it only
got better. On the bus going back to Cheltenham after the game, the
coach stood up and said, "Artie; I think this belongs to you. Then he
flipped the game ball to me. And at the dance in the high school gym that

night, Janet McPhee, who was very hot, slow-danced with me. You can put that in your article. But if you do, also put in that my wife and I have been married for thirty-one years and I'm the luckiest husband in the world.

TIM BRADLEY

It was at the district track meet when I was in seventh grade at Raymond Cree Middle School [in Palm Springs, California]. Every school in the district was there. Each team had three runners entered in the mile run. There were other guys who were favored over me. At first, I was in the pack and tried to work my way to the front but got blocked in. By the start of the last lap, I was running second. I was tired but I was used to pushing myself. I caught the leader on the final turn and we battled stride-for-stride to the very end. I was hurting; I could hardly breathe. But I wanted it so bad. It was like I gave everything I had and then I found something more to give. It was close but I edged him. I felt very proud of myself for winning that race. I felt like the man.

STEVE FARHOOD

I've been very involved in paddle tennis since I was in my teens. There are courts in the building complex that I've lived in since I was in junior high school. I love the game.

Paddle tennis is basically tennis. The difference is that you play with a paddle instead of a racket; the court is about one-third the size of a regulation tennis court; the ball, which is a regular tennis ball, is punctured with a needle to deaden it, and you serve underhand.

In 1981, when I was twenty-four years old, I played in the United States Paddle Tennis Association men's national doubles championship tournament. A friend named Dave Diamond was my partner. There were about twenty teams in the tournament. Dave and I were underdogs in every match, but we played well and made it to the semifinals. We were massive underdogs in that one, but we were in a zone. We won in straight sets. It was the best we'd ever played.

That was on a Saturday morning. After the match, I got on a plane and flew to Boston to cover Marvin Hagler beating Vito Antoufermo at

Boston Garden. Then I flew back to New York on Sunday for the tournament finals that afternoon.

In the finals, we played two guys from Brooklyn—Sol Hauptman and Jeff Fleitman. To give you an idea of what our chances were, Sol and Jeff won the national doubles championship thirteen of the fourteen years that they entered the tournament together. They're the greatest team to ever play the game. And Sol won ten more doubles championships with other partners.

Dave and I were the local boys and the crowd was rooting for us, but we were out of our league. Before the finals started, we told ourselves that we had to hold serve. If we could just hold serve in every game, good things might happen. Then we lost our first service game at love, which wasn't a good start. One of the things I remember about the match was, whenever Sol or Jeff made a mistake, the other would curse at him in Yiddish. They beat us 6–2, 6–3, 6–4.

Losing to Sol and Jeff is as much of a highlight for me as winning the semifinals. Sol is a legend, and I had the privilege of playing against him. Later, Sol moved to Southern California and taught paddle tennis to people like Wilt Chamberlain and Barbra Streisand. Word has it that he once shouted at Streisand, "Get your tuchus to the net."

BRUCE TRAMPLER

It was a Fourth of July track-and-field meet sponsored by the Chamber of Commerce or some group like that at Memorial Park in my home town [Maplewood, New Jersey]. There were no teams. It was just individual entries. I think I was thirteen years old. Ten or twelve of us were entered in the high jump competition.

I was a scissors-style jumper. The Fosbury Flop was way in the future. I lined up; got ready to make my approach to the bar; and saw my father, standing there, watching. I hadn't known he was coming. In fact, I don't think I'd known he was aware of the meet. We had an okay relationship, but it was pretty distant. It made me feel good, seeing him there. It was one of those moments like you had in *The Natural*, when Robert Redford looks into the stands and sees Glenn Close. Not really; but you get the point.

Then I focused on the bar and how many steps there were in my approach and cleared 5 feet, 4 inches or 5-6 or whatever it was and won the competition. It wasn't that I was good. I wasn't. I was just better than the rest of the field. They gave me a little medal attached to a red-white-and-blue ribbon which I still have, although I'm not sure where it is right now.

RONNIE SHIELDS

Back in 1992, I coached my oldest son's Little League baseball team. The kids were eleven and twelve years old. The first thing I did was take them to the gym and teach them a little about boxing. That way, I got to know them and they got some confidence in themselves.

My son—his name is Winston—played third base and shortstop and batted sixth or seventh in the line-up. The team had white uniforms with black trim. When Winston first got his uniform, he wouldn't take it off. That's how much it meant to him.

We lost our first few games, but I could see the team was getting better. I told them, "Don't get down. Do your best. Come back and win the next one."

Then everybody started hitting and we went on a winning streak. The first game we won, the kids were jumping up and down like they'd just won the World Series. I took them all out for pizza afterwards. That was such a great moment. It felt so good, the way the kids came together as a team and turned things around. I was so proud and happy for them.

WAYNE McCULLOUGH

I was eight years old, and they used me as goalkeeper for the eleven-year-old football [soccer] team at Spring Hill Primary School in Belfast. We played twenty or thirty games against other schools. Playing with bigger older boys the entire season was a thrill for me.

We won more than we lost. And there were games where I saved us from losing. I had quick reflexes and could jump like a monkey. I could catch and take the impact of the ball when it hit me. Football is a team game, but I loved the one-on-one challenge within the game. When you're the goalkeeper and the ball comes toward the goal, you're on your own.

My dream was to play goalkeeper at a higher level, but I didn't grow big enough. In high school, I was a defender. Then I gave football up to concentrate on boxing.

BRAD GOODMAN

I played ball lot when I was a kid; mostly baseball and football. When I got into my thirties, I turned to softball. I was a solid player, not great. I was playing for a team in a league in Queens [a borough of New York City] called The Bulls. We played every Sunday. This was a game we had to win to make the playoffs. The score was tied in the sixth inning. There were two outs and the other team had men on second and third base. The batter hit a shot to right field. I went to my left and made a diving catch. The next inning, we scored two runs and won the game.

My father was dying of cancer at the time. He liked watching me play, but he couldn't come to any of the playoff games because he was in hospice care by then. If your team won the championship, you got a jacket. I'd never won any kind of championship before. I'd always come up short. I can't tell you how badly I wanted to win this championship for him.

And we won. But it took a while to get the jacket. You had to order it and wait, and it didn't come until right after my father died. I remember the day it came. It was raining. I brought the jacket over to the funeral home and asked them to put it on my father. Then I put a letter in the coffin, telling him I loved him, and walked home in the rain.

MAX KELLERMAN

About twelve years ago, I was one of a bunch of guys from ESPN radio who played a team of former Major League Baseball players in a Minor League park in Connecticut. Brooks Robinson was our manager. I was playing left field. Ferguson Jenkins was pitching for the real players. He was just lobbing it in. Brian Kenny led off for us with a single. The next guy made an out, and I came up.

First pitch; I swung and missed. In fact, I swung so hard that I did a pinwheel. Jenkins looked at me and asked, "Did you try to take me deep?" I said, "No, sir," which, of course, I had.

Next pitch; a slow pitch down the middle. And I whacked it. I mean, I really got ahold of it. You know when you've smashed one. I'm thinking, "Line drive, deep in the gap, extra bases." It was as hard as I could hit a baseball. I'll remember that feeling until the day I die. And then George Foster, who was playing left field and was about a hundred years old, casually jogged over and caught it like a routine fly ball, which is all it was.

Later in the game, Pat Tabler hit a fly ball over my head. I went back for it and ran face-first into the wall. That was a three-run homer. And in my only other at bat that day, Rick Honeycut pitched to me like he was pitching batting practice and got me out on a pop up.

NONITO DONAIRE

It was in high school [San Lorenzo High School in the San Francisco Bay area]. At lunchtime, they'd have handball tournaments that lasted about an hour. There were a lot of guys; almost all of them were bigger than me; and some of them were good. But I made it to the finals and was up against this big tall kid. He was one of the guys who used to make fun of me all the time because I was so small. And I beat him. I've never won the lottery, but it must feel like what I felt that day. It felt so good. Then they gave me a T-shirt for winning the tournament. It was white with maroon trim, which were the school colors. And on the back, it said something about working hard to achieve your goals.

MICHAEL BUFFER

I had a good arm when I was young. I could throw a football fifty yards, although not with accuracy. I had no basketball skills at all. I couldn't make a lay-up. And I never had good hand-eye coordination, which meant I wasn't much of a hitter.

The Goossens used to put pick-up softball games together. They were good athletes. You had Greg Goossen, who had played Major League Baseball for the Mets. Dan was an athlete. There were brothers and sons and daughters and friends.

I played in a few of their games. One time, this was back in the 1980s, I was at bat. The pitch came in and I really got ahold of it. I knew it was gone the moment I hit it. It went out over the fence in left field. Running around the bases, I did the whole act. Dancing backwards, showing off. It was a little moment, but it meant something to me. I didn't hit a lot of home runs in my life, and that's the last home run I ever hit.

KEN HERSHMAN

I was a terrible baseball player. I was a pretty good guard in basketball, but I was too short. The sport I was best at was soccer.

In 1980, I played right forward on an all-star team from Long Island that was made up of sixteen and seventeen-year-olds. We were competitive at what I thought was a high level. Then we played against a team from Scotland. The Scottish kids were the same age we were. But it was no contest. I was in awe of their skills and the way they played the game. They were so much better than we were. They played at a completely different level.

We lost 5 to 0. There came a point where they were just toying with us and being merciful. They could have scored ten goals if they'd wanted to. Their replacement players were almost as good as their starters. But they stopped attacking. Instead of trying to score when they had the ball in front of our goal, they'd pass it back out again.

I'm a competitive person. If this had been a tournament final against a heated rival, I'm sure I would have felt differently about it. But I remember very clearly appreciating how good these guys were and appreciating the sport in a way that I never had before. To be on the field in the middle of that artistry was special for me. I remember it more vividly than any of the other games we won or lost that year. If someone told me that I could play against the New York Yankees for an inning, I'd do that too. It would be an incredible experience to share the field with athletes that good.

Despite its gravitas, there's a light side to boxing.

Fistic Nuggets

I was at ringside for eight consecutive Manny Pacquiao fights, starting with his eight-round demolition of Oscar De La Hoya in 2008. On five of those occasions, I was privileged to be in Manny's dressing room in the hours before and after the bout.

I watched Pacquiao-Marquez IV on television and, when it was over, thought back on the time I'd spent with Manny. One moment stood out on my mind.

On March 13, 2010, Pacquiao fought Joshua Clottey at Cowboys Stadium. Sports fans are familiar with the venue. It can accommodate 100,000 fans for boxing, has a retractable roof, and features a four-sided HDTV video board that's 160 feet long and weighs 600 tons.

Cowboys Stadium was close to empty when I arrived for the fight a little after 5:00 PM. I checked out my seat in the press section and made sure that my credential for dressing room access was in order. Then I explored the back corridors of the stadium, so I'd know how to make my way around. With time to spare, I sat for a while with John Duddy, who was readying to fight Michael Medina on the undercard.

I was in Pacquiao dressing room when Manny arrived at 7:50 PM. Over the next two hours, he went through his usual pre-fight rituals. Then it was time to leave for the ring, and I ran ahead to get to my seat.

Through the subterranean depths of Cowboys Stadium . . . Toward the tunnel that led into the . . .

Omigod !

The stadium had been a drab fluorescent gray with a few hundred people milling about when I'd arrived at 5:00 PM. Now a tunnel lined by Dallas Cowboys cheerleaders—sexual icons of our time—lay ahead. Beyond them, tens of thousands of fans were screaming. Music blared. Spotlights moved back and forth, casting everything in a silver other-worldly glow.

It was a bit intimidating.

I walked into the tunnel.

Then I said to myself, "Hauser, you've never been in a situation like this before and you'll never be in a situation like this again. So enjoy it for what it is."

The cheerleaders were bouncing up and down, their pom-poms and a lot more shaking. The crowd grew louder in anticipation of the fighters' ring entrance. Strobe lights flashed on and off.

As I walked through the tunnel, I said to myself, "This is how it feels to be the greatest fighter in the world."

★　★　★

Brad Goodman has become one of the premier matchmakers in boxing. Recently, he reminisced about the first professional fight he ever saw:

"I wasn't a boxing fan when I was a kid. But I had a cousin who was three years older than I was; and whatever he liked, I liked. I was eleven when Muhammad Ali fought Earnie Shavers at Madison Square Garden [on September 29, 1977]. My cousin was excited about the fight; so I asked my father to take me, and he did."

"My parents were divorced, so there was something special about a night out with my father. I'd never been to The Garden before. Walking into the arena, I could feel the excitement. We were there for all the preliminary fights, and I remember thinking how the sights and sounds were different from watching a fight on television."

"Reading the fight program, I decided that I was rooting for Shavers. He had all these knockouts and the program called him the hardest puncher in boxing history. I still remember how he looked, coming down the aisle to the theme music from S.W.A.T. Then Ali came down the aisle, and he looked invincible. The crowd had roared for Shavers, but that was nothing compared to the roar for Ali."

"When the fight started, my legs were shaking with excitement. I couldn't believe that I was there. It was a great fight. I was disappointed when they announced that Ali had won the decision. Most people think of that fight as Ali-Shavers; but for me, it will always be Shavers-Ali. I was hooked on Earnie."

"Two years later, Shavers fought Larry Holmes for the second time. That was the fight when he knocked Holmes down and almost killed him, and Holmes came back to win. I read that Shavers was training at the Concord Hotel and decided to go see him. I was thirteen by then. I cut school for a day, took a bus on my own to the Catskills, and actually met Earnie Shavers. His manager was a guy named Frank Luca, who also trained Earnie. Frank took a liking to me and gave me the T-shirt that he was wearing. I still have it. It says, 'Earnie Shavers—Next Champ.' That was the high point of my day. The low point was when I got home and saw police cars outside the apartment house we lived in. My mother thought I'd been kidnapped and had called the police. Believe me; I got punished."

★　★　★

Steve Albert has enjoyed a long and illustrious career in sports broadcasting as the voice of the New York Mets, New York Jets, Golden State Warriors, and New Jersey Devils. Boxing fans know him for his service as Showtime's blow-by-blow commentator for more than two decades.

Recently, Steve was reminiscing about a man who stopped him on the street and said, "I watch you all the time. I think you're wonderful."

Steve thanked his admirer and said it was gratifying whenever someone liked his work on television.

"Are you on television?" the man asked.

★　★　★

SOME WORDS OF WISDOM FROM LEGENDARY FIGHTERS

Joe Gans: "If you hit a man in a place that hurts, that's the place to hit him again. You only have to hit him half as hard there as any place else to finish him."

Willie Pep (on his victory over Sandy Saddler): "When I stepped on his toes, he said, 'Ouch?' So I stepped on his toes all night."

★　★　★

THINGS YOU'LL NEVER READ ON A BOXING WEBSITE

With fights like Povetkin-Rahman, boxing doesn't need Mayweather-Pacquiao this year.

Chuck Giampa is hosting *Saturday Night Live* tonight.

Al Haymon Speaks

★   ★   ★

An elevator operator named Ivan who works in the building I live in told me a story recently.

When Ivan was ten years old, his mother came back from visiting relatives in Puerto Rico. While she was waiting in the baggage claim area for her luggage, a crazy man jumped on the luggage carousel, started dancing, and gyrated his way through several 360-degree turns of the carousel. Then the crazy man picked up his luggage and left.

A week or so later, Ivan was watching a Hector Camacho fight on television when his mother came into the room and pointed at the screen.

"That's the crazy guy from the airport," she said.

This piece was part of a healing process.

A Letter from Emanuel Steward

Dear Tom,

I never got to say goodbye the way I wanted to. So I thought I'd say hello from here and bring you up to date on what's been happening lately.

I was in the hospital, not feeling good. Then I fell asleep. And the next thing I knew, I was in a car going through some pearly gates. I asked the driver where we were, and he said, "You'll see."

That night, there was a big welcome dinner for me. I couldn't believe all the people who were there. James Corbett, Bob Fitzsimmons, and Marcel Cerdan came over and introduced themselves. John L. Sullivan was at the next table. He's drinking again. What a character.

I was sitting next to Joe Louis. That was a real honor. I was so happy, I said to Joe, "This is fantastic. I feel like I've died and gone to heaven."

Joe told me, "That's exactly what you done."

It's amazing up here. The first fights I saw were Sam Langford against Gene Tunney and Benny Leonard against Joe Gans. Everyone goes in tough. Rocky Marciano has lost a few times. Joe Louis stopped him in the eleventh round. That was payback for what Rocky did to Joe at Madison Square Garden in 1951. But Marciano has won his share of fights and a loss on a fighter's record doesn't matter that much.

There are no sanctioning bodies. We've got same-day weigh-ins. All the fights are on free TV. It's boxing, so the only way a fighter can win is by hurting the other guy. But they fight more often here than down on earth because the recovery time is shorter.

Arturo Gatti fights mostly in the small clubs. Every time out, it's standing room only. He had a war against Lenny Mancini about a year ago that people are still talking about. Teddy Brenner made that match.

Joe Frazier got here, and the first thing he wanted to do was fight Jack Johnson. He said that Papa Jack reminded him of Ali.

Eddie Futch and Yank Durham told him, "Joe; hold off a bit. You have to get used to the altitude."

Joe said, "Fuck the altitude. I want to fight."

I'm training fighters with Luther Burgess and Bill Miller the way I did years ago. Ray Arcel has given me a lot of tips. What's really exciting is that Archie Moore asked me to work his corner when he fights Sugar Ray Robinson at Yankee Stadium at the end of the month.

That's the old Yankee Stadium. One of the things I love about this place is the venues. James Jeffries is scheduled to fight Jess Willard at the Polo Grounds later this year. Georges Carpentier is going up against Billy Conn at Boyle's Thirty Acres.

I've also been doing some television commentary. Last week, I called the fight between Henry Armstrong and Salvador Sanchez. It was my first time working with Don Dunphy, and I was a little nervous. But before the fight, Don told me, "You don't have to talk all the time. There are no network executives to please. Just sit back, enjoy the fight, and say what comes to mind when there's something important to say."

I learned so much over the years working with Jim, Larry, and Harold that I fit in fine with Don. The fight was amazing. I used to watch films of Henry Armstrong. And now I was watching him fight live.

Well, not exactly live. But he was right in front of me.

Armstrong didn't throw combinations as much as he threw punches all the time. When the bell rang, he got in Sanchez's face and banged away non-stop from every angle. It wasn't just bang! He was like a machine gun. Bang-bang-bang-bang-bang-bang! I started explaining to the TV audience all the subtle things that Henry was doing. He was keeping his chin close to his chest, so Sanchez couldn't hit him cleanly. He had a way of getting his elbows back against his body so, when he got inside, Sanchez couldn't tie him up. And his arms never got out to where Sanchez could clinch with him.

When the fight was over, Dunphy patted me on the shoulder and said, "You did just fine."

Jack Dempsey is fighting Rocky Marciano at the old Madison Square Garden in six weeks. I'm signed to work with Dunphy again on that one. Do you know how excited I am about that?

I was talking with A. J. Liebling the other day and told him I'd always dreamed of something like this. That night, Liebling gave me a poem by Robert Browning. There's a line in it that reads, "A man's reach should exceed his grasp, or what's a heaven for?"

Anyway; tell everybody you talk with that I appreciate all the nice things they've said about me. I can't believe Aretha Franklin sang at my memorial service.

Tell Wladimir that he'll do just fine without me.

Tell Lennox that I smile whenever I think of him.

Tommy Hearns was my first big star. Make sure he knows how much that meant to me.

Hilmer Kenty, Milton McCrory, Michael Moorer, all the champions I had; if you run into them, let them how much joy working with them brought me.

And the same goes for all the fighters I worked with who never made it beyond six-round club fights but were champions at heart.

I was blessed with an extraordinary group of friends and lived my life the way I wanted to live it.

Warm wishes,
Emanuel

Issues and Answers

This was the most important article I wrote in 2012.

The PED Mess

PART ONE

On December 30, 2009, Manny Pacquiao sued Floyd Mayweather Jr, Floyd Sr (Mayweather's father), Roger Mayweather (Floyd's uncle and trainer), Mayweather Promotions, Richard Schaefer, and Oscar De La Hoya for defamation. Pacquiao's complaint, filed in the United States District Court of Nevada, alleged that each of the defendants had falsely accused him of using, and continuing to use, illegal performance enhancing drugs.

Mayweather has gone to great lengths to position himself in the public mind as a "clean" fighter. For his three most recent fights (against Shane Mosley, Victor Ortiz, and Miguel Cotto), he has mandated that he and his opponent be subjected to what he calls "Olympic-style testing" by the United States Anti-Doping Agency (USADA).

USADA is an independent non-governmental sports drug-testing agency whose services are utilized by the United States Olympic and Paralympic movement. It receives approximately $10,000,000 annually in public funding; more in years when the Olympics are held. USADA was paid a reported $100,000 per fight for the drug-testing services that it performed in conjunction with Mayweather's outings.

Victor Conte is one of the most knowledgeable people in sports with regard to the use of, and testing for, performance enhancing drugs. In 1984, Conte founded the Bay Area Laboratory Co-Operative (BALCO), which was at the heart of several much-publicized PED scandals. In 2005, he pled guilty to charges of illegal steroid distribution and tax fraud and spent four months in prison. After being released from incarceration, Conte moved to the side of the angels and is now a formidable advocate for "clean" sport.

"Mayweather is not doing Olympic-style testing," Conte states. "I've never liked the use of that phrase. 'Olympic' means 24-7-365. To be effective, drug testing has to be twenty-four hours a day, seven days a week, 365 days a year. The benefits that an athlete retains from using anabolic steroids and certain other PEDs carry over for months. That means athletes can develop their strength and speed base early and the benefits of PED use will last after that use has been discontinued. If you wait to start testing until eight to ten weeks in advance of a fight, which is what Mayweather does, that's not Olympic-style testing. Who knows what Mayweather or his opponent has been doing during the previous six months."

Tests for a Mayweather fight generally begin around the time of the kick-off press tour heralding Floyd's annual ring appearance. Floyd and his opponent agree to keep USADA advised as to their whereabouts and submit to an unlimited number of unannounced blood and urine tests. Other details (such as which drugs are being tested for, how samples are analyzed, and what happens in the event of a positive test) are murky.

Mayweather and his promoter (Golden Boy Promotions) have gone to great lengths to propagate the notion that they're in the forefront of PED testing to "clean up" boxing. In return, they've reaped a public-relations bonanza. But some members of Team Mayweather haven't been content to simply disseminate a positive message with regard to Floyd's conduct. They've chosen instead to brand Pacquiao (Mayweather's chief rival) as a PED user.

Floyd Mayweather Sr declared, "He [Pacquiao] can't beat Clottey without that shit in him. He couldn't beat De La Hoya without that shit. He couldn't beat Ricky Hatton without that shit. And he couldn't beat Cotto without that shit. I don't even think he could beat that kid from Chicago [David Diaz] without that shit. He wouldn't be able to beat any of those guys without enhancement drugs."

Not to be outdone, Roger Mayweather proclaimed, "This motherfucker don't want to take the test. That's why the fight [Mayweather vs. Pacquiao] didn't happen. He got that shit in him. That's why he didn't want to take the test."

References to Pacquiao's alleged PED use by the other defendants in the defamation action were more subtle. But their message was similar.

The court case moved slowly, as litigation often does. Last year, the claims against Schaefer and De La Hoya were dismissed with the consent of Pacquiao's attorneys after Richard and Oscar apologized and stated that they had never meant to suggest that Manny was using performance-enhancing drugs.

The Mayweathers continued to fight the complaint. Floyd's conduct in failing to appear for a scheduled deposition on several occasions displeased the court and infuriated Pacquiao's attorneys. The case looked like it would be a long battle of attrition. Then things changed dramatically.

Under standard sports drug-testing protocols, when blood or urine is taken from an athlete, it's divided into an "A" and "B" sample. The "A" sample is tested first. If it tests negative, end of story. If the "A" sample tests positive, the athlete then has the right to demand that the "B" sample be tested. If the "B" sample tests negative, the athlete is presumed to be clean. But if the "B" sample also tests positive, the first positive finding is confirmed and the athlete has a problem.

On May 20, 2012, a rumor filtered through the drug-testing community that Mayweather had tested positive on three occasions for an illegal performance enhancing drug.

More specifically, it was rumored that Mayweather's "A" sample had tested positive on three occasions and, after each positive test, USADA had found exceptional circumstances in the form of inadvertent use and given Floyd a waiver. This waiver, according to the rumor, negated the need for a test of Floyd's "B" sample. And because the "B" sample was never tested, a loophole in USADA's contract with Mayweather and Golden Boy allowed the testing to proceed without the positive "A" sample results being reported to Mayweather's opponent or the Nevada State Athletic Commission (which had jurisdiction over the fights).

In late-May, Pacquiao's attorneys heard the rumor. On June 4, 2012, they served document demands and subpoenas on Mayweather, Mayweather Promotions, Golden Boy, and USADA calling for the production of all documents that related to PED testing of Mayweather for the Mosley, Ortiz, and Cotto fights.

The documents were not produced. There was a delay in the proceedings while Floyd spent nine weeks in the Clark County Detention Center after pleading guilty to charges of domestic violence and harassment. Upon his release from jail on August 2, settlement talks heated up.

On September 25, 2012, a stipulation of settlement ending the defamation case was filed with the court. The parties agreed that the terms of settlement would be kept confidential. Prior to the agreement being signed, two sources with detailed knowledge of the proceedings told this writer that Mayweather's initial monetary settlement offer was "substantially more" than Pacquiao's attorneys had expected it would be and that an agreement in principle was reached soon afterward.

As part of the settlement, the Mayweathers and Mayweather Promotions issued a statement that read: "Floyd Mayweather Jr, Floyd Mayweather Sr, Roger Mayweather, and Mayweather Promotions wish to make it clear that they never intended to claim that Manny Pacquiao has used or is using any performance enhancing drugs, nor are they aware of any evidence that Manny Pacquiao has used performance enhancing drugs. Manny Pacquiao is a great champion, and no one should construe any of our prior remarks as claiming that Manny Pacquiao has used performance enhancing drugs."

I don't know if Floyd Mayweather or Manny Pacquiao has used performance-enhancing drugs or not.

I do know that, if Mayweather's "A" sample tested positive for a performance enhancing drug on one or more occasions and he was given a waiver by USADA that concealed this fact from the Nevada State Athletic Commission, his opponent, and the public, we have an ingredient that could contribute to the making of a scandal.

Any analysis of PED use and boxing should start with the acknowledgement that chemistry is now part of sports.

We know certain things about the use of illegal performance enhancing drugs:

(1) PEDs offer more than a shortcut. They take an athlete to a place that he, or she, might not be able to get to without them. When undertaken in conjunction with proper exercise and training, the use of PEDs creates a better athlete.

(2) PED use is often difficult to detect. Sophisticated users evade detection in the face of rigorous testing. The more money an athlete spends, the less detectible PED use is. Also, in many instances, the testing is erratic, inadequate, and even corrupt. Three years ago, Victor Conte declared, "Boxing's testing program is beyond a joke. It's worthless. The loopholes are so big that you could drive a Mack Truck through them. Many of the people who are supposed to be regulating this don't want to know." Now Conte says, "In some respects, things have gotten worse."

(3) PED use is more prevalent in boxing now than ever before, particularly at the elite level. For many fighters, the prevailing ethic seems to be, "If you're not cheating, you're not trying." Fighters are reconfiguring their bodies and, in some instances, look like totally different physical beings. In a clean world, fighters don't get older, heavier, and faster at the same time. But that's what's happening in boxing. Improved performances at an advanced age are becoming common. Fighters at age thirty-five are outperforming what they could do when they were thirty. In some instances, fighters are starting to perform at an elite level at an age when they would normally be expected to be on a downward slide.

(4) The use of PEDs threatens the short-term and long-term health of the user. It's illegal and gives an athlete who uses them an unfair competitive advantage. It also endangers fighters who are getting hit in the head harder than before by opponents.

Earlier this year, a handful of high-profile cases became part of boxing's PED dialogue.

On May 4, 2012, WBA-IBF 140-pound champion Lamont Peterson learned that his "A" and "B" urine samples had tested positive for the presence of an anabolic steroid. Peterson had been scheduled to defend his titles in a rematch against Amir Khan. The fight was cancelled.

Two weeks later, the "A" and "B" urine samples of WBC 147-pound champion Andre Berto tested positive for norandrosterone (an anabolic steroid). Berto was slated to defend his belt against Victor Ortiz. That fight, too, was cancelled.

On June 22, it was revealed that, subsequent to Antonio Tarver's June 2 fight in California against Lateef Koyode, Tarver's pre-fight urine sample had tested positive for the anabolic steroid drostanolone. On fight night, the bout had been declared a draw. The result was changed to "no contest."

Finally, on October 18, two days before Erik Morales challenged Danny Garcia for the latter's WBA and WBC titles, word leaked to the media that Morales had tested positive for clenbuterol. Initially, the public was led to believe by the promotion that only Morales's "A" sample had tested positive and there was a need for his "B" sample to be tested (which couldn't be done until after the fight). Then it was learned that Morales had been tested on two occasions earlier in the month and, each time, both his "A" and "B" samples had tested positive. Despite that revelation, Garcia-Morales was allowed to take place.

In seeking out the truth behind the above-referenced matters, this writer interviewed dozens of participants and observers. Two people of note declined to be interviewed.

Golden Boy CEO Richard Schaefer sent a November 1, 2012, email that read in part, "We are trying to do something positive, and yet it seems that media and others are attacking us. It would be easy for us to do nothing just like all other promoters. But by trying to support the fighters' desire for additional testing, we are getting criticized."

Beyond that, Schaefer chose not to discuss the issues involved. Instead, his email referenced my relationships with Dr. Margaret Goodman and Gabriel Montoya and stated, "I consider you a friend and really don't want this Margaret Goodman, Gabriel Montoya vs. Golden Boy witch-hunt to affect our relationship. I have my opinion about Margaret and Gabriel, and you have yours. I respect your opinion, and I hope you respect mine."

Dr. Goodman was once chief ringside physician for the Nevada State Athletic Commission. She is now president and board chairperson of a drug-testing organization known as VADA (Voluntary Anti-Doping Agency). The drug tests on Lamont Peterson and Andre Berto that came back positive were carried out under the supervision of VADA.

Dr. Goodman is a friend. We've talked at length over the years about medical issues and boxing. She has been a valuable resource to me in my writing. We've also shared thoughts and offered advice to each other on a variety of subjects, both personal and professional.

Gabriel Montoya has written a series of significant articles on the use of PEDs in boxing. Earlier this year, I spoke with Schaefer on Montoya's behalf after Gabriel was denied access and credentials for certain Golden Boy events. I also spoke with Montoya about his problems with Golden Boy and what might be done to remedy the situation. Gabriel is a casual acquaintance.

I should add that, although I sometimes disagree with things that Richard Schaefer has done (just as he sometimes disagrees with what I write), I admire his skills and we've maintained a cordial relationship over the years

USADA CEO Travis Tygart also declined to be interviewed for this article and instructed that questions be addressed to USADA's media-relations manager, Annie Skinner. On November 2, this writer sent a series of preliminary questions to Ms. Skinner. There was no response.

At this point, it makes sense to take a closer look at the recent positive drug tests referenced earlier in this article.

In March 2012, Lamont Peterson and Amir Khan submitted applications to VADA pursuant to which their blood and urine were tested in conjunction with their scheduled May 19 fight. The first samples were taken on March 19, the only day on which the fighters knew in advance that they would be tested.

On April 12, VADA was advised by the UCLA Olympic Analytical Laboratory that Peterson's "A" sample had tested positive consistent with the administration of an anabolic steroid. On April 13, the Peterson camp was notified of that fact by FedEx and e-mail. In keeping with VADA's protocols, Peterson was given one week to challenge the "A" test result and ask for his "B" sample to be tested with one of his representatives present.

The Peterson team waited eight days (until April 21) to respond. Then it chose to challenge the positive test result, asserted its right to be present when the "B" sample was tested, and asked that the "B" sample be tested on Friday, April 27. The UCLA laboratory advised VADA that Friday was an inappropriate day to begin testing because four consecutive days were needed to complete the test.

The testing of Peterson's "B" sample began on Monday, April 30. On May 3, VADA was advised by the laboratory that this sample had also tested positive. The Peterson camp was so notified by FedEx and e-mail on May 4. That same day, VADA also sent a letter by FedEx and fax to Keith Kizer (executive director of the Nevada State Athletic Commission) stating the facts of the matter.

The Peterson-Khan rematch was cancelled.

Richard Schaefer was livid at the way in which drug testing for Peterson-Khan unfolded. Golden Boy was to have promoted the fight, and he felt that VADA should have notified him as soon as Peterson's "A" sample tested positive.

Margaret Goodman says that, after Peterson's "A" sample tested positive, she asked Lamont's attorney (Jeff Fried) whether there was an agreement between Peterson and Golden Boy that authorized VADA to release the "A" test results to the promoter. Fried told her that no such authorization existed.

Ryan Connolly is counsel for VADA. In the late 1990s, he was the business manager for the UCLA Olympic Analytical Laboratory. He's now an attorney in private practice with an expertise in PED testing in the context of competitive sports. In that role, he oversaw the process outlined in a May 10, 2012, document entitled "Statement of VADA."

"When VADA became involved with the Peterson-Khan fight," that statement reads, "the individual athletes signed up for the VADA program and executed the proper documentation. VADA was told that GBP [Golden Boy Promotions] also wanted a contract so that GBP would be authorized to receive the testing results, including the preliminary results from an 'A' sample analysis. In order for VADA to release the preliminary 'A' sample results to a third party such as GBP, VADA requires an executed authorization allowing us to do so. VADA sent GBP a draft contract for its signature which would have authorized the preliminary 'A' sample results to be released to GBP. This initial draft, which was never signed, contained a clause pursuant to which GBP would have represented that it had obtained the necessary authorization from the fighters. GBP's legal team rejected this clause and instead suggested making the fighters signatories to the contract with their signatures being the necessary authorization. VADA's counsel made it clear to GBP that, if GBP wanted to handle it this way, GBP must take responsibility for obtaining the athlete's signatures. Unfortunately, GBP never obtained the signatures. The bottom line is that VADA had no contract with GBP. This is not a mere technicality. It involves issues of medical ethics. VADA needed a signed contract in order to deviate from its Results Management Policy (posted on our website) and release the preliminary and personal medical information to a third party. VADA would have been happy to inform GBP of the preliminary 'A' results. But we needed a signed authorization allowing us to do so, which we never received. VADA has complied in every way with all signed contracts that we had and will continue to do so."

Dr. Goodman elaborates on that theme, saying, "As per our contracts and protocols, VADA gives certain test results to the athletic commission in any jurisdiction where the fighter holds a license or a request for a license is pending. We also release certain results to FightFax, the Asso-

ciation of Boxing Commissions, and whomever else the athlete asks us to
release them to. We'd be happy to release any and all results to a fighter's
promoter, but we need an authorization from the fighter to do so. That's
the law and those are the terms in the Results Management Policy posted
on the VADA website."

As a postscript, the Peterson camp later claimed that Lamont had
tested positive because of the surgical implantation of "testosterone pellets" to correct a testosterone deficiency known as hypogonadism.

That led Ryan Connolly to observe that more than a few elite athletes suffer from hypogonadism and note, "This may seem odd since these
athletes are physical specimens. How can they be so muscular and fit but
have natural testosterone production deficiencies at a higher rate than
ordinary people? The dirty little secret is not necessarily that these athletes
are lying about their hypogonadism. The dirty little secret is the likely cause
of the hypogonadism in the first place—past anabolic steroid abuse."

Meanwhile, even before the Peterson controversy subsided, a new
controversy was brewing. Andre Berto and Victor Ortiz had submitted
applications for VADA testing in advance of their scheduled June 23, 2012,
fight. On May 11, Dr. Goodman was advised by the UCLA Olympic
Analytical Laboratory that an "A" sample urine specimen taken from
Berto had tested positive for norandrosterone (an anabolic steroid) at a
level above the permitted amount.

On May 12, following VADA protocols, Goodman notified the
Berto camp. Berto was advised by FedEx. Tony Morgan (Berto's trainer,
who had been listed on notice forms as a designated recipient of information) was advised of the finding by e-mail, as was Al Haymon (Berto's
manager).

Dr. Goodman's e-mail to each recipient read in part, "VADA urges
you to immediately notify Golden Boy Promotions [the lead promoter
on the fight], DiBella Entertainment [Berto's promoter], and the
California State Athletic Commission of this positive "A" sample finding
by forwarding each party a copy of this notification so that it is received
by each party as quickly as possible but no later than 3:00 PM on
Monday, May 14. Please confirm to VADA in writing that you have forwarded a copy to each party by that time."

The requested confirmation was not forthcoming. Instead, on May

14, Dr. Goodman received a letter from Howard Jacobs (an attorney retained by Berto), who warned that telling anyone other than Berto's representatives about the "A" sample positive could result in "civil liability on the part of VADA."

On May 15, Goodman sent an e-mail to Al Haymon that read, "Dear Al, As you are aware, Mr. Berto has asserted a medical privilege insofar as VADA is concerned. I would think that you will be held personally accountable by Golden Boy Promotions and DiBella Entertainment for your failure to notify them of this issue in a timely manner. Please advise us with regard to whether or not you have notified GBP and DBE. Thank you, Margaret Goodman."

There was no response.

That same day, Ryan Connolly sent an email to Howard Jacobs urging similar notification.

On May 18, Dr. Goodman was advised by the UCLA Olympic Analytical Laboratory that Berto's "B" sample urine specimen had tested positive. VADA then notified Berto, his designated representatives, and the California State Athletic Commission.

Haymon, in turn, notified Richard Schaefer. Lou DiBella says that, despite the fact that he was Berto's promoter, neither Schaefer nor Haymon advised him that Andre's "A" and "B" samples had tested positive until plans were underway to replace Berto as an opponent for Victor Ortiz with Josesito Lopez (another Haymon fighter, who was promoted by Golden Boy in conjunction with Goossen-Tutor).

"How do you think that makes me feel," DiBella asks rhetorically. "I raised the issue with Al afterward, and he didn't say anything. That told me all I needed to know."

Haymon, like Richard Schaefer and Travis Tygart, declined to be interviewed for this article.

Berto later told RingtvOnline, "To all of my fans who have been supportive, you know, everybody who knows me; they know that everything that I've always accomplished has just been through hard work. And when it comes to the positive test, that was just a situation that was unfortunate. It was a situation that didn't get properly explained to the public on what it was and what caused it. I believe that's what really made an uproar about everything. You know, like I've said, I've never been a cheater. Never have and never will. I've never injected anything in any type of situation at all. So when it comes up as a positive test, it didn't have anything to do with any type of drug enhancement or any type of testosterone or EPO or none of that type of stuff that a lot of guys probably use. It was, after we got the positive test, we just needed to know what it was because we knew that everything that we were doing was straightforward. After they put the news out, that's when we found out exactly what it was. Then I had to go through all of the right processes and the hiring of the lawyers and things like that. So it was basically just taking my sample test and just really proving the fact that it was a contamination of something. I couldn't believe it happened the way it did with no explanation for it to the press or the public. The way it was put out there without explaining exactly what it was and how much upset me. Nothing was really explained to the public."

There's a bit of hypocrisy there. Berto expressed unhappiness that news of his positive tests "was put out there without explaining exactly what it was . . . to the public." But as previously noted, his own lawyer had made it clear to VADA that the dissemination of information to third parties should be kept to a minimum under threat of civil liability on the part of VADA.

Given Golden Boy's professed commitment to making boxing a clean sport, Richard Schaefer might have been expected to commend VADA for its findings with regard to Peterson and Berto. Instead, he seemed intent on attacking Dr. Goodman and VADA.

On May 22, Arnold Joseph (counsel for Golden Boy) sent a letter to Goodman stating Golden Boy's intention to sue VADA for not notifying the promoter that Peterson's "A" sample had tested positive; a failure that Joseph claimed was magnified by VADA reporting the "B" sample positive to the Nevada State Athletic Commission and not to Golden Boy.

To date, no lawsuit has been filed. But three days later, Golden Boy terminated a column on medical issues that Goodman had written monthly for *The Ring* (now owned by Golden Boy) since 2004.

"I guess the only question I have is why it took so long for Richard to fire me," Dr. Goodman said afterward. "Once Golden Boy bought the magazine, I was told I couldn't cover certain topics like more insurance coverage for catastrophic injuries suffered by fighters. Michael Rosenthal [the editor who replaced Nigel Collins at *The Ring*] is a great guy. He's been very supportive. But I could see the writing on the wall. You know; the first column I wrote for *Ring* eight years ago was about Fernando Vargas testing positive for Winstrol. It was called 'JUICED!' How ironic is that?"

At the same time Golden Boy was attacking Margaret Goodman, it also took aim at Gabriel Montoya.

Montoya, as previously noted, has written a number of articles on the use of PEDs in boxing. On May 20, 2012, a source with extensive knowledge in the area of drug testing told him that he believed Floyd Mayweather had tested positive on three occasions for performance enhancing drugs and that, in each instance, the test results had been covered up by Golden Boy and USADA.

Montoya did what a responsible journalist is supposed to do. He began to question people in boxing and the world of PED testing about the rumors. On May 23, he received a letter from Jeffrey Spitz (an attorney for Golden Boy).

Montoya says that the Spitz letter mischaracterized the nature of his investigation. There was no mistaking the fact that the letter accused him of making false and defamatory statements with regard to Golden Boy and threatened legal action against him.

"There was an earlier time when Golden Boy wouldn't credential me for its fights because I sent out some tweets that Oscar didn't like," Montoya recounts. "But I spoke with Schaefer and we worked past that. Then I started looking into the issue of Floyd's drug tests. I got the threatening letter from Spitz, which I posted on Maxboxing. And I was banned again from Golden Boy fights."

For example, Montoya was told that he would be credentialed for the June 30, 2012, fight card headlined by Cornelius Bundrage vs. Cory Spinks at Fantasy Springs Resort Casino. Then, on June 29, he received an e-mail from Anndee Laskoe (public-relations manager for the Cabazon Band of Mission Indians), who wrote, "I have been asked by Golden Boy Promotions to remove your name from the press credential list for the June 30th fights at Fantasy Springs. I am sorry for any inconvenience this may have caused you."

Golden Boy publicists Monica Sears and Ramiro Gonzalez were copied on the email.

Meanwhile, other troubling incidents were brewing.

In mid-May 2012, Winky Wright was preparing to fight Peter Quillin in a June 2 bout promoted by Golden Boy at the Home Depot Center in Carson, California.

"Everybody kept popping up positive for all this stuff," Wright told Montoya. "Boxing isn't always a fair game. I figured I should get this [testing] too. So I called Golden Boy and said 'Why we ain't doing it?' They was like 'Uh, etcetera, etcetera, this and this and that, and someone didn't want to pay.' I said 'Okay; I'm going to pay for it. I just want to play on the same field.'"

Wright and Quillin entered into a May 21, 2012, contract with Golden Boy and USADA pursuant to which USADA was to provide drug-testing services in conjunction with their fight.

"I didn't know the difference between [USADA and VADA]." Wright says. "I just told Golden Boy I wanted to be tested and they came back with USADA."

On or about May 23, USADA collected blood and urine samples from Quillin. Wright gave samples on May 24.

"They came to my house at six in the morning," Winky recalls. "They took urine, blood, everything."

Then, without warning, Wright was told that the testing was off.

"I think it was like two days later," Winky told Montoya. "Golden Boy called and told Damian [Damian Ramirez, Wright's manager], and Damian told me. I don't understand it. All I'm asking is 'How do you take urine and take blood and then, all of sudden, you say you aren't going to test it?' Then they tried to make up an excuse and say they wanted to teach us. There ain't nothing to teach. They took blood. They told us we would take a test and either come up positive or negative. That's it. All I want to know is, are we playing on the same field. So my lawyer called and asked for it to be tested, and they told him they threw it out. They told my attorney they threw it out. That's crazy. Why would they throw it out? They just finished [taking samples] and they're going to throw it out already? Does this sound crazy? We gave samples. Let's test that and let me see the result. They threw it out. I just don't understand that."

Quillin-Wright went ahead as planned with Quillin winning a unanimous ten-round decision. Quillin, like Andre Berto and Floyd Mayweather, is managed by Al Haymon.

The contract that Wright and Quillin entered into with Golden Boy and USADA specifically provided, "USADA will be responsible for storing the samples after collection and transporting them safely and securely to a laboratory for analysis . . . USADA will send all samples for analysis to a WADA [World Anti-Doping Agency] accredited laboratory under contract to USADA . . . USADA shall maintain Sample Collection Documentation, including test results for testing conducted under this Master Agreement, for a period of six years."

"The destruction of samples isn't supposed to happen," Ryan Connolly states. "If that happened in an Olympic context, it would set off alarms in a lot of places. There would likely be a thorough investigation by the International Olympic Committee and WADA."

Victor Conte adds, "The trend in drug-testing now is to save samples longer than before, not pour them down the drain."

But the worst was yet to come.

PART TWO

Scott Hale runs a small website called HaleStormSports.com. On Thursday, October 18, 2012, at approximately 8:30 AM Pacific Coast time, Hale got a telephone call from a source in New York who told him that Erik Morales (who was scheduled to fight Danny Garcia two days later on a Golden Boy card at Barclays Center in Brooklyn) had tested positive for a banned substance.

"I knew they were about to start the [final pre-fight] press conference," Hale recalls. "And I assumed the fight would be cancelled. Four hours later, I went online and saw that the fight was still on and the story hadn't broken. So I made some follow-up calls and a second source confirmed the story. Then a third source called me to confirm, but I still didn't know what the drug was."

"At that point," Hale continues, "I called USADA and Golden Boy. Neither of them would confirm the story. One of my partners called the New York State Athletic Commission. They said they didn't know anything about it. But our sources were solid. All three of them are reliable. So we decided to go with the story."

The snowball rolled from there.

Initially, Golden Boy and USADA engaged in damage control.

Dan Rafael of ESPN.com spoke with two sources and wrote, "The reason the fight has not been called off, according to one of the sources, is because Morales's 'A' sample tested positive but the results of the 'B' sample test likely won't be available until after the fight. '[USADA] said it could be a false positive,' one of the sources with knowledge of the disclosure said. 'But from what I understand, they won't know until the test on the 'B' sample comes back. That probably won't be until after the fight.'"

Richard Schaefer told Chris Mannix of SI.com, "USADA has now started the process. The process will play out. There is not going to be a rush to judgment. Morales is a legendary fighter. And really, nobody deserves a rush to judgment. You are innocent until proven guilty."

Also on Thursday, Schaefer told Rick Reeno of BoxingScene.com, "I think what is important here is that there is not going to be a witch hunt against Erik Morales. Let's allow the process to play out."

The New York State Athletic Commission was blindsided on the Morales matter. The first notice it received came in a three-way telephone conversation with representatives of Golden Boy and USADA after the Thursday press conference. In that conversation, the commission was told that there were "some questionable test results" for Morales but that testing of Morales's "B" sample would not be available until after the fight.

Then, on Friday (one day before the scheduled fight), Keith Idec revealed on BoxingScene.com that samples had been taken from Morales on at least three occasions. Final results from the samples taken on October 17 were not in yet. But both the "A" and "B" samples taken from Morales on October 3 and October 10th had tested positive for clenbuterol. In other words, Morales had tested positive for clenbuterol four times.

Clenbuterol is widely used by bodybuilders and athletes. It helps the body increase its metabolism and process the conversion of carbohydrates, proteins, and fats into useful energy. It also boosts muscle growth and eliminates excess fats caused by the use of certain steroids.

Under the WADA code, no amount of clenbuterol is allowed in a competitor's body. The measure is qualitative, not quantitative. Either clenbuterol is there or it's not. If it's there, the athlete has a problem.

After the positive tests were revealed, Morales claimed that he'd inadvertently ingested clebuterol by eating contaminated meat. No evidence was offered in support of that contention.

Nor was any explanation forthcoming as to why USADA kept taking samples from Morales after four tests (two "A" samples and two "B" samples from separate collections) came back positive. Giving Morales those additional tests was like giving someone who has been arrested for driving while intoxicated a second and third blood test a week after the arrest. The whole idea behind "cycling" is that it enables an athlete to use illegal PEDs, stop using them at a predetermined point in time, and then test clean in the days leading up to an event. A fighter shouldn't be given the opportunity to test again and again until he tests clean.

Also, Richard Schaefer vigorously attacked Margaret Goodman and VADA for not advising him that Lamont Peterson's "A" sample had come back positive. But not only did Schaefer fail to notify Lou DiBella (Andre Berto's promoter) in a timely manner that Berto had tested positive for norandrosterone; Schaefer didn't tell the New York State Athletic Commission in a timely manner that Morales had tested positive for clenbuterol. Rather, it appears as though the commission and the public were deliberately misled with regard to the testing and how many tests Morales had failed.

The moment that the "B" sample from Morales's first test came back positive, that information should have been forwarded to the New York State Athletic Commission. The fact that USADA had positive test results from two "A" and two "B" samples and didn't transmit those results to the NYSAC raises serious questions regarding USADA's credibility.

WOULD USADA HANDLE THE TESTING OF AN OLYMPIC ATHLETE THE WAY IT HANDLED THE MORALES TESTING?

"The Erik Morales case is a travesty," says Victor Conte. "Golden Boy and USADA seem to have made up a new set of rules without telling anyone what they are. What are the rules? Explain yourself, please! In 'Olympic-style testing,' you don't have an 'A' sample and a 'B' sample test positive, and then another 'A' sample and 'B' sample test positive, and keep testing until you get a negative. What happened with Erik Morales should put everything that USADA and Golden Boy have done in boxing under a microscope. This is more than suspicious to me. It's outrageous."

Incredibly, Garcia-Morales was allowed to proceed. This, in effect, amounted to a "get out of jail free" card for Garcia. Morales, a heavy underdog, was knocked out in the fourth round. But had Erik won the fight, the positive drug tests (which had been concealed prior to the leak on Hale Storm Sports) could have been used to overturn the result and give Garcia back his belts.

Garcia is managed by Al Haymon and is considered by Golden Boy to be one of its stars of the future.

Since the Morales incident, people in the PED-testing community have begun to question the curious role played in boxing by USADA. When someone hears "USADA testing," the assumption is that it's legitimate. In that light, the reports that Erik Morales's "A" and "B" samples tested positive for clenbuterol on two occasions without notification to the New York State Athletic Commission are extremely troubling.

Don Catlin founded the UCLA Olympic Analytical Laboratory in 1982 and is one of the founders of modern drug testing in sports.

"USADA should not enter into a contract that doesn't call for it to report positive test results to the appropriate governing body." Catlin states. "If it's true that USADA reported the results [in the Morales case] to Golden Boy and not to the governing state athletic commission, that's a recipe for deception."

When asked about the possibility of withholding notification because of inadvertent use (such as eating contaminated meat), Catlin declares, "No! The International Olympic Committee allowed for those waivers twenty-five years ago, and it didn't work. An athlete takes a steroid, tests positive, and then claims it was inadvertent. No one says, 'I was cheating. You caught me.'"

But more importantly, Catlin says, "USADA is a testing organization. USADA should not be making decisions regarding waivers and exemptions. That would make USADA judge and jury."

Ryan Connolly is in accord and adds, "There is no such thing in the Olympic world as an inadvertent use waiver. Athletes are strictly liable for what they put in their bodies. Inadvertent use might affect the length of an athlete's suspension, but the athlete would still be disqualified from the competition that he, or she, was being tested for."

"I'm not sure what rules USADA is following," Connolly continues.

"But under WADA protocols, you wouldn't see samples being destroyed and you wouldn't see re-tests for clenbuterol positives."

In other words, USADA seems to have one set of rules for testing Olympic athletes and another set of rules when it tests fighters for Golden Boy.

"It looks to me like USADA and Golden Boy are making up the rules as they go along," says Victor Conte. "One of the things that enables them to do it is that there's no transparency to USADA's testing for any of the fighters. What drugs are they testing for? What tests have been performed? What were the results? Why is Travis Tygart doing this?"

One might also ask why Golden Boy and Richard Schaefer are doing this.

"I think that Richard really wanted to be in the forefront on drug testing when he first got involved," one Golden Boy employee (who, for obvious reasons, wishes to remain anonymous) says. "He knew it would ingratiate him with Floyd. It would get him some good PR. And it was a way to stick it in [Bob] Arum's ear. But talking with him, I also felt that he thought it was the right thing to do. Then he realized that things were a lot more complicated and, probably, a lot dirtier than he'd thought. And at that point, his priorities changed."

It would be a stretch to say that Schaefer is trying to install himself as boxing's drug tsar. But he certainly doesn't want drug testing to interfere with Golden Boy's fights. That's evident from his assault on VADA and Margaret Goodman after Lamont Peterson and Andre Berto tested positive.

"Richard Schaefer saw what happened when somebody tests impartially with sophisticated testing methods," HBO blow-by-blow commentator Jim Lampley observes. "I haven't spoken with him about these issues. But it would certainly appear as though he has decided to stay away from Margaret Goodman."

Stripped of its rhetoric, Schaefer's main objection to VADA and Dr. Goodman appears to have been that they wouldn't empower him in the testing process. He talks about VADA failing to notify him of Peterson's positive "A" test in a timely manner. But if early notification is so important, why didn't Golden Boy advise the New York State Athletic Commission that Erik Morales's "A" and "B" samples had tested positive for clenbuterol? Twice.

In fairness to Golden Boy, no other promoter has made a serious effort to rid boxing of PEDs, or even pretended to. And Schaefer himself acknowledged recently, "I think that ultimately it should be up to the athletic commissions to adopt a more updated drug testing protocol and really not up to a promoter."

That latter point is particularly well taken. The problem is that the state athletic commissions, as presently constituted, are woefully unsuited to the task. In many instances, boxing is barely governed at the state level. Everything has a loophole. Illegal PED users vs. the state athletic commissions is one of the biggest mismatches of all time.

Most state athletic commissions don't have the resources, the technical expertise, or the will to deal effectively with the PED problem. People go along to get along. No one wants to make waves.

There's no uniformity with regard to standards, degree of testing, or punishment from state to state. Testing on the day of a competition is notoriously ineffective in the face of sophisticated drug use. But that's the only testing that most states utilize. Some states don't drug test at all.

The Nevada State Athletic Commission has long been considered to have one of the best drug-testing programs in the country. Two years ago, Travis Tygart was asked, "How easy is it to beat a testing program like Nevada's?"

"As simple as walking across the street," Tygart answered. "It's good for PR, to give the appearance that you're testing, but nothing more."

After Lamont Peterson tested positive with VADA, Zach Arnold of FightOpinion.com spoke with Keith Kizer (executive director of the Nevada State Athletic Commission).

"Kizer admits that a standard Nevada State Athletic Commission drug test would not have caught Peterson using synthetic testosterone," Arnold reported afterward. "He admits that the reason the VADA test caught Peterson is because they use the Carbon Isotope Ratio standard for urine testing, which does in fact catch synthetic testosterone usage."

The Peterson camp, as earlier noted, says that Lamont tested positive because of the surgical implantation of testosterone pellets to correct a testosterone deficiency known as hypogonadism. Jeff Fried (Peterson's attorney) says that the implantation occurred on November 12, 2011.

Four weeks later, on December 10, 2011, Peterson fought Amir Khan in Washington, DC. The tests administered by the local commission failed to detect the testosterone. That's a pretty good indication that PED testing in Washington, DC, is deficient.

California hosts more fight cards than any other state in the country. On October 9, 2012, the California State Athletic Commission upheld a one-year suspension imposed on Antonio Tarver in the wake of his testing positive for drostanolone.

"The Commission heard both sides of the issue and upheld Mr. Tarver's suspension," Kathi Burns (interim executive officer of the CSAC told ESPN.com). "I think the commission's actions speak for itself. It's well-known that the commission has among the toughest anti-doping standards in the world, and that we have zero tolerance for doping."

Not true.

California then turned 180 degrees and, without a full hearing, licensed Andre Berto for a November 24, 2012, fight (to be promoted by Golden Boy) against Robert Guerrero despite the fact that Berto tested positive for norandrosterone in May of this year. The explanation given by commission personnel was that Berto's positive drug tests were administered by VADA and not by the commission itself.

"How can they not recognize VADA?" Margaret Goodman asks. "Our program is in accord with WADA protocols. Our scientific director was recommended to us by WADA's medical chief. We use internationally-recognized sample collectors. We even use the same laboratory [the UCLA Olympic Analytical Laboratory] that the California commission uses."

Then there's the case of Julio Cesar Chavez Jr. Following his November 14, 2009, fight against Troy Rowland in Las Vegas, Chavez tested positive for Furosemide (a diuretic and steroid-masking agent). He was fined $10,000 by the Nevada State Athletic Commission and suspended for seven months. Four of his next six bouts were in Texas, one in California, and one in Mexico. Texas has a reputation for being lax in the area of drug-testing. Mexico is Mexico.

On September 15, 2012, Chavez returned to Las Vegas to fight Sergio Martinez. After the bout, it was revealed that Julio had tested positive for marijuana.

Marijuana is illegal, but it's not a performance-enhancing drug. Chavez's explanation for the positive test was as follows: "I have never smoked marijuana. For years, I have had insomnia; so I went to the doctor and he prescribed some drops for me that contained cannabis. I stopped taking them before the fight with Martinez, and I didn't think I was going to test positive."

That explanation strains credibility. Chavez might have been better off claiming that he ate tainted beef from a cow that ate a marijuana plant. Still, before the NSAC rules harshly on Julio, it should consider testing all commission personnel (including the five commissioners) for recreational drugs. Boxing has a drug problem. But the drug isn't marijuana.

As for Erik Morales and New York; on the day of Garcia-Morales, the New York State Athletic Commission issued the following statement: "The New York Athletic Commission has taken into consideration the testing of Erick [sic] Morales conducted by USADA, an independent non-governmental organization contracted by Golden Boy Promotions to conduct testing on its boxers. Based upon currently available information and the representations made by Mr. Morales that he unintentionally ingested contaminated food, it is the Commission's opinion that at this time there is inconclusive data to make a final determination regarding the suspension of Mr. Morales's boxing license. The Commission will continue investigating the allegations and will wait until official laboratory results are available before making a final decision."

Let's give the NYSAC the benefit of the doubt and assume that enormous political pressure from above was brought to bear on well-intentioned administrators. Garcia-Morales was the main event on the first fight card at the new billion-dollar Barclays Center, which is an anchor for economic redevelopment in Brooklyn.

Still, Keiran Mulvaney summed up nicely when he wrote on ESPN.com, "The way in which the situation was handled was borderline farcical. Morales failed tests twice, yet was allowed to take a third, which he passed, and faced no real consequences. Why have a drug-testing program if testing positive means nothing? If commissions are going to stand on the sideline, will failing a drug test become like missing weight: an inconvenience that can be smoothed over with some extra money changing hands?"

It should also be noted that the world sanctioning organizations are part of the problem, not part of the solution.

Four days after Garcia-Morales, World Boxing Council president Jose Sulaiman declared, "The time of getting urine samples for the antidoping tests is absolutely none other than in the dressing rooms before going into the ring or after the fights. The WBC only wants to test how a fighter is at the time of his performance and no other time unless it is a special circumstance. The tests are done by the local boxing commissions, most with which we have excellent relations and amicable agreements of mutual cooperation. We are, and have been, testing against drugs in boxing since 1975 and we have had only fifteen positives in thirty-seven years and about 1,600 fights. Boxing is a clean sport, as our data proves."

If Sulaiman weren't so adept at gobbling up sanctioning fees and crushing reform movements within the WBC, one would be inclined to dismiss him as a buffoon.

As for what comes next; the signs aren't promising. On November 24, Andre Berto will fight Robert Guerrero in Ontario, California, on a card promoted by Golden Boy.

Guerrero asked that the fighters be tested for PEDs by VADA. Walter Kane (Guerrero's attorney) says that Richard Schaefer and Al Haymon (Berto's manager) refused and would only allow testing by the California State Athletic Commission and USADA.

In other words, Berto said he'd do drug testing, but not with the people who caught him earlier this year.

Guerrero had two options. He could accept USADA and a career-high payday or lose the payday.

"I'm not happy about it," Kane says. "But in the end, we really didn't have a choice. Golden Boy controls the purse strings, and they're calling the shots."

Would the National Football League let Dallas Cowboys owner Jerry Jones dictate drug testing-terms for games that the Cowboys play? Of course, not. But in essence, Golden Boy (which has a vested interest in the outcome of the fights it promotes) is doing just that.

Once again, the playing field has been tilted. There are times when it appears as though, not only does Golden Boy dictate which drug-testing organization is utilized, it can also influence whether or not there is random blood and urine testing for a fight.

Indeed, Golden Boy might even be able to use its influence over the drug-testing process as a bargaining chip in signing fighters. Andre Berto tested positive and, soon after, was licensed to fight in California in a big-money fight. Erik Morales tested positive and New York said, "No problem. He can fight here right now."

Meanwhile, Golden Boy is refusing to use a drug-testing agency that plays by the reporting rules (VADA) and is giving its business to an agency (USADA) that appears to have ceded a certain amount of reporting authority to the promoter.

The problems are overwhelming and there are no easy answers. Even state-of-the-art tests often fail to uncover PED use.

Olympic gold medalist Marion Jones was tested more than 160 times during her track-and-field career and none of the tests came back as a confirmed positive. As the BALCO investigation widened, she admitted that she'd used steroids prior to the 2000 Olympics and lied to federal investigators about it. She pled guilty to federal charges and spent six months in prison. The tests have gotten more sophisticated since then, but so have the cheaters.

Should boxing even try to curtail PED use?

"Yes," says Victor Conte. "There will always be athletes who escape detection. But when there's a desperate need, half a loaf of bread is better than none."

One might look to Major League Baseball for parallels. No sport wants to tarnish its image, let alone its major stars. But as baseball found out, if a sport looks the other way, the use of PEDs can come back to haunt it.

Baseball got a huge bounce when Barry Bonds, Mark McGwire, and Sammy Sosa rewrote its record book. Now an entire era has been disgraced, and baseball's most hallowed records (which link fans from one generation to the next) are in limbo.

Baseball made significant strides when it decided, finally, to crack down on PED use. Home-run statistics are evidence of that. For eight consecutive seasons (between 1995 and 2002), the MLB home run leader hit at least fifty home runs. In the past five years, that mark has been reached only once. In the past two seasons, the four league leaders hit 44, 41, 43, and 39 home runs. Compare that with 1998, when Mark McGwire hit 70, Sammy Sosa hit 66, and Ken Griffey Jr hit 56.

In boxing at present, the users are way ahead of the testers and the distance between them is growing. The only thing that can possibly close the gap is a national approach with uniform national standards and a uniform national enforcement mechanism. If additional federal legislation is necessary to achieve that end, so be it. The notion that boxing can clean itself up one state athletic commission at a time is frivolous.

To make real headway, it should be a condition of granting a license in any state that a fighter can be tested for PEDs at any time. Logistics and cost would make mandatory testing on a broad scale impractical. But unannounced spot testing could be implemented.

All contracts for drug testing (such as Golden Boy's contracts with USADA) should be filed immediately with the Association of Boxing Commissions and the supervising state athletic commission for the fight at issue. The ABC and supervising commission should be notified when each test is performed and also of each test result.

For a state athletic commission to say (as is the case in some jurisdictions) that it won't recognize any tests but its own is ridiculous. It shouldn't matter who does the testing as long as the tests are reliable. Whether it's a police officer or a private security guard who sees a bank being robbed, the offense is prosecuted.

The implementation of sophisticated, unannounced, impartially administered, random drug testing is the only way to turn the tide.

That said; one has to acknowledge that we live in the real world. If a megafight is cancelled two days before its scheduled date because one of the combatants has tested positive for PEDs, it isn't like saying, "Number 94 won't be playing defensive tackle on Sunday." In boxing, if a fighter is suspended, the fight doesn't go on.

Big events are the economic engine that drives boxing. Cancelling a megafight, particularly at the last minute, will result in tens of millions of dollars in lost income.

For that reason, it's not unreasonable suggest that, in certain instances if a fighter tests positive for PEDs before a fight: (1) his opponent should have the choice of proceeding with the fight or not; (2) if the fight takes place, the fighter who has tested positive should forfeit 50 percent of his purse; and (3) the fighter who has tested positive should be suspended for a minimum of one year after the fight with the suspension being recognized by every jurisdiction in the United States.

Meanwhile, one has to ask: How many positive test results similar to those for Erik Morales (and possibly Floyd Mayweather) are there that we don't know about? How many other samples have been destroyed in the manner of the samples taken from Peter Quillin and Winky Wright? What would happen if federal investigators put key players in boxing's ongoing PED drama under oath?

Victor Conte says flatly, "I think the relationship between USADA and Golden Boy needs to be investigated."

An Internet website isn't the place to make judgments as to whether or not USADA has acted properly. Congress is. There's an open issue as to whether USADA has become an instrument of accommodation. For an agency that tests United States Olympic athletes and receives in excess of $10,000,000 a year from the federal government, that's a significant issue.

If USADA has violated appropriate protocols, the consequences could be enormous. If, in fact, USADA has made special accommodations for Golden Boy, one has to wonder how many times it has made similar accommodations for other athletes in the past.

This isn't about a handful of athletes. It's about the integrity of boxing and the well-being of all fighters.

Someday, if it hasn't happened already, a fighter who has been using PEDs will kill his opponent in the ring. Thus, in closing, it's worth remembering the thoughts of Emanuel Steward.

"Boxing isn't like other sports," Steward said several months before his death. "In boxing, a human being is getting hit in the head. None of us like to talk about it, but there's a very real risk of brain damage. So to my way of thinking, anyone in boxing who's part of using performance-enhancing drugs—I don't care if it's the fighter, the trainer, the strength coach, the conditioner, the manager, the promoter—that person is ruining the sport and doing something criminal."

Sometimes it seems as though nonsense is the only type of sense that boxing has.

It's Sixty Seconds Between Rounds, Not Sixty-Seven

At times, there seems to be a maxim in boxing: "If it ain't broke, fix it until it is."

One of the few things in boxing that ain't broke is the time-honored rhythm of the sport; three minutes a round with sixty seconds between rounds. Much of the integrity that has existed in professional boxing since the 1800s comes from that rhythm and the conduct of the fights themselves.

NBC Sports Network is airing a series of fights that run occasionally on Saturday night. Earlier this month, Jon Miller (president of programming for NBC Sports and NBC Sports Network) wrote to the Association of Boxing Commissions and asked that promoters be allowed to increase the time between each round of a televised fight from sixty to sixty-seven seconds.

Miller believes that the extra time between rounds is a concession that boxing should make to adapt to a business reality. More specifically, in his letter to the ABC, he declared, "NBC has a major concern with the rigid timing between rounds set forth by the Boxing Commissions in each state. We feel strongly this mandate negatively impacts the quality of television production. The Fight Night Series will simply not survive without advertising support and allowing us to be storytellers. We must run two thirty-second commercial units between each round. The inability to come back from a one minute commercial break without any additional time to show highlights from the previous round and set up the next round is a disservice to the boxing viewer and most importantly the athletes who are giving their all in the ring."

It's nice that Miller is concerned "most importantly" with "the athletes who are giving their all in the ring." His letter closes with the declaration, "This change will make the sport more broadcast friendly and substantially increase a boxer's ability to make a living on a platform other than the pay channels of HBO, Showtime, and PPV. The NFL, NBA, MLB and NHL all have adapted to this broadcast friendly model and, with their network partners, customized mutually beneficial television timings. This timing change will not negatively impact the integrity of competition but only enhance the content in building stars and elevating the great sport of boxing."

NBC wants the Association of Boxing Commissions to issue a policy statement in support of the proposed change. It would then be up to individual state athletic commissions to implement the sixty-seven-second rule or decline to do so. Presumably, other networks that are supported by advertising (such as ESPN) will follow NBC's lead if the change is approved.

Tim Lueckenhoff (president of the Association of Boxing Commissions) told this writer (on July 19, 2012), "I will speak in favor of the proposal. Anything we can do to promote boxing is a positive."

Sports change. That's a given. Boxing has changed too.

In bare-knuckle days, a round lasted until a fighter was knocked down. He then had one minute to return to the center of the ring and continue the battle. Fighters now wear gloves instead of fighting with bare knuckles. Championship fights have evolved from "fights to the finish" to fifteen rounds to twelve. A fighter must now go to a neutral corner in the event of a knockdown rather than stand over a fallen opponent and throw punches as soon as his foe rises from the canvas. Weigh-ins have moved from the day of a fight to the day before to allow a fighter to replenish his body. Fighters now enter the ring to their own ring-walk music; something that was not contemplated by John L. Sullivan or Joe Louis.

Through it all, the sixty-second period between rounds has been sacrosanct.

Boxing is different from other sports. Breaks in the action are carefully calibrated. Three-minute rounds with a one-minute rest period between rounds is at the core of professional boxing. In gyms across the country, an automatic bell sounds the familiar cadence that becomes second-nature to a professional fighter.

No matter how supporters of the sixty-seven-second rule style it, they're asking for a seven-second television timeout between rounds. TV timeouts don't alter the nature of the game in football, basketball, baseball, or hockey. They would in boxing.

Dr. Margaret Goodman is a neurologist who served previously as chief ringside physician and medical director for the Nevada State Athletic Commission. She is currently president and chairperson of the Voluntary Anti-Doping Association.

"Absolutely, the extra seven seconds could change the outcome of a fight," Dr. Goodman says. "It would give a tired fighter extra time to recover. It would give his cutman an extra seven seconds to work on a cut. If a fighter is hurt, the extra time might allow him to keep fighting; but to me, that's bad. If a fighter needs those extra seven seconds, he's likely to be hurt more seriously as the fight goes on."

Alex Ariza has earned a reputation as one of the foremost strength and conditioning coaches in boxing.

"It definitely could affect the outcome of a fight," Ariza states. "Obviously, a fighter who is hurt or a fighter who is poorly conditioned would benefit to a degree from the extra seven seconds. But it goes beyond that. The most important measure of a fighter's conditioning is how fast the fighter can get his heart rate down between rounds. With sixty-seven seconds, you're talking about a fighter getting his heart rate down significantly more than if he has just sixty seconds between rounds. In some instances, you could see a fifteen-to-twenty-percent better recovery with those seven extra seconds. For me, everything is based on recovery time. I train fighters based on the sixty seconds that I have. Sixty-seven seconds between rounds would change the way I train a fighter. If I have an extra seven seconds to work with, I would condition the fighter differently."

Would forty-nine-year-old Evander Holyfield like an extra seven seconds between rounds if he fights again? I think so. Ask Bernard Hopkins if he would have liked an extra seven seconds between rounds when he fought Joe Calzaghe.

Also, not only could an extra seven seconds between rounds change the outcome of a fight; there would be a perception by fans in certain instances that it changed the outcome of a fight whether it did or not.

Greg Sirb is past president of the Association of Boxing Commissions and current executive director of the Pennsylvania State Athletic Commission.

"I understand the point that NBC is making," Sirb notes. "But one minute between rounds has been the standard for a long time and it works. We've given an extra one or two seconds on a few occasions in Pennsylvania. But even that troubles me because, once you start, it's a slippery slope. Seven seconds is too much. And what happens if someone comes back after that and asks for ten seconds?"

Should boxing have one set of rules for fights that are televised on advertising-supported television and another set of rules for all other fights?

Can the sport tolerate a situation where New Jersey says that there's sixty seconds between rounds, Ohio says sixty-five, and Texas says seventy?

How much can NBC really accomplish in those extra seven seconds?

How do we know that, over time, viewers won't simply get an additional station break or commercial plug: "Watch the news on NBC after the fights . . . SportsCenter on ESPN at eleven o'clock."

What if a network says that it will put a REALLY BIG fight on broadcast television? "We can get Floyd Mayweather. But to do it, we'll need ninety seconds between rounds for commercials."

Boxing didn't disappear from broadcast television because the networks had trouble getting their commercials in. Boxing disappeared from broadcast television because there weren't enough commercials. Advertisers didn't want their product identified with a sport that was perceived by the public as brutal and corrupt.

Fans today have a lot of complaints about boxing on television. The most common complaint is, "The fights sucked." Another complaint is that some commentators say stupid things and don't understand the sport. I don't recall hearing a fan complain, "My viewing experience was unsatisfactory because of the transition from the commercial break to the live action."

Boxing is now being asked to change one of its most fundamental rules. This shows a lack of respect for the history, traditions, and essence of the sport.

The World Cup is one of the most popular televised sports events on the planet. Games are played in forty-five-minute halves WITHOUT STOPPING PLAY FOR COMMERCIALS in either half. The television networks deal with it.

Television networks should adhere to the rules of boxing; not the other way around.

Boxing is the only major sport in which the officials are often presumed to be incompetent or biased. That might be why, in the minds of many, it's no longer a major sport.

Bad Judging: A Case Study

I don't know Ruben Garcia. He might be a very nice man. I do know that Garcia was in the wrong place at the wrong time last Saturday night (February 4, 2012). More specifically, Garcia was sitting in a judge's chair scoring the fight between Nonito Donaire and Wilfredo Vazquez Jr.

It wasn't a hard fight to score. Donaire outlanded Vazquez in eleven of twelve rounds en route to a 231-to-163 show of superiority. Donaire also landed more power punches in every single round for a 147-to-56 advantage.

Judges Levi Martinez and Don Trella scored the fight 117–110 for Donaire. Every ringside report of the fight that I've read had Donaire winning by a comfortable margin. For the record, watching at home, I scored the fight 117–110 for Donaire.

Garcia scored the fight 115–112 for Vazquez.

In other words; the consensus among knowledgeable observers was that Donaire won nine of twelve rounds. Garcia gave eight rounds to Vazquez.

"Gave" is the proper word for most of those rounds. Vazquez didn't earn them.

What was Garcia watching? It was almost as though fans could have checked out "early results from San Antonio" on a boxing website before the bout and read that Garcia had Vazquez ahead by four points at the opening bell.

No doubt, some people are saying today, "What's the big deal? It doesn't matter. The other two judges got it right."

Trust me. It's a big deal.

Suppose Donaire–Vazquez had been close, with Levi Martinez scoring the bout for Donaire and Don Trella scoring the fight for Vazquez (or vice versa). Garcia would have cast the deciding ballot.

Also; think of all the fights out of the spotlight that Garcia has scored over the years. How many fighters have been deprived of a victory that might have made a difference in their lives because of his scoring?

I'm not familiar with the body of Ruben Garcia's work. It might be that he's a capable unbiased judge who simply had a (very) bad night.

That said, Texas is a state that takes pride in its sports heritage. I doubt that it wants to become known as "The Bad Officiating Capitol of America."

Al Bernstein once wrote, "Justice is not always served in boxing. Months of work and sweat and blood can be trivialized and wasted by incompetent or biased judges."

People in boxing would do well to remember Ruben Garcia's scorecard in Donaire-Vazquez.

★ ★ ★

Two weeks ago, I referenced Ruben Garcia's absurd 115–112 scorecard favoring Wilfredo Vazquez Jr over Nonito Donaire in San Antonio and posited, "No doubt, some people are saying today, 'What's the big deal? It doesn't matter. The other two judges got it right.' Trust me. It's a big deal. Suppose Donaire-Vazquez had been close, with [the other two judges splitting their vote]. Garcia would have cast the deciding ballot."

I told you so.

On Saturday night (February 18, 2012), Gabriel Campillo got robbed in Corpus Christi.

Campillo survived two first-round knockdowns at the hands of Tavoris Cloud, fought his way back into the fight, and appeared to have won the IBF 175-pound title. This writer scored the bout 114–112 in Campillo's favor. Judge Denny Nelson had it 115–111. Joel Elizondo raised eyebrows with a 114-112 scorecard favoring Cloud.

Then came the shocker.

David Robertson scored the bout 116–110 for Cloud.

That led Showtime analyst Al Bernstein to declare, "How he could have arrived at a 116–110 scorecard is beyond my comprehension."

Bernstein was being polite. I can think of several ways that Robertson arrived at his verdict; none of them pretty.

Elizondo's scorecard was an embarrassment. Robertson's was worse. Sampson Lewkowicz (Campillo's co-promoter) put the matter in perspective, saying, "These fighters are risking their lives. They spend hundreds of hours preparing for a fight. And when a fighter like Gabriel comes to a foreign country against a well-respected champion and puts on the kind of performance he did, he deserves to win fairly. These judges need to be removed so that they cannot ruin any more fights and tarnish boxing with their incompetence."

Near the end of the Showtime telecast, Bernstein noted that, prior to Cloud-Campillo, Elizondo and Robertson had judged only one world title fight between them. They shouldn't judge another.

The February 18, 2012, fight between Vitali Klitschko and Dereck Chisora made headlines. But not for the fight itself.

Klitschko-Chisora: Sucker Slap

In the past, I've referred to the fighter staredowns at weigh-ins as "a publicity-seeking ritual that has become an idiotic incendiary part of boxing." The truth of that critique was on display yet again at the February 17, 2012, weigh-in for Vitali Klitschko vs. Dereck Chisora.

Chisora had been chosen as the challenger for Klitschko's WBC heavyweight crown on the basis of his coming out on the short end of an atrocious decision against Robert Helenius last December.

A loss, however unfair the verdict, is not a sterling credential for a title fight. A loss to Helenius is worse. As Carlos Acevedo observes, "Helenius has just enough speed and coordination to rise from his stool before his corner man pulls it out from under him. He's as mobile as a stalactite and looks like he could be chased out of a bar by Chuck Wepner."

As for Chisora, Acevedo references him as "the only passenger on his own personal Crazy Train" and "a vulgar non-sportsman with little talent and lots of mouthiness." Acevedo then notes for the record, "Over the last couple of years, Chisora has bitten a fighter in the ring, kissed one at a weigh-in, and been found guilty of assaulting his ex-girlfriend."

At the weigh-in for Klitschko-Chisora, Dereck disgraced himself by slapping Vitali during the staredown. That breach of decency threatened the physical well-being of everyone within shoving distance.

Then WBC president Jose Sulaiman got into the act, announcing that the WBC would fine Chisora $50,000, and declared, "This is definitely a lack of respect for the sport and completely unacceptable. He's no gentleman at all, and he's failed in what we expect of boxers."

Sulaiman's outrage would be more convincing were it not for his own past history. After Floyd Mayweather Jr was found criminally guilty of beating up a woman for the third time, the WBC president said that Mayweather should not be stripped of his WBC title and proclaimed, "Beating a lady is highly critical, [but] it is not a major sin or crime."

Stung by the widespread negative reaction to his remarks, Sulaiman then issued a "clarification" which read in part, "I am a devoted husband and father of two daughters, and have three wonderful granddaughters, as well. The Virgin of Guadalupe is my superior saint. I just meant to say that I know Floyd Mayweather personally, and I know that he's a good human being with a good heart. I just wanted Floyd to know that the WBC will always stay strongly in his corner."

Apparently, Sulaiman believes that slapping a 6 feet, 7 inch, 243-pound fighter is a more egregious act than beating a women in front of her children.

As for the $50,000 fine; Sulaiman said that 50 percent of the money would go to an unnamed children's charity in Germany and the other 50 percent to World Boxing Cares.

There's considerable doubt as to whether the WBC has the authority to levy and collect a fine of this nature.

Also, it's worth noting that World Boxing Cares is a boxing-related charity that does some good work but is also a de facto public relations arm of the WBC. World Boxing Cares chairperson Jill Diamond has been identified on the organization's website as a "media representative" for the World Boxing Council and chairperson of the WBC and NABF women's divisions. Speaking on behalf of the WBC at the kick-off press conference for Floyd Mayweather Jr vs Shane Mosley last June, Ms. Diamond declared that Mayweather "bleeds green" but has "a heart of gold."

A more appropriate punitive measure against Chisora would have been for the WBC to withdraw its recognition of him as a valid challenger and hence its sanction of Klitschko–Chisora. But that would have cost the organization a sanctioning fee.

When fight night for Klitschko vs. Chisora arrived, dressing room antics delayed Dereck's ring entrance by twenty minutes. Once in the ring, he spat water in Wladimir Klitschko's face.

Then, to the surprise of many, Chisora waged a credible fight.

Vitali isn't a counter-puncher. The best way to neutralize his power is by throwing punches. Also, Klitschko likes to fight at a distance. The best way for an opponent to get inside is to punch his way in.

Chisora threw punches throughout the night, forcing Vitali out of his comfort zone. He aimed for every legal body part that he could hit. One of his blows may well have damaged Klitschko's left shoulder, inasmuch as

Vitali seldom threw his jab with authority during the latter stages of the fight. Each man showed a good chin.

"It's never easy in a fight," Klitschko has said.

That was particularly true this time. This observer scored the bout 116–112 in Vitali's favor. The official judges were more pro-Klitschko, rendering a 119–109, 118–110, 118–110 verdict.

Chisora fought like a professional fighter. It's too bad that he didn't act like one before the bout.

Too often in boxing, medical issues involving fighter safety go unaddressed.

Chad Dawson's KO by

The Greek dramatist Aeschylus (525–456 BC) wrote, "The first casualty of war is truth."

Boxing is war. And while the essence of ring combat is truth, a lot of what goes on behind the scenes is neither honorable nor honest. With that in mind, there's an issue relating to the September 8, 2012, fight in Oakland between Andre Ward and Chad Dawson that should be explored.

Ward entered the fight with an unblemished 25-and-0 record. By virtue of his "Super Six" tournament conquests, he was widely recognized as super-middleweight champion of the world. Dawson sported a 30-and-1 ledger and was the #1 light-heavyweight in boxing.

Prior to the bout, rumors circulated that Dawson had been knocked down and badly hurt by Edison Miranda in a sparring session. Team Dawson denied the rumors. Walter Kane (Chad's attorney) says that, to his knowledge, no one from the California State Athletic Commission asked anyone in the Dawson camp about them. Dawson underwent the usual pro forma pre-fight medical examination, but that's all.

In the fight itself, Chad looked tentative and weak. He'd been knocked down twice before in his career; by Eric Harding in 2006 and Tomasz Adamek a year later. Each time, he'd gotten up and won a unanimous decision by a comfortable margin.

Ward knocked Dawson down in the third, fourth, and tenth rounds en route to a tenth-round stoppage. Andre is a superb fighter, but he's not a knockout puncher. In Ward's previous eight outings, the only opponent he'd KO'd was Shelby Pudwell (who was knocked out by John Duddy in one round). In the entire "Super Six" tournament, Andre didn't knock an opponent down.

After Ward-Dawson, the rumors multiplied. Miguel Diaz told BoxingScene.com that, in the ninth round of a ten-round sparring session, "Miranda executed something that I'd been telling him to do the whole workout—left, right hand, left hook—and he knocked him [Dawson] down. It was devastating for me because I don't want to see something like that, but it happened. He was hurt. He tried to get up. He went down again and got up. I screamed to Rafael Garcia [Dawson's assistant trainer], 'Come and help him.'"

On September 14, Diaz told this writer that Dawson was knocked down by Miranda, fell on his face, tried to get up, and pitched face-first into the ring ropes.

On September 19, John Scully (Dawson's trainer) added fuel to the fire when he sent out a mass e-mail that read, "Just a note for future reference: If before a big fight—or ANY fight, really—it doesn't matter if my boxer has gotten hit by a tractor trailer three days ago, been dropped seven times in sparring, lost 42 pounds in the steam room over the course of one week, and just got dropped to his knees in the gym five minutes before you ask . . . I'm still telling you he feels great. What else can a fighter or his trainer be expected to say?"

So what really happened?

This past week, I spoke with Kane, Scully, and Dawson. They all told me the same thing.

"I got knocked down," Chad acknowledged. "But it was a flash knockdown. I wasn't hurt. I got back up right away and finished the rest of the sparring session. Stuff like that happens all the time in boxing. The only reason we didn't talk about it was, I knew people would make a big deal out of it and it wasn't a big deal."

Scully elaborated on that theme, saying, "Chad was sparring ten rounds that day. He got hit with a left hook in the ninth round. He went down. He got up. He was fine. He finished the round and then he finished the next round, so he sparred all ten rounds, which was what we planned for the day."

"There's some self-serving talk in what Miguel Diaz is saying," Scully added. "That might be why he's exaggerating. If you read what Miguel said, it was Miranda hit Chad with a combination that Miguel was telling him to throw. Do you really think that we would have allowed Chad to finish the round and then spar another round after that if he'd been hurt like Miguel says?"

"I wasn't in the gym," Kane told me. "But I heard the rumors and I asked about them. I believe what Chad and Scully are saying."

I believe Chad and Scully too.

But that raises another issue. Suppose Dawson had been dazed or, worse, concussed? What would have been the proper course of action to follow?

The issue might be defused insofar as Chad is concerned. But it's still out there for incidents involving other fighters in the future.

Boxing is about making money. The bigger the fight, the more money will be lost if a fight is cancelled because a fighter has suffered a debilitating blow to the head in training.

Here, the thoughts of Dr. Margaret Goodman (former chief ringside physician and chairperson of the medical advisory board for the Nevada State Athletic Commission) are instructive.

"You don't have to be knocked unconscious to suffer a concussion," Dr. Goodman says. "That's one reason a ring doctor evaluates each fighter immediately after every fight. There's only one thing to do if a fighter is dazed in the gym. You take him to an emergency room or a comparable facility with similarly skilled doctors to be evaluated immediately. And you keep him there for a while after he has been examined so he can be observed by trained professionals."

"There are no studies that I'm aware of on this point," Dr. Goodman continues. "But my educated guess is that, more often than not when a fighter dies in a fight, it comes after he was hurt in the gym. If someone suffers a concussion, even a minor concussion, and is hit in the head again a week or two afterward, the damage can be additive, permanent, and even life-threatening. If a fighter is knocked out in a fight, he isn't allowed to take punishment to the head for at least forty-five days. You can't have a different safety standard for a fighter who suffers head trauma in the gym. And you certainly can't have a bunch of lay people in the fighter's camp saying, 'It's okay; he can still fight.' That's a recipe for disaster."

For those who think that Dr. Goodman is overly cautious and overly protective of fighters, the thoughts of Freddie Roach are equally instructive. Asked what he'd do if one of his fighters suffered a debilitating blow to the head while preparing for a megafight, Roach answered, "The trainer's job is to protect his fighter. You report something like that to the proper authorities. If you don't, that's how fighters get killed."

All of this leads to one last issue: If Dawson wasn't thrown off his game by head trauma suffered in sparring, why was he so outclassed by Ward? Is Andre that good?

John Scully thinks he knows the answer.

"After the fight, Chad was a gracious loser," Scully says. "He told everyone that Ward is a great champion and the better man won. I respect Chad for that, but I want to tell you something. And this isn't an excuse, because when someone tells the truth, it isn't an excuse."

"Chad is a light-heavyweight," Scully continues. "Chad has fought for years at 175 pounds. And to get this fight, he had to go down to 168. Chad had trouble making weight, a lot of trouble. The weight didn't come off like he thought it would. Making weight weakened him badly. He had to lose something like nine pounds the last two days. That's why he looked the way he did in the fight. It wasn't about being hurt in the gym because that didn't happen. When a fighter goes down to a weight division lower than the one he's been fighting in for years, he's not the same fighter. Look at Chris Byrd against Shaun George. Byrd went from heavyweight to 175 pounds for that fight, and Shaun knocked him all over the place before he knocked Byrd out. Byrd beat Vitali Klitschko, David Tua, and Evander Holyfield. None of those guys even knocked him down. And no disrespect to Shaun George; are you telling me that he hits harder than those guys hit? Andre Ward is good. But it was the weight, man. It was the weight."

As for Dawson, he won't talk about the weight other than to say, "I don't expect to fight at 168 pounds again. I'll be back at 175 and I expect to be successful."

As a contrast to "Fistic Nuggets," these "Notes" were on the serious side.

Fistic Notes

Time moves slowly for a young fighter on the rise. He's anxious to climb to the next level, become a world champion, reach elite-fighter status.

But when a fighter gets old, time moves quickly on his downward slide.

"Old masters of boxing don't paint epic scenes," Patrick Kehoe notes. "They become part of the canvas. Time wins."

I thought of that recently when word came that Shane Mosley will be Canelo Alvarez's next opponent. And my mind drifted back to the night of November 14, 1998, at Foxwoods Resort Casino.

Roy Jones Jr and Shane Mosley were on the same HBO card. No one in boxing had more physical talent than they did at the time.

Mosley (the IBF 135-pound champion) entered ring at 29-and-0 and demolished Jesse James Leija in nine rounds.

Jones followed. The sole blemish on his thirty-eight-fight ledger was a questionable disqualification against Montel Griffin (avenged four months later on a first-round knockout). Roy was defending multiple 175-pound belts against Otis Grant.

Jones was "pound-for-pound" at the time. Everyone, including Grant, knew it.

"It's rare that an athlete gets the opportunity to compete against the best in his sport," Otis said before the fight. "It's the opportunity of a lifetime, and I can't afford to let it pass me by. If I can stay in there and fight well for twelve rounds, that's a victory in itself. I can't do much worse than the other thirty-eight guys he fought."

Jones stopped Grant in round ten. Like Mosley, he won every round.

After the bouts, I wrote, "Watching Roy Jones, Jr. and Shane Mosley on the same fight card was the equivalent going to a concert where the Rolling Stones opened for the Beatles."

Shane is now forty years old. He hasn't won since January 2009 and is winless in his last three outings. In his next fight, he'll be a measuring stick for a young fighter who the powers that be hope is good enough to beat him.

Roy is forty-three. His record since August 2009 is 1-and-3 with two of those losses coming by knockout. The party ended for Roy years ago, and everybody but Roy knows it.

It's better to be a has-been in boxing than to be a never was. Still, I can't help but remember the words of Budd Schulberg, who wrote, "It's heart-breaking to see a great fighter just stand there, unable to get away from the punches. Old fighters don't fade away. They die slowly in front of our eyes."

We all know a lot of fighters who fought too long. I've never had a fighter tell me after his ring days were over, "Tom, I quit too soon."

★   ★   ★

Obsessed with Manny Pacquiao (and by extension, Pacquiao's Asian heritage), Floyd Mayweather Jr tweeted yesterday (February 13, 2012), "Jeremy Lin is a good player but all the hype is because he's Asian. Black players do what he does every night and don't get the same praise."

Hey, Floyd; listen up.

The hype is also because Lin (1) was undrafted and cut by two teams before the Knicks picked him up (the quintessential underdog story); (2) plays in New York (still the media capitol of the world); (3) led a moribund franchise to five consecutive victories (with teammates Amare Stoudemire and Carmelo Anthony out of action); and (4) went to Harvard (think education, Floyd).

Maybe Floyd could reframe his tweet to read, "Jeremy Lin is a good player, but all the hype is because he went to Harvard. Guys like Kobe and LeBron who never went to college do what he does every night and don't get the same praise."

★   ★   ★

Nine years ago, I authored an article entitled "Professional Losers" that recounted the travesty of fighters who travel from state to state for the purpose of serving as cannon fodder.

"These fighters are different from perennial losers in other sports," I wrote. "We're not talking about a high school basketball team that loses forty games in a row. Athletes 'play' sports like baseball, football, tennis, and golf. No one plays boxing. These men are getting punched in the head, hard. They're prime candidates for brain damage. And when they enter the ring, the spectators aren't paying to watch a competitive fight. They're paying to see someone get beaten up. There's a difference."

One of the fighters I referenced in that article was Bradley Rone, who had lost twenty-five bouts in a row. On Friday, July 18, 2003, three days after the article appeared online, Rone collapsed in the ring after the first round of a bout against Billy Zumbrun in Cedar City, Utah. Within hours, he was pronounced dead.

That bit of history came to mind this past week when I learned that Deontay Wilder was slated to fight Marlon Hayes on the undercard of Devon Alexander vs. Marcos Maidana in St. Louis on Saturday night.

Wilder (a 6 foot, 7 inch heavyweight) was a bronze medalist at the 2008 Olympics). He's 20-and-0 as a pro with 20 knockouts. That record is deceiving, since most of his bouts have been against soft touches. Still, Hayes was particularly soft.

Hayes is forty years old and hadn't been in the ring since 2007. He's 5 feet, 9 inches tall and came in against Wilder having lost eight of his last nine fights. Worse, Marlon campaigned for most of his career as a super-middleweight.

Wilder-Hayes was a mismatch from the start. Predictably, the bout ended in a knockout for Wilder; his twenty-first in twenty-one pro fights. But as trainer Don Turner has said, "You build a record that way. You don't build a fighter."

One of the people I quoted in "Professional Losers" was Tim Leuckenhoff (president of the Association of Boxing Commissions).

"We wish we had the power to suspend some of these fighters," Leuckenhoff told me in 2003. "But under federal law, we don't. Unfortunately, a fighter can only be suspended by a state in which he has a license. Sometimes that happens. But a month or two later when the suspension expires, they're back in the ring again. And most of these guys are smart enough to steer clear of states that would put them on a permanent suspension list."

That quote is relevant now because Leuckenhoff is also executive director of the Missouri Office of Athletics, which regulates boxing in Missouri. In that capacity, Leuckenhoff approved Deontay Wilder vs. Marlon Hayes.

Not good.

★   ★   ★

Some fighters are legendary champions. Others are footnotes to history. Often, the two are linked.

On August 16, 1965, Woody Goss was a club fighter with a 2-and-2 record. The two guys he'd lost to had seven losses in seven fights. The two guys he'd beaten would retire from the sweet science without a victory to their credit.

Goss was slated to fight Johnny Deutsch, a local prospect with a 5-and-1 record, on the undercard that night. But the main-event opponent fell out and Woody was pressed into emergency service. For a few more dollars, he agreed to fight a twenty-one-year-old heavyweight who was making his pro debut.

At least Goss was paid. The guy he fought didn't get anything but a handful of tickets that he sold for $125.

That guy, by the way, was Joe Frazier.

Frazier knocked Goss down with a left hook in the first round. Referee Zack Clayton called a halt to the action 102 seconds into the fight. Goss protested the stoppage and said afterward, "Lee Phillips [a local light-heavyweight] hit me with harder shots in the gym."

"He came to win and he lost," Frazier countered. "He ran into a left hook like everyone else."

★   ★   ★

FROM AND ABOUT JOE LOUIS

Max Baer: "Fear is standing across the ring from Joe Louis and knowing he wants to go home early."

Barney Ross (on the beating that Louis gave to Tony Galento): "It made my skin crawl. Nobody who ever lived could stand much more of a beating like that. Galento won't be right for weeks. A beating like Joe gave him isn't something you get over with a night's sleep."

Art Rooney (before the rematch between Louis and Billy Conn): "Billy is like every guy who's been knocked out by Joe Louis. Sure, Billy was great the first time. He'd never been tagged by Joe before and he never knew how hard Joe could hit. He knows now, and it's not good. No guy going in against Louis the second time has the same confidence."

King Levinsky: "Joe Louis finished me. In one round, he turned me from a fighter to a guy selling ties."

Joe Louis (when Art Sykes was taken to the hospital after a Louis knockout punch): "They come in there to give it to me. I have to give it back. I can't say it's a sorry feeling, but I don't like to do it."

★ ★ ★

Bernard Hopkins and James Toney never met in the ring, which is a shame. Each man is a master craftsman. And each man is a talker. The prefight press conference would have been memorable in and of itself. Yet over they years, they've voiced respect for one another. Listen to what they've had to say about each other in the past.

James Toney: "I'm a natural born fighter. Everybody else was taught to fight. But Bernard learned his lessons well. He's a professional, and there aren't enough professionals in boxing today."

Bernard Hopkins: "James Toney in his whole career had problems with his weight. You take that away, Toney was the most defensive, the hardest to hit fighter in my era. He had a style, the roll with your shoulders, the roll with your head. I adopted that style and added it on to what I've been doing over the years. I'm not the easiest guy to hit. James Toney contributed to that, whether he knew that, whether he believes that. The difference between me and James Toney was that I always took care of my body the correct way."

★   ★   ★

Muhammad Ali and Larry Holmes will be joined forever as sparring partners, ring adversaries, and great champions. The tie between Tunney Hunsaker and Rodell Dupree is more tenuous.

Hunsaker was the opponent when Cassius Marcellus Clay Jr made his pro debut at Freedom Hall in Louisville, Kentucky, on October 29, 1960. Tunney was big, white, and slow; a part-time fighter whose primary job was serving as police chief in Fayetteville, West Virginia. Clay won a six-round decision.

Decades later, Hunsaker looked back on that moment in time and declared, "I'm honored to have been the first person Muhammad Ali fought in his professional career. It was an honor for me to have been in the ring with him, a real honor."

But Hunsaker's own life after that historic encounter was hard. In his final fight, a 1962 bout against 3-4-1 Joe "Shotgun" Sheldon, he was knocked out in the tenth round and suffered a subdural hematoma. After nine days in a coma, he recovered and was able to resume his duties as police chief. He died on April 25, 2005, at age seventy-five, in an extended care facility after a long battle with Alzheimer's disease.

Hunsaker knew that he was fighting an Olympic gold-medalist. Rodell Dupree had no foreknowledge of what he was in for.

On March 21, 1973, Jimmy Dupree (Rodell's uncle) battled to a ten-round draw against Bobby Cassidy in the main event at the Catholic Youth Center in Scranton, Pennsylvania. Rodell had a 2-and-2 record and fought on the undercard against Holmes, who was making his pro debut.

Holmes won a four-round decision. His purse was $100. Manager-trainer Earnie Butler, took a third and also deducted the three-dollar boxing license fee. Larry went home with $63.

"Dupree came at me smoking," Holmes later recalled. "I had to use my jab and footwork to keep him away. I was worried about my stamina. While I was fighting him, a phrase kept going through my mind: 'Come on, body; don't fail me now.'"

Dupree now lives in Jersey City, New Jersey. "We was both coming up and trying to get to the same place," he recalls. "Holmes got there; I didn't. It was a good fight, a rough fight. He deserved the decision. I have no regrets about it. I wish I'd been able to fight him again. But to be honest with you, I couldn't beat the man he become."

★ ★ ★

SOME REMEMBRANCES FROM HEAVYWEIGHT CHAMPIONS

Jack Johnson [on Jess Willard knocking out two of his gold-capped teeth in their 1915 championship fight]: "Jess ruined my golden smile. It was a left crack that did it. I felt them drop down on my tongue and my pride wouldn't let me spit them out. I knew what a howl would go up from the crowd if they saw them in the sunlight, so I did the next best thing. I swallowed them."

Jim Jeffries [on coming out of retirement to fight Jack Johnson]: "There was no reason for my fighting again. I had a good home, many friends, a good business, everything a man could want. And I had been out of the ring for over five years. I had lost the ambition that a great champion must have. But the pressure became too great."

Max Schmeling [on walking to the ring for his first fight against Joe Louis]: "Do you know what was on my mind? A curiosity and an excitement. I knew my body was right. I had thought something out. I had made a plan. Soon I was going to find out how good my thoughts were; whether I was right or wrong."

James Braddock [on signing to fight Max Baer for the heavyweight championship. Nine months earlier, Braddock (a fighter with twenty-three career losses) had been on welfare, collecting twenty-four dollars a month. He beat Baer to claim the most coveted prize in sports]: "That's the way it is in boxing. You get the breaks, and then sometimes you don't get the breaks. If you get the breaks, then you're getting a shot at the top. If you don't, you're at the bottom. I know a lot about both places."

★ ★ ★

Jimmy Cannon, the hall-of-fame boxing writer, died in 1973 at the much-too-young age of sixty-four. It was Cannon who labeled boxing "the red-light district of professional sports" and characterized Joe Louis as "a credit to his race, the human race."

Cannon also opined, "If Howard Cosell were a sport, he'd be roller derby." But some of his harshest words were reserved for fellow boxing writers.

"The reporter who covers games immediately appoints himself an authority on courage," Cannon wrote. "No other group in the newspaper business is as severe in its judgments of a man's behavior as we are. We demand that the athlete be perfect in competition and proceed on the theory that he should be exempt from fear. We denounce a young man because he was not brave according to the standards we have established for his sport. We can be timid and frightened in our personal lives. We move down the bar when a guy gets stormy. We cross the street or walk in the gutter when a man approaches us late at night, and our excuse is that he may be a stickup guy. But we are cruel judges of human behavior when we settle down to play our pieces on the typewriter."

★   ★   ★

Some of boxing's finest writers have had moments when they questioned their devotion to the sport. A sampling of their thoughts follows:

* Pierce Egan: "No men are more subject to the caprice or changes of fortune than pugilists. Victory brings them fame, riches, and patrons. Their bruises are not heeded in the smiles of success. Basking in the sunshine of prosperity, their lives pass on pleasantly until defeat comes and reverses the scene. Then, covered with aches and pains, distressed in mind and body, they are assailed by poverty, wretchedness, and misery. Their friends forsake them. Their towering fame expired and no longer the plaything of fashion, they fly to inebriation for relief, and a premature end puts a period to their misfortunes."

* Hugh McIlvanney: "My own attitude toward the issue of whether any decent society should tolerate fist-fighting has been ambivalent for

years. But I must admit that, as I get older, my enthusiasm for the game is increasingly under siege from my misgivings."

★ John Schulian: "The fight racket seems as repugnant as a sport could be. There is the violence, of course; the furious destruction of scar tissue, brain cells, even lives. And there are also the little murders committed with ballpoint pens in smoky back rooms."

★ Jim Murray (on Mike Tyson biting off part of Evander Holyfield's ear): "It was boxing's lowest moment. There are many things wrong with the manly art of self-defense. But we always thought those mouthpieces were in there to protect the teeth of the wearer, not the ear of an opponent."

★   ★   ★

Earlier this month (March 2012), a poll asked the question, "What would happen if the best thirteen middleweights in the world fought a round-robin tournament against one another? Ten matchmakers and three expert analysts participated in the deliberations. When the polling was done, 1,014 fight predictions were entered into the data base.

As expected, Sergio Martinez finished first. Two other middleweights separated themselves from the rest of the field. One of them (the second-place finisher) was Gennady Golovkin.

Golovkin had more than three hundred amateur fights in his native Kazakhstan and lost only a handful. He says that he has never been knocked down as an amateur or pro and is willing to fight at any weight from 154 to 168 pounds. He won a silver medal at the 2004 Olympics and a World Amateur Boxing Championship the year before. His victims in the amateur ranks included Andre Dirrell, Lucian Bute, Andy Lee, Daniel Geale, and Matt Korobov.

Gennady now lives in Germany and has compiled a professional record of 22-and-0 with 19 knockouts. In the convoluted world of professional boxing, he is one of several WBA middleweight champions.

It's unclear how good Golovkin is, or might become, because his record is devoid of world-class opponents. But the manner in which he has performed to date has given rise to great expectations.

Abel Sanchez (Golovkin's trainer) says, "Gennady is very patient. He's like a sniper. He waits for the right moment to go for the kill; and when it comes, he's deadly. I've been around a lot of fighters who were motivated by anger. Gennady is motivated by the pursuit of excellence. He's the whole package. Power, patience, conditioning, a cerebral approach. Fighters call out other fighters all the time. But you don't hear anyone saying 'I want Golovkin.'"

Gennady has a soft voice, easy-going manner, and warm welcoming smile. He looks younger than his thirty years and speaks with a rapid cadence. Among the thoughts he offered in a recent interview were:

★ "My father was a coal miner. My mother worked as an assistant in a chemical laboratory. I have a twin brother named Max. We started boxing when I was ten. Almost always, we were in the same weight division. Max was technically better than I was. I was more aggressive and the harder puncher. We decided from the beginning that we would never fight each other. Three times, we were in the finals of the same important tournament; and each time, one of us stepped aside. At the 2004 Olympic trials, Max stepped aside so I could go to the Olympics. After that, I took the risk to leave Kazakhstan and turn professional. Max stayed in Kazakhstan to take care of our parents and look after my financial interests."

★ "I was nine years old when the Soviet Union disintegrated and Kazakhstan became an independent country. It was depressing at first. The economic and social condition of the country went into crisis. We lacked things that people take for granted and we lived our lives within a limited framework. There was a lot of worry about what would happen next. We didn't know what the future would hold. Now things are better. There is more for the people to enjoy and life is good."

★ "The best thing about being a fighter is taking everything I've learned and applying it to real life. In the ring, that is hard. You can't always do what you want to do. I know that perfection will never come to me as a boxer, but I keep striving to achieve it."

★ "Courage is the responsibility of every boxer. When a boxer is in the ring, he cannot feel fear. But I don't think that being a boxer requires cruelty. For me, boxing is a sport. It isn't about cruelty. Does a soldier have to be cruel to do his job?"

★ "Sergio Martinez is a very good boxer. Right now, he deserves to be called the middleweight champion of the world. I think I am better, but I do not know that for sure. I would like to fight him to find out."

Last week, Golovkin came to New York to attend the championship bout between Martinez and Matthew Macklin. On his first night in the Big Apple, he went to a restaurant, where the doorman looked at him and asked, "Do you remember me?"

"No," Golovkin answered honestly.

"Well, my chin remembers you very well."

Gennady looked more closely. Then the two men embraced.

The doorman was Ramadan Nasser, who Golovkin defeated in the second round of the 2004 Olympics.

"He is from Egypt," Gennady said afterward. "Now he lives in New York. The restaurant is his sponsor. He is part owner of a gym and is a professional fighter [with a 7-and-0 record]. We never know what life holds for us. But so far, that is not a bad result."

★   ★   ★

Stung by criticism that WBC officials are doing a lousy job, WBC President Jose Sulaiman announced on March 15, 2012, that the WBC has created a ring-officials supervision committee. The committee will be headed by eighty-three-year-old Tom Kaczmarek, who last judged a fight three years ago. The other judges on the panel are Ken Morita (who had Mike Tyson leading Buster Douglas in Tokyo when Iron Mike was knocked out), Larry O'Connell (who scored Lewis-Holyfield I a draw), and Angelo Poletti (whose scorecard in Leonard-Duran I read three rounds for Duran, two rounds for Leonard, and ten rounds even).

Any questions?

★   ★   ★

SOME MORE WORDS OF WISDOM FROM GREAT FIGHTERS

Jack Johnson: "I learned from all my opponents. When I was in the ring, my opponent was a teacher."

Benny Leonard: "The toughest fighter to fight is a stupid fighter. When you feint him, he doesn't know you're doing it."

Carmen Basilio: "Some people have to learn everything the hard way. That's me. I learn hard, but I learn good."

Billy Conn: "I fought Fritzie Zivic when I was eighteen years old; ten rounds in Dusquesne Garden. He was a real experienced fighter. Fighting fellows like that is how you learn to box. That was like going to college for five years, just boxing him."

★   ★   ★

It was sad watching Hasim Rahman in the ring against Alexander Povetkin in a bogus WBA "championship" fight on Saturday afternoon (September 29, 2012).

Rahman caught lightning in a bottle on April 22, 2001, when he knocked out Lennox Lewis in South Africa to become heavyweight champion of the world. He could have parlayed that victory into a $20,000,000 payday to fight Mike Tyson or a $15,000,000 rematch against Lewis. Each offer guaranteed that, win or lose, there would be more multi-million-dollar television paydays for future fights.

Instead, seduced by the siren call of Don King and a duffel bag filled with $400,000 in cash, Hasim signed with King, lost a subsequent court battle, and received a reported $4,000,000 for the privilege of being knocked out by Lennox in the fourth round of their November 17, 2001, rematch.

The money that Rahman got for fighting Lewis is long gone. Hasim has now fought sixty times as a pro. Throw out his one shining moment in South Africa and he has never beaten an elite fighter. On Saturday, weighing in at 256 pounds, he was knocked out by Povetkin in the second round.

After the knockout, Freddie Roach (who was commentating on the fight for Epix) opined, "He's not respecting the sport. He's not respecting himself. He came into the fight just for the paycheck."

That certainly appeared to be true.

Six years ago, Tim Smith wrote, "There is something fundamentally wrong with Rahman. Perhaps that's why the guy has had nine trainers in his career. He comes up small in big spots. You don't want him on the mound trying to save a one-run lead or at the plate trailing by three in the bottom of the ninth with two outs and the bases loaded."

That said; there's something inherently likeable about Hasim. So it's particularly sad that there's now cotton in his voice when he talks.

As for Povetkin; he's hardly a world-beater. In his only other fight this year, he eked out a controversial majority decision over WBO cruiser-weight beltholder Marco Huck. It wouldn't be a surprise if Alexander continues to avoid the Klitschkos and moves in to pick at the carcass of the heavyweight division only after Vitali and Wladimir are gone.

★   ★   ★

In the 1960s, Muhammad Ali stood as an exemplar of black pride and beacon of hope for oppressed people around the world. In recent years, he has been a symbol of tolerance and understanding.

Ali taught his children to rid their hearts of prejudice. The lessons took hold. One of his grandchildren, Jacob Wertheimer, was recently bar mitzvahed.

Coming of age rituals are an important part of every religion. Under Jewish law, when a boy reaches the age of thirteen, he accepts full responsibility for his actions and becomes a man. The ceremony commemorating this occasion is known as a bar mitzvah.

Jacob (the son of Khaliah Ali-Wertheimer and her husband, Spencer) turned thirteen on January 21, 2012. The bar mitzvah took place on April 28 at Congregation Rodelph Shalom in Philadelphia. One hundred fifty people were in attendance. Jacob's grandfather was among them.

"I was born and raised as a Muslim," Khaliah says. "But I'm not into organized religion. I'm more spiritual than religious. My husband is Jewish. No one put any pressure on Jacob to believe one way or another.

He chose this on his own because he felt a kinship with Judaism and Jewish culture."

"The ceremony was wonderful and very touching," Khaliah continues. "The theme of Jacob's presentation was inclusiveness and a celebration of diversity. My father was supportive in every way. He followed everything and looked at the Torah very closely. It meant a lot to Jacob that he was there."

Khaliah says proudly that Jacob is an "A" student and a good athlete with Ivy League aspirations. She also notes that the bar mitzvah of Muhammad Ali's grandson is "a wonderful tale of what's coming in the world."

Ali, one assumes, would agree. Shortly before lighting the Olympic flame at 1996 Olympics in Atlanta, Muhammad proclaimed, "My mother was a Baptist. She believed Jesus was the son of God, and I don't believe that. But even though my mother had a religion different from me, I believe that, on Judgment Day, my mother will be in heaven. There are Jewish people who lead good lives. When they die, I believe they're going to heaven. It doesn't matter what religion you are, if you're a good person you'll receive God's blessing. Muslims, Christians and Jews all serve the same God. We just serve him in different ways. Anyone who believes in One God should also believe that all people are part of one family. God created us all. And all people have to work to get along."

Deconstructing a hero and putting him back together again.

Ray Mancini for Real

I started reading *The Good Son: The Life of Ray "Boom Boom" Mancini* by Mark Kriegel with a jaundiced eye. There are a lot of mediocre books about fighters who were embraced by the media and whose fame outweighed their ring accomplishments. But from the prologue on, it's clear that *The Good Son* is far more than a "golly gee" biography.

Ray Mancini was marketed to the American public as the All-American boy. Or as Top Rank publicist Irving Rudd proclaimed, "the All-American boy with a touch of mozzarella." He represented Youngstown, Ohio, to the United States the way Manny Pacquiao represents the Philippines to the world.

Mancini received what Kriegel calls "the highest blessing in American sports, that consecrating kiss of network television." In 1984, *Sport* magazine ranked him as the second-highest paid athlete on the planet in terms of performance income, ahead of superstars like Mike Schmidt and Kareem Abdul-Jabbar. But Ray paid a heavy price before, during, and after his glory years.

The Good Son begins with the story of Ray's father. Lenny Mancini turned pro in 1937 and was a promising lightweight. "He gave the fans what they wanted," Bill Gallo of the *New York Daily News* told Kriegel. "Kept throwing punches, never quit. He took a shellacking even when he won."

Describing a post-fight photograph of Lenny at age twenty-one, Kriegel observes, "His face is undergoing the inevitable inexorable transfiguration from puckish to pugilistic. Its supple features have begun to flatten and purple. His lips are bruised and split. A cut sack of swollen tissue hangs over his left eye. The right eye is completely closed, clenched like the seam of a mussel shell."

Lenny went into the Army after Pearl Harbor. He came out a physically broken man, who fought for four more years as a ticket-selling club fighter and, when the money was right, as an opponent. "He might have become the lightweight champion if he hadn't gone into the Army," legendary trainer Ray Arcel said in 1945. As Kriegel notes, "That was just another way of saying Lenny Mancini would never be a champion. He had the stink of 'what if?' about him."

The younger Mancini idolized his father. Looking at photographs in old scrapbooks, Kriegel recounts, "Raymond didn't see a club fighter with a busted eye and dried blood on his lips. He saw a hero. It might as well have been Christ on the cross."

Ray Mancini's career was in significant measure a tribute to his father. His journey through the sweet science was guided by two of the smartest men in boxing. Manager Dave Wolf was knowledgeable, tenacious, a pain in the ass to deal with, and devoted to the best interests of his fighter. Promoter Bob Arum was well-connected and built stars better than anyone else in the business. With their help, Mancini (who was already a matchmaker's dream) became, in Kriegel's words, "The Last White Ethnic, more valiant than violent, a redemptive fable produced by CBS Sports."

Ray turned pro in 1979 at age eighteen. On October 3, 1981, he challenged Alexis Arguello for the WBC lightweight crown. Asked by a reporter if he was ready to fight an opponent of Arguello's caliber, Ray answered, "Why don't you ask my father how many title shots you get?" In private, he was more to the point: "How the fuck can you call yourself a fighter and say 'no' to a world title? How is anyone going to believe in me if I don't believe in myself?"

Arguello broke Mancini down round by round en route to a fourteenth-round stoppage. Seven months later, Ray got a crack at WBA beltholder Arturo Frias.

"It's bullshit that I control the WBA," Arum said after Mancini kayoed Frias in the first round. "When I want something done, I have to pay off [Pepe] Cordero. Anytime you want a fix in the WBA, you bribe Cordero and he takes care of it. Cordero took me to the cleaners. Half a million bucks [in various inducements to make Frias-Mancini]."

On November 13, 1982, at age twenty-one, Mancini defended his WBA title against Deuk-Koo Kim. It was a brutal back-and-forth slugfest. Kim collapsed in the fourteenth round and died four days later. Kriegel explores the fight and its emotional impact on Mancini in detail. There were also economic repercussions.

"Ray Mancini," Kriegel writes, "was boxing's equivalent of the boy next door. Now [Americans] had to reconcile their trust and affection with the idea that he had taken a life. Negotiations for his endorsements came to an abrupt end. There would be no soft-drink deal, no shoe deal, no apparel deal. The Mancini fable had been corrupted. The all-American boy, a televised icon of righteousness and redemption, now engendered conversations of money and murder."

Arum has similar recollections, noting, "To have him associated with this tragedy cast a pall on the sport. A lot of sponsors had second thoughts, and once that happens, there's no money. If you're an advertiser, you don't want to see death."

More ring conquests followed, but boxing was taking a toll on Mancini.

"You feel like Hercules," he'd once said of knocking out an opponent. "You always want the guy to get up after the count of ten. But when you knock him down, it's the greatest feeling in the world. There ain't nothing better than to stand over a man and see him down on the canvas. Nothing."

Now, more and more often, Ray was on the receiving end of the punishment. Looking at his face in the mirror in his dressing room after a victory over Orlando Romero, he told himself, "Oh, God. I don't want this. You can't buy a face."

Mancini lost his title at age twenty-three when Livingstone Bramble stopped him on cuts in the fourteenth-round. Numerologists might note that the three worst rounds of Ray's life (his knockout losses at the hands of Arguello and Bramble and the punch that sent Deuk-Koo Kim to the grave) were all numbered "14."

There were three more fights, all of them losses, spread out over the next seven years. It was during this time that Ray turned to acting on the theory that it might be better to play a fighter on film than to be one.

Kriegel is honest about his subject's strengths and limitations as a fighter. The crossroads fights are dramatically recounted and put in context. Kriegel also explores the underside of the Mancini narrative.

Youngstown, when Ray lived there, was referenced in the national media as "Murdertown" and "Crimetown USA."

"Where else in America," Kriegel asks, "would the chairman of the county Democratic Party call the police to arrest FBI agents for trespassing at a mob boss's restaurant?"

There's no suggestion in *The Good Son* that Ray did anything illegal insofar as organized crime was concerned. But more than one of Ray's older relatives was affiliated with the mob. And there were times when Ray showed a fascination for the company of fringe mob figures. The "feel-good" stories about the All-American boy didn't mention those associations. Nor did they reference the fact that Ray's older brother was found dead in bed with a bullet that entered his head an inch and a half behind his right ear.

"Neilsen families didn't want to hear that," Kriegel writes. "'Boom Boom' was a family show serialized for Saturday afternoons."

The most gripping portions of *The Good Son* describe Mancini in retirement. "I was in the light," he said. "But the light moved."

Ray cheated on his wife, which led to the end of their marriage. Worse; violence had been passed down from generation to generation in the Mancini home. Kriegel describes in painful detail how Ray became physically abusive toward his own children. To his credit, he eventually confronted the issue and appears to have resolved it.

"Ray broke a pattern of violence that has been in his family for generations," his ex-wife, Carmen, told Kriegel. "Nobody recognizes that. Nobody celebrates it. But that takes a real man."

Kriegel is a good researcher and a good writer. *The Good Son* treats Ray Mancini with respect but acknowledges his flaws. It also conveys an admirable understanding of the sport and business of boxing.

Raging Bull was a great movie because it wasn't just about Jake LaMotta. It explored the generic soul of a fighter. *The Good Son* isn't just a book about Ray Mancini. It's a look into a fighter's soul.

I've read several books about Joe Gans. This one brought him to life for me.

Joe Gans Comes to Life

Joe Gans was relegated long ago to a seldom-visited corner of boxing history.

Knowledgeable fight fans know that Gans was the first American-born black champion and perhaps the most technically advanced fighter of his time. Between October 23, 1893, and March 12, 1909, he had 191 professional bouts, scored an even 100 knockouts, and (including newspaper decisions) lost only 12 times. Fifteen months after retiring from the ring, he died of tuberculosis, which had almost certainly hindered him late in his career.

Now, thanks to *The Longest Fight* by William Gildae (Farrar Straus and Giroux), Gans comes to life again.

The Longest Fight will enhance any reader's appreciation and understanding of Gans. Gildae crafts a sense of time and place and a moving personal portrait of his subject. The heart of the story, he writes, "is what it was like a century ago to be black in America, to be a black boxer, to be the first black athlete to successfully cross the nation's gaping racial divide, to give early-twentieth-century African Americans hope."

The book is keyed to the historic first fight between Gans and Battling Nelson, which took place in Goldfield, Nevada, on September 3, 1906. Gans was lightweight champion by virtue of having knocked out Frank Erne in one round four years earlier. At age thirty-one, he was past his prime. Nelson was twenty-four and peaking. Gans-Nelson was contracted as a fight to a finish. It was to continue until one of the combatants was counted out or quit on his stool.

There had been "mixed race" fights before Gans-Nelson, but never one of this magnitude. The bout attracted national attention. Arrangements were made for round-by-round summaries to be disseminated by telegraph throughout the country.

Gans was a gracious well-spoken man, gentle outside the ring, meticulous in appearance and partial to three-piece suits. Nelson was a thug.

The champion, in contrast to his opponent, showed such good sportsmanship in the days leading up to the fight (and during the fight itself) that a substantial number of white spectators found themselves openly rooting for him.

The bout lasted two hours forty-eight minutes, making it the longest championship fight of the twentieth century. It began in the Nevada desert at 3:23 PM under a broiling sun with temperatures in excess of one hundred degrees and ended at 6:11 PM.

Gans dominated for most of contest. The granite-jawed Nelson committed virtually every foul in the book while being beaten to a bloody pulp and was disqualified by referee George Siler for repeated deliberate low blows in the forty-second round. Most likely, the champion would have knocked his foe out earlier but for the fact that he broke his right hand in the thirty-third round.

Gans emerged from the Nelson fight as a national figure.

"People had begun to take boxing seriously, even though it was illegal in most places," Gildae writes. "Its appeal was in its simplicity, its violence, and the glamorous figures it produced. Beating Nelson made Gans prominent in a way no other black athlete had been. Money followed the fame. White fighters suddenly realized that a black man could make them a good payday. Promoters vied to gain his attention. Newspaper editorial page writers, who had ignored not only black boxers but virtually the entire black American experience, gave space to Gans."

After beating Nelson, Gans became the first black man in his hometown of Baltimore to own an automobile; a bright red Matheson touring car with a canvas top that he parked outside a hotel and saloon named The Goldfield that he opened in 1907. A half-century later, emulating Gans, Sugar Ray Robinson would park his own fuchsia Cadillac convertible outside Sugar Ray's Café in Harlem.

Gans also accepted an offer of $6,000 a month for a midwestern vaudeville tour. Putting that number in perspective, Ty Cobb was paid $4,800 for the entire 1908 season one year after he led the American League in hits, batting average, and RBIs.

Gans lost his championship in a rematch against Nelson on July 4, 1908. He receded further into the background with the ascendance of Jack Johnson to the heavyweight throne at the end of that year. But by then, the ripples from his life had spread throughout America.

In Gildae's words, "Gans was the first African American, after horse racing's early black jockeys and the cyclist Major Taylor, whose athletic ability even hinted at the possibility that sports could be a springboard for racial justice in American life."

How good was Gans?

Bob Fitzsimmons called him "the cleverest fighter, big or little, that ever put on a glove." And Sam Langford said of Joe Louis at his peak, "He can hit. He is fast and is no slouch at employing ring craft. He is the marvel of the age. I consider him another Gans."

It should also be noted that Gans inspired people in many ways. Goldfield was America's last mining boomtown. It was short on hotel accommodations, leaving thousands of fight fans to sleep in tents or on hard ground under the starry sky. But it had fifty-three saloons to keep them well-lubricated.

One of those saloons was owned by George Lewis Rickard, better known as "Tex." It was Rickard who had first suggested to local businessmen that the publicity flowing from a major fight would attract investment capital to Goldfield for mining-related ventures.

Gans-Nelson was Rickard's maiden voyage into big-time promoting. "I never knew what the fight game offered until then," he acknowledged later. "I wasn't a boxing expert. But what happened in the Gans-Nelson show made me think."

In later years, Rickard would promote the first five fights in boxing history with gates in excess of $1,000,000; build Jack Dempsey into a superstar before the term existed; head a group that financed construction of a new Madison Square Garden on Eighth Avenue between 49th and 50th Streets in Manhattan; and play a key role in making New York City the boxing capital of the world.

Books like this one about Ray Arcel keep boxing history alive.

Ray Arcel: Behind the Façade

The image of Ray Arcel that exists today is that of a sage old trainer who knew the science of boxing and was a gentleman. He preached patience as the foundation of training and never made himself the center of attention.

Ray Arcel: A Boxing Biography by Donald Dewey (McFarland and Company) explores Arcel's life in detail. The author has an appreciation of boxing and boxing history. His writing is a bit ponderous at times, but the book is intelligent and insightful.

Arcel was born in Terre Haute, Indiana, in 1899. His family moved to New York when he was young so that his dying mother could be near her parents. Dewey questions the veracity of certain stories that Arcel told about himself that were repeated by others so often that they came to be accepted as true. For example, Arcel told people that he graduated from Stuyvesant High School in New York (a school for gifted students). The school records don't support that claim.

Stephanie "Steve" Arcel (Ray's second wife, who was married to him for thirty-nine years) told Dewey that her husband "wasn't really much of a family man." The facts appear to support that statement. Arcel's daughter attempted suicide at age twenty-three by taking an overdose of sleeping pills. He didn't talk much about that or the death of his first wife from cancer. Indeed, Steve was married to him for more than three decades before she learned that Ray's father had remarried after Ray's mother died. Even then, he didn't tell her about a half-sister and step-brother that he had.

One thing that Arcel did talk about, though, was boxing. He often emphasized the following themes:

★ "A trainer can only work with the talent that's there. He can't give some kid a talent for boxing. What he can give him are the moves and steps that will help him give a good performance in the show when it counts."

★ "Just to train your fighters, to have them hit the bag and skip rope and develop stamina; that doesn't mean anything. Get it out of your head that this is just some blooming gymnasium."

★ "Every young man that came to me, I made a complete study of his personal habits, his temperament. There are some people you can scold and some people you have to be careful with. No two people are alike. Unless a kid was obviously not cut out for the ring, I always took my time figuring him out."

★ "Never overestimate yourself or underestimate the other guy. See what the other guy has. See what his strengths are. See what his weaknesses are. See how you can overcome anything he has to offer."

★ "The name of the game has always been outsmarting the other fighter, not beating him to a pulp. If you can't outsmart him, if you don't use your brain, you're going to be a loser."

★ "One thing you see far too often is a fighter coming back to his corner after a round and immediately being manhandled by everybody there. This one has this to say; that one has that to say. I always kept in my mind that the fighter came back to rest. The last thing he needed was all that screaming at him."

During the course of Arcel's career, he trained champions in each of boxing's eight classic weight divisions. At various times, he worked with Benny Leonard, Jackie "Kid" Berg, Barney Ross, James Braddock, Max Baer, Tony Zale, Kid Gavilan, and Ezzard Charles. There came a time when he was in the corner for a succession of charter members of Joe Louis's "Bum of the Month Club." Johnny Paycheck, Al McCoy, Paulino Uzcudun, Nathan Mann, Abe Simon, Buddy Baer, and Lou Nova were all knocked out with Arcel in their corner. Before one of those bouts, when the fighters met in the center of the ring for the referee's final pre-fight instructions, Louis looked at Arcel and blurted out, "You here again?"

Arcel was most active as a trainer during the years that organized crime was a commanding presence in boxing. Dewey acknowledges that Ray trained fighters who were controlled by mob figures like Owney Madden and Frankie Carbo. In that regard, Arcel once said of Madden,

"Any other business he was involved in; that was his business, not mine." Carbo's fighters fell under the umbrella of, "When a manager asked me to train a fighter, the first thing I asked was to see his manager's license. If he had a license, that meant he'd been approved by the licensing commission. If the commission didn't have a problem with the people behind that manager and his fighter, why should I?"

That said; Arcel was aware of the moral ambiguities of his position. "All I know is the boxing business," he said. "There's nothing else I can do. Nothing else I'd want to do. But sometimes . . ."

Sometime came in the 1950s. On September 14, 1953, Arcel was knocked unconscious on the streets of Boston by a man wielding a lead pipe. He was taken to Massachusetts Memorial Hospital in critical condition and remained there for nineteen days. It was widely assumed that the assault resulted from his involvement on the business end of a *Saturday Night Fights* series televised by ABC that threatened the TV monopoly established by James Norris and the IBC.

Thereafter, Arcel took a job in the purchasing department of Meehanite Metal (a company that blended alloys for foundry use). He returned to boxing in 1972 to work with Roberto Duran, who challenged Ken Buchanan at Madison Square Garden for the lightweight crown.

Arcel stayed with Duran through some glorious highs and one particularly heartbreaking low. The worst moment in the trainer's career came in New Orleans on November 25, 1980, when Duran pled "no mas" is his rematch against Sugar Ray Leonard.

Dewey writes, "For all his insistence that every fighter had to be handled differently and no two boxers were the same, all of Arcel's perceptions answered to very fixed laws. The first of these laws, inscribed more deeply the longer his career stretched, was that he simply didn't want to be surprised by anything that happened. Whatever he had assured himself of with Duran over years of professional collaboration, 'no mas' had never been an ingredient of it."

Longtime friend Jerry Izenberg accompanied Arcel back to his hotel after the fight and described him as "looking like a heart attack." Later that evening, Arcel broke down in his room and cried. "The whole situation was more than I could take," he admitted later. "It took a long time for me to get over it, if I ever did."

Yet Arcel never asked Duran why he quit. "I didn't think it was my business," he said.

Nineteen months later, at age eighty-three, Arcel notched his last victory in a fighter's corner when Larry Holmes knocked out Gerry Cooney at Caesars Palace in Las Vegas.

Dewey's book is filled with anecdotes. One of my favorites involves the time that Arcel was training Charlie Phil Rosenberg, who was struggling to make the 118-pound limit for a bantamweight title fight against Eddie Martin in 1925.

Arcel had some strange ideas, including the belief that a person shouldn't drink water or anything else during meals. For a fighter struggling to make weight, water was rationed in particularly sparse quantity.

"I always had to sleep with one eye open," Arcel said of the nights leading up to Rosenberg's fight against Martin. "Charlie would get up in the middle of the night to go to the bathroom, and I would stand there with the door open. He kept cussing me. 'I just want to gargle,' he'd say. And I'd tell him, 'I'm watching your Adam's apple, Charlie. Don't swallow that water.'"

"After this fight is over," Rosenberg told Arcel, "I'm going to kill you."

Rosenberg beat Martin on a fifteen-round decision.

Arcel lived another sixty-nine years.

The parade of biographies continued.

The Rise and Fall of Alexis Arguello

I met Alexis Arguello in 1986, six months after *The Black Lights* (my initial foray into boxing writing) was published. The book tracked the career of WBC 140-pound champion Billy Costello and culminated in his successful title defense against Saoul Mamby. In his next bout, Billy suffered the first loss of his career at the hands of Lonnie Smith.

Meanwhile, Arguello was nearing the end of a hall-of-fame career that had seen him dominate in three weight classes. His place in history as a Nicaraguan icon and one boxing's great fighters was secure.

Arguello and Costello met in the ring on February 9, 1986, in Reno, Nevada. That morning, I had breakfast with Eddie Futch, who trained Alexis. James Shuler (an undefeated middleweight also trained by Futch) joined us. Four weeks later, Shuler was knocked out in the first round by Thomas Hearns. Seven days after that, he was killed in a motor-cycle accident.

After breakfast, Futch brought me upstairs and I spent some time with Arguello. He had movie-star looks with an elegance and grace that conjured up images of Omar Sharif.

Arguello-Costello was scheduled for ten rounds. Alexis was a 2-to-1 favorite. Billy won the first three stanzas on each judge's scorecard. One minute into round four, Arguello landed a textbook righthand followed by a left hook that separated Billy from his senses and deposited him on the canvas. Forty seconds later, the fight was over.

I have many memories from the decades that I've been writing about boxing. Most of them are good. One of the most painful is the recollection of Billy sobbing in his dressing room after the fight. Twenty-six years later, I can still see it; I still hear him. His heart was broken.

Those thoughts came flooding back when I read *Beloved Warrior: The Rise and Fall of Alexis Arguello* by Christian Giudice.

Arguello was born in Nicaragua in 1952 and turned pro at age sixteen. Giudice notes that Alexis and Roberto Duran were immediate forerunners of the Latino dominance of boxing in the United States. He adds that Duran was "a tough street kid" while Arguello was cast in the role of "a Spanish gentleman."

In reality, they both came from the streets.

Arguello lost four fights early in his career and won his first world championship at 126 pounds with a thrilling thirteenth-round come-from-behind knockout of Ruben Olivares in 1974. Victories over the likes of Alfredo Escalera, Bobby Chacon, Ruben Castillo, Cornelius Boza-Edwards, James Watt, and Ray Mancini followed.

As a fighter, Arguello was a consummate professional. He was tall with superb technique and power and deployed his weapons with consistency and patience. In the ring, Giudice notes, "he pondered each punch, carefully analyzed each open space, and never rushed to get to the finish line."

He also conducted himself like a champion should, never mocking an opponent or disrespecting the sweet science. "Boxing is a beautiful sport," Arguello said.

"No one could prepare you for how hard he hit," Mancini (a fourteenth-round knockout victim) added.

The magic carpet ride came to an end for Arguello with a brutal fourteenth-round knockout loss at the hands of Aaron Pryor in 1982.

"Arguello fought a winning fight," Steve Farhood said of that night. "There was nothing he didn't do." But Pryor was greater. The bout ended with Alexis battered into submission, lying unconsciousness on the ring canvas.

"That was his night," Arguello said later, "like it was my night against Olivares. It happened to Sugar Ray Robinson; it happened to Muhammad Ali; and it happened to me. That is a life cycle that none of us can avoid. What we do when we come in, they do to us when we go out."

Ten months later, Arguello and Pryor fought again with Aaron ending the contest on a tenth-round knockout. Alexis's final record was 77 wins against 8 losses with 62 knockouts. After retiring from boxing, he fell victim to liquor and drugs. During the course of his life, he had five stormy marriages and numerous children.

There's a wealth of information in *Beloved Warrior*, although the writing is a bit flat and there are too many protracted fight reports.

The most interesting portions of Giudice's book detail Arguello's involvement in Nicaraguan political life and his relationship with Sandanista leader Daniel Ortega. After the Sandanistas overthrew Nicaraguan dictator Anastasio Samoza in 1979, Arguello's financial assets and real estate holdings were confiscated. Eventually, he reconciled and aligned with Ortega, who, for his own political ends, engineered Arguello's 1994 election as vice mayor of Managua.

"Arguello was reduced to a punch-drunk journeyman when he decided to allow Daniel Ortega back into his life," Giudice posits. "Although he told himself his decision had to do with aiding the poor and resolving bitter conflict, when he made his final pact with this devil, failure was the only outcome. In the ring, few could match his boxing IQ. In the political arena, he was clearly overmatched."

Then, in 2008, Ortega engineered a campaign by Arguello for the mayoralty of Managua. "I gave you three titles," Alexis told the voters. "I represented you honestly. Now I need you."

He was narrowly elected amidst widespread allegations of voting fraud. Thereafter, Giudice writes, "All Nicaraguans knew that Arguello was involved in an illegitimate election. A clearly frustrated Arguello had to live with the reality that, having cemented his role with the Sandanista Party, he had to blend in with its ugly charade. Thirty years earlier, Arguello, a champion, had the power to question authority. He no longer had leverage. As a former addict rescued by the Sandanista Party, Arguello was powerless, a puppet for Daniel Ortega and First Lady Rosario Murillo to control at their behest."

"Alexis knew that the Sandanistas were manipulating him," journalist Edgar Tijerino told Giudice. "During his several months as mayor of Managua, he knew he was handpicked because he could be controlled. No longer was Arguello allowed to think for himself or act on his own accord."

On July 1, 2009, Arguello was found dead in his bedroom, killed by a single shotgun wound to the chest. The official explanation was suicide. Recounting and weighing the evidence, Giudice finds this explanation more likely than not and concludes that Alexis "fell victim to the self-pity and recklessness" that characterized much of his life after he retired from boxing.

Is there a moral to the story?

Arguello carried the Nicaraguan flag at the opening ceremonies of the 2008 Olympics in Beijing. The standard-bearer for the Philippines at the same games was Manny Pacquiao.

Recounting the death of a fighter and an institution.

The End of College Boxing

Boxing took hold on a handful of college campuses in the 1870s as an intramural sport. Theodore Roosevelt boxed as a student at Harvard and later wrote, "I like to see a bout between two evenly-matched men. There can be no harm in such an exhibition. In my opinion, it is much better for a man to know how to protect himself with his fists than to resort to firearms, knives, or clubs. I believe the sport should be encouraged. It is a manly sport."

In *Lords of the Ring* (University of Wisconsin Press), Doug Moe explores the long-ago days of college boxing through the prism of the University of Wisconsin boxing team.

Wisconsin was the center of the college boxing universe. Starting in the 1930s, fifteen thousand fans packed the Wisconsin Field House on a regular basis to watch the Badgers compete.

"The fans—young and old, men and women—would begin to arrive two hours before fight time," Moe writes. "The University of Wisconsin band would play rollicking tunes such as *The Beer Barrel Polka*, and necks would crane as people spotted their friends and neighbors in the throng."

On March 29, 1940, Joe Louis defended the heavyweight championship of the world against Johnny Paycheck at Madison Square Garden with 11,620 spectators in attendance. That same night, more than 15,000 fans crowded into the Wisconsin Field House to watch a dual competition between Wisconsin and Washington State.

Over the years, Wisconsin won eight NCAA team championships in boxing and thirty-five NCAA individual titles. "I liken boxing at Wisconsin to football at Notre Dame," Cal Vernon (a 1948 NCAA champion) later said. "We were the Notre Dame of boxing."

But by 1960, college boxing was under attack. Mob scandals had tarnished the professional ranks. College faculties were questioning whether an athletic competition founded on the intent to physically incapacitate an opponent belonged on campus. More and more universities were dropping the sport. The University of Wisconsin was one of the few major colleges that still had a boxing team.

In April 1960, the Wisconsin Field House hosted the NCAA championship boxing tournament for the seventh time. Six Badgers made it to the final round. One of them was middleweight Charlie Mohr.

Mohr could have sprung from the pages of a Horatio Alger novel. He'd won an individual NCAA championship the previous year, but had no intention of turning pro. He boxed because the sweet science was his passport to a college scholarship.

Local newspaper accounts of Mohr's ring exploits and personality described him as "handsome" and "soft-spoken" with "bewitching charm."

"Charlie had a way about him," columnist Bonnie Ryan wrote in the *Capitol Times*. "When he talked to you, he made you feel that you were the best friend he had in the world. Never, never would he think of saying a bad word against anyone."

Bill Urban (one of Mohr's teammates at Wisconsin) told Moe, "He was just so very very kind. I always enjoyed being with him. Everybody did."

But as Moe writes, "The pure and simple truth is rarely pure and never simple."

Although the information was kept secret at the time, Mohr had been hospitalized for depression early in his senior year of college and given electroshock therapy.

Years later, Jim Doherty (a classmate) acknowledged in an article written for *Smithsonian Magazine*, "There was a lot more going on with Charlie than many of us realized. The legend was true as far as it went. He was a hero, for sure. But not the one we all thought we knew. Concealed beneath the jaunty facade he beamed at the world was a tormented young man who had the misfortune to end up in a place where he didn't want to be but who never quit fighting and always tried to do the right thing."

Mohr was ambivalent about boxing by his senior year but continued to box to keep his scholarship. On April 9, 1960, he entered the ring to face Stu Bartell of San Jose State in the finals of the 165-pound division at the NCAA championship tournament. The bout would determine both the NCAA individual title and team championship.

Bartell stopped Mohr in the second round. The fight ended with Charlie on his feet.

Earlier in the day, a young Nevadan named Mills Lane (yes, that Mills Lane) had beaten Gary Wilhelm of Wisconsin to capture the 147-pound NCAA championship. Lane later recalled, "I remember the Wisconsin Field House being a gigantic place. I was standing in back near my dressing room because I had already completed my fight. I saw Charlie walk back to his corner and sit down on his stool, and I saw him talking to his coach. I later found out that Charlie was apologizing for having lost the fight. Charlie felt he had let the school down because the defeat enabled San Jose State to win the team trophy. After a minute or so, Charlie got up off his stool, slipped through the ropes, and started walking back to the dressing room. Under any circumstances, that is a long walk. It's even longer when you have been defeated. Charlie signed autographs all the way back to the locker room. I remember how bad I felt for Charlie. I watched Charlie step toward the Wisconsin dressing room, then turned away, lost in my own thoughts. Within minutes, word spread through the Field House that Charlie had collapsed."

Mohr had suffered a massive subdural hematoma. He died eight days later, on Easter Sunday, without regaining consciousness.

"What's really sad," Wisconsin boxing coach John Walsh later said, "is that Charlie had planned on retiring from boxing after the tournament. He was about two-and-a-half minutes away from never boxing again."

Lords of the Ring is well-researched. It's bit tedious at times, as Moe tends to fall into a tournament-by-tournament, fight-by-fight recounting of the history of Wisconsin boxing. But the story of Charlie Mohr and his tragic death adds an underlying drama to it all.

There's also a poignant footnote.

On May 19, 1960, the University of Wisconsin faculty voted to discontinue boxing as a varsity sport. That led to a ripple effect. San Jose State, Sacramento State, and Washington State (three of the few other major universities with credible boxing programs) followed suit. On January 7, 1961, the executive committee of the NCAA voted to discontinue boxing as an NCAA sport.

Boxing's literary tradition continues to grow.

Literary Notes

There are no first-rate biographies of Floyd Patterson. *Floyd Patterson: Boxing's Invisible Champion* by W. K. Stratton (Houghton Mifflin Harcourt) tries to fill that void, succeeds in some ways, and falls short in others.

The outlines of Patterson's story are known to older fans. At age ten (after an early-childhood filled with self-flagellation, petty crime, and school truancy), he was sent to the Wiltwyck School for Boys in upstate New York. From there, he segued into boxing. Cus D'Amato oversaw his early development in tandem with Frank Lavelle (an amateur trainer who began the process of molding the young fighter). Eventually, D'Amato pushed Lavelle out and replaced him with Dan Florio. During Patterson's championship reign, D'Amato was jettisoned.

Stratton calls Patterson "an overachiever who bootstrapped his way to the top." That description could apply to most boxing champions. He also regards Patterson as an important figure in the civil rights movement because of his support for integrationist ideals in the face of opposition from racist whites and, later, the Nation of Islam as personified by Muhammad Ali.

Stratton's book benefits from some good research on the early stages of Patterson's life and his amateur years. The writing flows nicely and there are some poignant scenes, such as Patterson visiting Sonny Liston in the latter's dressing room after Liston was knocked out in the first round by Ali in Lewiston, Maine. But *Floyd Patterson: Boxing's Invisible Champion* is wanting in several respects.

Patterson won a vacant title by beating forty-year-old Archie Moore after Rocky Marciano retired. He defended it against a series of non-entities (losing to Ingemar Johansson, before besting Johansson in a rematch). He avoided credible challengers like Cleveland Williams and Zora Folley, and was dropped like a bowling ball by Sonny Liston in their two encounters. Later in his career, he was knocked out twice by Muhammad Ali.

In the face of this historical record, Stratton writes hyperbolically that Patterson had "a left hook as powerful as any ever seen in boxing" and that "no one had ever seen faster hands." He calls the Patterson-Johansson trilogy "one of the most celebrated rivalries boxing has known" and Patterson-Liston I "the most talked-about heavyweight title bout since Louis-Schmeling." He also devolves into fantasy with the claim that the "real reason" Rocky Marciano retired was fear that, if he fought Patterson, he would "suffer a humiliating defeat." Indeed, Stratton writes, "Word spread that some people close to the champ feared Marciano risked getting killed in the ring with Floyd."

Authors are entitled to their opinions, but there are also nagging factual inaccuracies in the book. At one point, Stratton says that Johansson was a "heavy favorite" over Patterson in their rematch. Two pages later, he reports that the odds were 8 to 5. He writes that a decision by the New York State Supreme Court paved the way for Ali to return to the ring in the Empire State against Oscar Bonavena and Joe Frazier after his exile from boxing. In truth, it was a decision by a federal court (the United States District Court for the Southern District of New York) that opened the door.

Presenting an idealized version of Patterson, Stratton recounts how, prior to fighting Chester Mieszala in Mieszala's hometown of Chicago, he refused to train in the same gym as his opponent because "Floyd feared he might inadvertently pick up some tips by watching Mieszala that would give him an unfair advantage in the fight."

Isn't it more likely that Patterson (and D'Amato) feared Mieszala's camp would learn by watching him?

As for D'Amato; too often, Stratton opens doors that might lead to a thorough exploration of his life but doesn't walk through them.

The book raises questions regarding D'Amato's relationship with several mob figures at the same time he was self-righteously feuding with James Norris and Frankie Carbo. But it doesn't answer them. It follows Patterson's tumultuous relationship with D'Amato to the end of Cus's life, but never mentions Mike Tyson.

And the book touches on the issue of D'Amato's sexuality but then drops the subject.

More specifically, Stratton references "D'Amato's peculiar behavior," including the fact that he sometimes slept in the same bed as Patterson.

He then quotes author Gay Talese as saying, "I remember a story that Patterson told me. I got the impression that D'Amato had a sexual thing for Patterson. Patterson told me he was lying in bed and D'Amato was lying next to him. This one time in bed, D'Amato had his foot on Patterson's foot, sort of playing with his toes."

Also, Stratton references Patterson's tenure as chairman of the New York State Athletic Commission and the dementia that had begun to creep into his life by then. He ignores the fact that Patterson was already mentally impaired at the time of his appointment and that putting him in the job was a cynical ploy by New York governor George Pataki and Senator Alfonse D'Amato to use the former champion as cover for a scheme that turned the commission into a cesspool of political patronage, incompetence, and corruption.

Floyd Patterson reigned at a time when the heavyweight championship was the most coveted title in sports. Some champions have added stature to the crown by virtue of their extraordinary ring skills and persona. Others were less gifted and came along at the right time.

Floyd Patterson was a good fighter (not a great one) who came along at the right time.

★   ★   ★

Billy Miske was born in 1894, and fought professionally from 1913 through 1923. His life in and out of the ring is painstakingly re-created by Clay Moyle in *Billy Miske: The St. Paul Thunderbolt* (Win by KO Publications).

Miske fought in an era when bouts that went the distance were often ruled "no decision" and fans relied on newspaper reports (known as "newspaper decisions") to determine who had "won." Factoring newspaper decisions into the equation, Miske had 73 career victories against 14 losses and 16 draws. The six best fighters he faced and his record against them were Jack Dempsey (0-2-1), Harry Greb (0-2-1), Tommy Gibbons (1-3-1), Battling Levinsky (2-2), Jack Dillon (4-1), and Kid Norfolk (0-2). In other words, Miske was good but a shade below the best of his era.

That said; one has to wonder how much a kidney disease diagnosed in 1919 affected his performance in some of those encounters.

Miske is best known for his three fights against Jack Dempsey. The first two culminated in newspaper verdicts and occurred before Dempsey became champion. A still-raw Dempsey came close to knocking Miske out in round seven of their initial bout but was forced to settle for a draw. The Manassa Mauler later conceded, "At the start of the fight, and I think in most of the rounds, Miske outboxed me."

In their second confrontation, Dempsey prevailed on a six-round decision but admitted afterward, "I was hitting harder, but he was landing so often that my punches were weakened."

Dempsey-Miske III was contested on September 6, 1920; fourteen months after Billy was diagnosed with the kidney disease that would kill him. Miske was fighting because he needed the money to provide for his wife and two young children.

It was Dempsey's first title defense. Years later, the champion acknowledged, "Miske was through as a serious contender. I knew full well that he would give me no real fight. But I was hearing stories from other fighters that he was broke and needed the money badly."

Three undercard bouts preceded the main event. Two of them featured Harry Greb and Sam Langford. That's quite an undercard. Adding to the historical import of the moment, updated telegraph reports of Dempsey-Miske III were broadcast live on radio.

In round two, a vicious body shot put Miske on the canvas for the first time in his ring career. He was counted out in the third round.

Still in need of money, Miske fought for three more years. His final fight, a maudlin affair, was a fourth-round knockout of Bill Brennan on November 7, 1923. He died on January 1, 1924.

Kudos to Clay Moyle for illuminating a piece of boxing history.

★   ★   ★

There's a tendency to assume that everything that could be written about Jack Johnson has already been published. Biographers like Geoffrey Ward and Randy Roberts have mined the mother lode of research material. Other historians have had their say. Johnson himself put his own recollections into writing. But Theresa Runstedtler, who calls Johnson "the most famous discontent of his time," brings new perspectives to bear in *Jack Johnson: Rebel Sojourner* (University of California Press).

Runstedtler moves the study of Johnson's impact from race relations in the United States to the global debate over race and imperialism in the early 1900s. Two decades earlier, John L. Sullivan had elevated the heavyweight championship to an internationally recognized crown. Hence, Johnson wasn't just defying white America. He was, in the author's words, taking on the whole white world.

Runstedtler notes that, when Johnson journeyed to Australia in 1908 to challenge Tommy Burns for the heavyweight throne, "the athletic body had become an all important medium through which white men expressed their mutual interest in the maintenance of global white domination. The image of an ideal citizen was a muscular white male. Johnson and other black boxers publicly disrupted not only the mainstream ideals of the white male body and the white body politic but also the racial fictions of the degenerate stage darky. Thanks in part to the growing popularity of prizefighting, their powerful black bodies became the visual portents of racial Armageddon."

Johnson's victory over Burns, in Runstedtler's words, "helped to unleash a rising tide of color across the globe." And his 1910 decimation of James Jeffries in history's most anticipated prizefight up until that time inspired celebratory displays of racial pride and anti-colonialism in non-white nations.

"Johnson fought a great fight," African American scholar James Weldon Johnson (a contemporary of Jack Johnson's) wrote after Johnson-Jeffries. "It was the fight of one lone black man against the world. Before the fight, the papers were full of statements to the effect that the white man had the history of Hastings and Agincourt behind him, while the black man had nothing but the history of the jungle."

Johnson gave people of color their own battle hero. And equally important, as Runstedtler states, "he encouraged people of color to view their own oppression as part of a worldwide race problem [and] empowered them to imagine a future of freedom and solidarity stretching beyond their local circumstances."

Jack Johnson: Rebel Sojourner is virtually devoid of ring action. It's not a "boxing book" per se. But it's well worth the read.

★   ★   ★

Joe Layden wrote an exceptionally good book entitled *The Last Great*

Fight about James "Buster" Douglas's historic upset of Mike Tyson. Micky Ward was as honest in and out of the ring as any fighter ever. The problem with their collaboration on Ward's autobiography—*A Warrior's Heart*—is that it often fails to capture Micky's voice.

That's clear from the prologue, which reads in part, "Adrenaline-soaked cotton swabs protrude from your nostrils. An enswell struggles to flush blood pooling along the harsh ridges of your cheekbones and eyebrows . . . Like anybody else, I have my own narrative—history and circumstance that go a long way toward shaping the person I am and the man I still hope to be."

That's good writing. But it's not how Micky thinks, speaks, or writes. And there are also a number of nagging factual inaccuracies in *A Warrior's Heart* (such as placing NBC's *Contender* series before, rather than after, Ward's fight against Shea Neary).

That said; there's some nice material in the book. A sampler follows:

★ "You can put it any way you want, choose flowery language that makes you feel better about it. But the truth is this. Professional boxing is about trying to inflict as much damage as possible on your opponent. Every fighter who steps in the ring understands his mission: Hurt the other guy."

★ "Losing your first fight is like losing your virginity. You can't ever get it back. It's a rite of passage."

★ "If you get knocked out, your career is sure to take a turn for the worse. You're damaged goods, literally and figuratively. Once your brain gets scrambled like that, you're more susceptible to further deterioration down the road. The brain never fully recovers. With each concussion, there is residual damage. And there's something else that happens in the wake of a knockout. People look at you differently. And you look at yourself differently."

And then there's Ward on his money punch: "As bad as it is to get knocked out with a shot to the head, it's nowhere near as painful as a perfectly placed body shot. You draw the left in tight and you pivot hard, rotating your hips like a golfer on the tee. Then you drive right through the man, sinking your fist deep into his tissue so far and clean that you swear, if you weren't wearing a glove, you could grab his liver with your fingers. Drive a left hook deep into a man's belly right below that floating rib, and he is instantly incapacitated. There is something elegant about it; the delayed reaction, the way the punch lands and the fight continues until suddenly, after a second or two, the man who has been hit drops to one knee in a display of utter submissiveness. He can wait five seconds, ten seconds, a minute. It doesn't matter. The paralyzing pain isn't going away."

★ ★ ★

Al Bernstein has been calling fights on television, most often as an expert analyst, for more than thirty years. The job requires an understanding of the sweet science and the ability to communicate well. But the most successful analysts have an additional quality. Viewers think that it would be fun to sit next to them on a sofa and watch a fight on television.

Al Bernstein: 30 Years, 30 Undeniable Truths about Boxing, Sports, and TV (Diversion Books) reads like a conversation on the sofa. It's a collection of recollections and anecdotes about Al's life and the sport he loves. There's a moving section about Connie Bernstein's long battle with cancer and the strength of the marriage that she and Al share. And there are portraits of boxers, from legendary greats to four-round club fighters.

In one of my favorite anecdotes, Bernstein recounts how he and Charley Steiner covered the weigh-in for Mike Tyson's 1995 comeback bout against Peter McNeeley. Al was on-camera and told his ESPN audience, "Let's see if we can hear from former heavyweight champion, Mike Tyson. Mike, can we talk to you now?"

"No fucking way," Tyson answered.

Bernstein reflected for a moment and said calmly, "I'll take that as a 'no.' Back to you, Charley."

"After more than two decades of trying to explain Tyson's chaotic behavior," Bernstein writes, "we are left with the simple explanation—he's a nut."

In the most interesting passage in the book, Al recalls hall-of-fame announcer Don Dunphy telling him, "The best advice I can give you as a sportscaster is to remember, when you are on the air, it's not about you."

Bernstein then casts aside his non-confrontational persona and declares, "The majority of sportscasters working today believe it is always about them. Amazingly, they do so with the endorsement and even encouragement of their networks and their producers. We live in a time when most networks value argument over discussion, opinion over information, and loudness over intelligence. While I don't take myself too seriously, I take sportscasting very seriously. My claim that sportscasting has changed dramatically, and not for the better, is not some idle statement or sentimental bromide about 'the good old days.' It's a well-considered assessment of my profession. I am hardly known as a combative personality. I have steadfastly refused to criticize my colleagues over the years, so writing this is out of character for me. I hope that my reputation will give my words in this chapter even more meaning."

"We have seen many major boxing matches," Bernstein continues, "where three broadcasters are debating amongst themselves something only vaguely related to the match we are all watching. This debate has been known to extend for almost an entire three-minute round, while the action in the ring goes virtually unnoticed. An offshoot of this is the use of opinion to replace analysis. 'Analyst' is the title of the person sitting next to the host or play-by-play announcer. The title is not 'opinion giver.' Opinions may be part of some type of analysis, but pure opinion is never to be confused with analysis. Using opinion under the guise of calling it analysis is often the sign that a color commentator is too lazy to do the homework necessary to provide real analysis. Anyone can have an opinion on anything. Analysis is using knowledge of an athlete or team to explain something that has just happened or foreshadow something that might happen. Being considered an expert does not give you the right to do nothing but blurt out opinions to viewers. More than that is required from an analyst of a sporting event."

★   ★   ★

Henry Cooper, who died last year, was a good heavyweight, not a great one. Over time, his courage, generosity, and inherent decency led the people of England to recognize him as a national treasure. Their good will peaked in 2001, when he was knighted by Queen Elizabeth in a ceremony at Buckingham Palace.

"I was busting with pride," Cooper said afterward. "Just wished my mum and dad and [manager] Jim Wicks had been there to share the moment. We were ordinary people. And here I was, kneeling before the Queen of England and being told, 'Arise, Sir Henry.'"

Cooper deserves a major biography. *Henry Cooper: A Hero for All Time* by Norman Giller (The Robson Press) falls short of that goal. There's some nice material in the book. But it's essentially an adoring uncritical look at a complex man who merits more.

Cooper began fighting professionally in 1954. He won the British and Commonwealth heavyweight titles in 1959 and held them for a record ten years. By the time he retired in 1970, his ledger showed 40 wins, 14 losses, and 1 draw.

Cooper was a small heavyweight (generally weighing in around 188 pounds) and the lighter man in 47 of his 55 fights. His most potent weapon was a devastating left hook, known to British boxing fans as "'Enry's Hammer."

"To be honest," Cooper acknowledged, "I couldn't hurt a fly with my right hand."

His greatest liability was a tendency to cut, particularly around the eyes. "I often wonder what I could have achieved but for the cut eye curse," he said. "But it's no use crying over spilt blood."

The high point of Cooper's ring career came on June 18, 1963, at 2 minutes, 55 seconds of round four, when 'Enery's Hammer landed flush on the jaw of Cassius Marcellus Clay Jr. It was the most famous punch in British boxing history.

Clay hit the canvas like he'd been shot. "There was pandemonium," Giller recounts. "Those of us used to being at Wembley for FA Cup finals and England football internationals were convinced we had never heard a roar like the one that greeted Clay's knockdown."

Only the bell kept Cooper from finishing his foe on the spot. Between rounds, Angelo Dundee revived his fighter with the help of illegal smelling salts. He also sought to extend the one-minute rest period by pulling at a pre-existing split along the seam of Clay's right glove.

"Now we enter the world of myth and mystery," Giller writes, "Many observers claimed that Dundee's chicanery earned Clay an extra twenty to thirty seconds of recovery time. Much as I would like to perpetuate the legend, I have been in the BBC archives department and watched the unedited version of the fight in real time. The interval between the fourth and fifth rounds actually lasted sixty-six seconds, which means that the Dundee gamesmanship gained just an extra six seconds."

Clay stopped Cooper on cuts in the next round. "At least we shut him up for a while," Henry said afterward.

There are some poignant passages in Giller's book that detail Henry's love match with his wife of forty-eight years, Albina Genepri Cooper. Albina died in 2008 from a sudden heart attack at age seventy-one.

"I am lost without her," Cooper confided. "To be honest, I am really struggling. I've got a candle in front of my favorite photograph of her and I light it every night in her memory. I take her ashes in an urn with me if I am staying somewhere overnight. I know that sounds morbid, but it just sort of keeps me in touch. I don't know how I'm going to manage without her. Life is just not the same anymore. Always thought I'd go first. I'm in shock. Just can't take it in."

Here I should add a note regarding my own personal experience with Henry Cooper. I was fortunate to spend time with him on three occasions, the last of them in December 2001. Sir Henry had been knighted by then, and we talked over tea and crumpets for three hours. As always, he was warm, open, and charming.

I remember the day well. That remembrance leads me to the thoughts of Terry Baker, who arranged many of Cooper's public speaking engagements.

"Henry really was the nicest man you could wish to meet," Baker said. "How he ever hit anybody is hard to imagine."

★　★　★

Howard Schatz is an ophthalmologist by training. In an earlier professional incarnation, he was one of the foremost retinal specialists in the world. In 1995, he began a second career in photography. He now makes his living as a commercial photographer, which pays well but isn't as artistically satisfying as he'd like it to be.

Six years ago, Schatz began a remarkable journey. *At the Fights: Inside the World of Professional Boxing*, (Sports Illustrated Books) is the end product of his work. It's a monumental book in more ways than one, printed on heavy glossy fourteen-by-eleven-inch stock with faithful photographic reproductions and splendid production values.

Before Schatz embarked on his project, he studied hundreds of sports photo books, looked at classic George Bellows paintings, and talked with a wide range of creative artists. As the years passed, he invested hundreds of thousands of dollars in addition to his time and emotional input.

"I wanted to make images that said 'boxing' but said it differently from the way anyone had said it before," Schatz recounts. "My studio is like a research lab. We work at other ways of seeing. The idea was to use a still photograph, not as a frozen moment but to show movement and, if possible, to show who the fighters are. These are violent vulnerable men with needs and ambitions. They're physical marvels. They're courageous, passionate, determined. The challenge was to convey all of that in a photograph."

Schatz was at ringside for numerous club shows and high-profile fights. But his most impressive work was undertaken in his studio. Dozens of fighters posed beneath as many as eleven lights while three assistants facilitated the photo shoots. A handful of boxing luminaries who were on Schatz's wish list eluded his grasp. He was never able to land a studio session with Floyd Mayweather Jr, Don King, or Oscar De La Hoya.

That's their loss.

Monet captured the essence of water lilies better than a photograph. The same can be said of Schatz's computer-styled images. Light and shadow are distorted to show movement. The images convey strength and power, motion and emotion.

Also, many photo books have a text that's serviceable at best. This one is worth reading. Schatz interviewed most of his photo subjects at length. Then he and Beverly Ornstein (his wife, business partner, and best friend) fashioned the text.

Among the most telling quotations in *At the Fights* are:

Steve Cunningham: "Before a fight, you're nervous; you're scared. Every emotion goes through your body, When you're in that locker room, that's the crazies, the jitters. Like you seriously do not want to go out there. You have to tell yourself you're good. You have to talk to yourself. Any fighters that tells you he's not nervous or scared before a fight; either he doesn't have it anymore or he's lying."

Ann Wolfe: "I love boxing because it's the only thing I've ever done in my whole life that I was good at."

James Kirkland: "In that ring, you get to do absolutely what you want to do. If you want to head-butt somebody, knee somebody; hell, you can actually do it. They may take a point away, but you can do what you want to do. And being able to break a man down, take control over him, make him bleed, bang his face up; it feels good."

Andre Ward: "Kobe Bryant can have a bad night and he can shrug it off. He's still Kobe Bryant. You lose one fight in boxing, and the whole world is scratching their heads, saying, 'This guy is not what we thought he was.'"

Tim Bradley: "I never feel for my opponent after a fight. He's in there trying to knock my head off. He's in there trying to kill me."

Michael Schwartz: "There is really only one person who gives a damn about these kids, and that's the doctor. Everybody else to different degrees has other motives. The doctor is there to make sure the kid lives."

John Duddy: "The dream is a lot different from the reality of it."

Jim Lampley: "We watch. But we don't really know. Only they know."

Contemplating his journey through the sweet science, Schatz says, "I look at boxing, and the whole thing thrills me."

The same can be said of *At the Fights*.

The ritual "ten count" tolled for some good people in 2012.

In Memoriam

Today (January 17, 2012) is Muhammad Ali's seventieth birthday. But a poignant note accompanies the tributes that he's receiving. Wali Muhammad died this morning at Calvary Hospital in the Bronx where he was in hospice care after a long battle with cancer.

Wali (formerly known as Walter Youngblood or "Blood") was one of the people who worked behind the scenes in Muhammad Ali's training camp. He was also in Ali's corner from the first Ali-Frazier fight on.

I met Wali in 1989, when I was researching *Muhammad Ali: His Life and Times.* We became friendly and kept in touch from that point on.

Wali lived a good life. He made a lot of people happy and was very much loved.

★   ★   ★

The world is paying homage to Angelo Dundee, who died on February 1, 2012, at age ninety. But the boxing community suffered another loss that day. Referee Wayne Kelly died after a massive heart attack at age sixty-three.

Kelly served with the United States Army in Vietnam and fought professionally in the 1970s. His career record was a modest four wins and three losses with two knockouts. The composite record of his opponents at the time he fought them was one win against eight losses and a draw.

"I'd like to think that I'm a better referee than I was a fighter," Wayne said years afterward.

He was.

Kelly began refereeing in 1988. He didn't play the political game with the world sanctioning organizations to the extent that he might have. That cost him some high-profile assignments, but he had his share of big fights.

Wayne was the third man in the ring for Arturo's Gatti's first championship victory (against Tracy Harris Patterson). Three months later, he oversaw Gatti's dramatic comeback triumph over Wilson Rodriquez on the night that the Arturo Gatti legend was born. A less-knowing referee might have stopped that fight in the early going when Arturo was in trouble.

Kelly was also the New York State Athletic Commission's go-to guy for big heavyweight bouts. Wayne presided over three Wladimir Klitschko championship contests (vs. Chris Byrd, Calvin Brock, and Sultan Ibragimov) and, most notably, the infamous confrontation between Riddick Bowe and Andrew Golota at Madison Square Garden that ended in an ugly riot on July 11, 1996.

"Golota was clearly winning the fight," Kelly later recalled. "He was out jabbing Bowe. He was outboxing Bowe. He was outpunching Bowe. And he kept throwing low blows. I don't know why. It was so unnecessary and stupid. How many warnings can I give and how many points can I deduct? Enough is enough. Finally, I had no choice but to disqualify him."

Thereafter, Wayne occasionally joked, "Great! My legacy will be that I'm the guy who started a riot at Madison Square Garden."

Wayne Kelly was a class act and one of the many people who do their part to make boxing a great sport. He knew that the fighters, not the referee, are the story. When giving instructions before a bout, he never called attention to himself by uttering a signature phrase or doing anything else to grab the spotlight. He had a smile and kind word for everyone he met and was always willing to offer advice to young referees who were learning their craft.

He was also a terrific referee; a blue-collar guy who got in the ring and did what he was supposed to do. He had great positioning and great judgment. He didn't stop fights too soon, and he didn't let them go on too long. The boxing community could always count on Wayne Kelly to do his job right.

★   ★   ★

I met Whitney Houston in 1992 at Muhammad Ali's fiftieth birthday party. Ella Fitzgerald was Queen that night. But Whitney was a beautiful princess who glowed.

Houston was a star by then with countless Grammy Awards and other honors to her credit. Her stirring rendition of "The Star-Spangled Banner" at the 1991 Super Bowl shortly after the start of the Persian Gulf War had further enlarged her following. And she was about to get bigger, having just completed filming *The Bodyguard* with Kevin Costner.

Houston was associated with Ali in the public mind by virtue of having recorded "The Greatest Love of All" (written for the soundtrack of *The Greatest,* which starred Ali, Robert Duvall, James Earl Jones, and Paul Winfield). I spoke with her briefly at Ali's birthday party. She was more interested in talking with Muhammad, which was fine with me because I was more interested in talking with Ella.

I don't know what Whitney Houston was like as a person, other than what I've experienced through the media over the years. Still, listening to the outpouring of emotion following her death on February 11, 2012—a death linked to chronic cocaine abuse—I can imagine her saying, "Learn from what I did right. But also learn from what I did wrong."

★   ★   ★

Emanuel Steward, who died on October 25, 2012, at age sixty-eight, was an important part of my professional life and also my friend.

He was one of my "go-to" guys. Whenever I was researching a major article—whether it was on fighters from the past or the contemporary boxing scene—I'd call Emanuel. We'd talk about what made this fighter great or how an upcoming bout shaped up. He was unfailingly generous with his time and knowledge. Over the years, we fell into a routine of getting together for lunch or dinner whenever I was on-site for an *HBO World Championship Boxing* or HBO-PPV fight. He wasn't a snob like some major players on the boxing scene. He treated low-level Internet writers, career club fighters, and everyone else he met with respect.

Emanuel won a national Golden Gloves title in the bantamweight division at age eighteen. After that, he worked as an electrician, an insurance salesman, and a cosmetics distributor. Along the way, he began training fighters and turned the Kronk Gym in Detroit from a neighborhood recreational center into one of the most famous gyms in the world. He was as good behind the microphone as any expert boxing commentator ever. But his greatest impact on the sweet science was as a trainer.

"There's a special bond between a fighter and his trainer," Emanuel told me years ago. "Often, they're the closest two people in camp. Look at the young men who become fighters. Many of them never had a father at home when they were growing up. Or if the father was there, he wasn't a positive influence. So when the relationship between a fighter and his trainer is right, oftentimes the trainer becomes a father figure and the fighter's best friend. The two men develop similar thought patterns and become spiritually synchronized with one another."

"Emanuel had some good teachers," fellow trainer Don Turner observes. "Men like Bill Miller and Luther Burgess. But you can have the best teachers in the world and it won't make you good if you're a poor student. Emanuel was a great student. Unlike a lot of people in boxing, he gave back to the sport. And he looked after the people who worked for him. We didn't always get along, but I always respected him."

Like many great trainers, Emanuel had a gentle exterior. But a fierce competitive fire burned within. Recently he told photographer Howard Schatz, "The worst experience, not just in boxing, in my life of pain I experienced was Thomas Hearns losing the first fight with Ray Leonard. That was really the most painful experience I've ever had. For about a week, I would sit at home and I would cry almost like a baby. I was a mess. I'm a very very hard loser. I may seem gracious as a loser, but losing is hard on me. It's harder than even on the fighters."

Hilmer Kenty was Emanuel's first champion. The first superstar that he developed from scratch was Thomas Hearns. Lennox Lewis and Wladimir Klitschko sought Emanuel's counsel after hitting bumps in the road, and he helped elevate them to new heights. Hundreds of fighters have borne his imprint over the years.

Michael Buffer summed up the feelings of these fighters and everyone else in boxing when he said of the ritual ten-count for Emanuel, "I don't know how I'm going to get through it."

Emanuel loved boxing. And boxing is better for his contribution to it.

Most likely, I'll write about Joe Frazier for the rest of my life.

Remembering Joe Frazier

I've been thinking a lot lately about Joe Frazier, who died one year ago, on November 7, 2011.

I met Joe at the Sahara Hotel in Las Vegas on December 1, 1988. I'd just signed a contract to become Muhammad Ali's official biographer. Two days of taping were underway for a documentary entitled *Champions Forever* that featured Ali, Frazier, George Foreman, Ken Norton, and Larry Holmes. I was there to conduct interviews for my book.

On the first morning, I sat at length with Foreman; the pre-lean-mean-grilling-machine model. George was twenty months into a comeback that was widely regarded as a joke. Six more years would pass before he knocked out Michael Moorer to regain the heavyweight throne.

"There was a time in my life when I was sort of unfriendly," George told me. "Zaire was part of that period. I was going to knock Ali's block off, and the thought of doing it didn't bother me at all. After the fight, for a while I was bitter. I had all sorts of excuses. The ring ropes were loose. The referee counted too fast. The cut hurt my training. I was drugged. I should have just said the best man won, but I'd never lost before so I didn't know how to lose. I fought that fight over in my head a thousand times. Then, finally, I realized I'd lost to a great champion; probably the greatest of all time. Now I'm just proud to be part of the Ali legend. If people mention my name with his from time to time, that's enough for me. That, and I hope Muhammad likes me, because I like him. I like him a lot."

Then I moved on to Ken Norton, who shared a poignant memory.

"When it counted most," Norton reminisced, "Ali was there for me. In 1986, I was in a bad car accident. I was unconscious for I don't know how long. My right side was paralyzed; my skull was fractured; I had a broken leg, a broken jaw. The doctors said I might never walk again. For a while, they thought I might not ever even be able to talk. I don't remember much about my first few months in the hospital. But one thing

I do remember is, after I was hurt, Ali was one of the first people to visit me. At that point, I wasn't sure whether I wanted to live or die. That's how bad I was hurt. Like I said, there's a lot I don't remember. But I remember looking up, and there was this crazy man standing by my bed. It was Ali, and he was doing magic tricks for me. He made a handkerchief disappear; he levitated. I said to myself, if he does one more awful trick, I'm gonna get well just so I can kill him. But Ali was there, and his being there helped me. So I don't want to be remembered as the man who broke Muhammad Ali's jaw. I just want to be remembered as a man who fought three close competitive fights with Ali and became his friend when the fighting was over."

Larry Holmes held out for cash, so our conversation was short: "I'm proud I learned my craft from Ali," Larry said. "I'm prouder of sparring with him when he was young than I am of beating him when he was old."

End of conversation.

That left Joe.

Frazier wouldn't talk with me because I was "Ali's man." But at an evening party after the second day of taping, Joe approached me. He'd been drinking. And the bile spewed out:

"I hated Ali. God might not like me talking that way, but it's in my heart. First two fights, he tried to make me a white man. Then he tried to make me a nigger. How would you like it if your kids came home from school crying because everyone was calling their daddy a gorilla? God made us all the way we are. He made us the way we talk and look. And the way I feel, I'd like to fight Ali-Clay-whatever-his-name-is again tomorrow. Twenty years, I've been fighting Ali, and I still want to take him apart piece by piece and send him back to Jesus."

Joe saw that I was writing down every word. This was a message he wanted the world to hear.

"I didn't ask no favors of him, and he didn't ask none of me. He shook me in Manila; he won. But I sent him home worse than he came. Look at him now. He's damaged goods. I know it; you know it. Everyone knows it; they just don't want to say. He was always making fun of me. I'm the dummy; I'm the one getting hit in the head. Tell me now; him or me, which one talks worse now? He can't talk no more, and he still tries to make noise. He still wants you to think he's the greatest, and he ain't. I don't care how the world looks at him. I see him different, and I know him better than anyone. Manila really don't matter no more. He's finished, and I'm still here."

Twenty-one months later, when I finished writing *Muhammad Ali: His Life and Times*, I journeyed to Ali's home in Berrian Springs, Michigan. Lonnie Ali (Muhammad's wife), Howard Bingham (Ali's longtime friend and personal photographer), and I spent a week reading every word of the manuscript aloud. By agreement, there would be no censorship. Our purpose in reading was to ensure the factually accuracy of the book.

In due course, Lonnie read Frazier's quote aloud.

There was a silent moment.

"Did you hear that, Muhammad?" Lonnie asked.

Ali nodded.

"How do you feel, knowing that hundreds of thousands of people will read that?"

"It's what he said," Muhammad answered.

Ali's thoughts ended that chapter of the book.

"I'm sorry Joe Frazier is mad at me. I'm sorry I hurt him. Joe Frazier is a good man. I couldn't have done what I did without him, and he couldn't have done what he did without me. And if God ever calls me to a holy war, I want Joe Frazier fighting beside me."

On the final day of our reading, Muhammad, Lonnie, Howard, and I signed a pair of boxing gloves to commemorate the experience. I took one of the gloves home with me. Howard took the other.

The following spring, I was in Philadelphia for a black-tie gala celebrating the twentieth anniversary of the historic first fight between Ali and Frazier. This was Joe's night. It was a fight he'd won. But his hatred for all things Ali was palpable.

Early in the evening, Howard suggested that I pose for a photo with Muhammad and Joe. I stood between them. Joe wrapped his arm around my waist in what I thought was a gesture of friendship. Then, just as Howard snapped the photo, Joe dug his fingers into the flesh beneath my ribs.

It hurt like hell.

I tried to pry his hand away.

You try prying Joe Frazier's hand away.

When Joe was satisfied that he'd inflicted sufficient pain, he smirked at me and walked off.

Muhammad Ali: His Life and Times was published in June 1991. Thereafter, Joe decided that I'd treated him fairly in the book. In the years that followed, when our paths crossed, he was warm and friendly. A ritual greeting evolved between us.

Joe would smile and say, "Hey! How's my Jewish friend?"

I'd smile and say, "Hey! How's my Baptist friend?"

Fast forward to January 7, 2005. Joe was in my home. We were eating ice cream in the kitchen.

Three boxing gloves were hanging on the wall. The first two were worn by Billy Costello in his victorious championship fight against Saoul Mamby. That fight has special meaning to me. It's the subject of the climactic chapter in *The Black Lights*, my first book about boxing.

The other glove bore the legend:

> Muhammad Ali
> Lonnie Ali
> Howard L. Bingham
> Thomas Hauser
> 9/10—9/17/90

Joe asked about the gloves. I explained their provenance. Then he said something that surprised me.

"Do you remember that time I gave you the claw?"

"I remember," I said grimly.

"I'm sorry, man. I apologize."

That was Joe Frazier. He remembered every hurt that anyone ever inflicted upon him. With regard to Ali, he carried those hurts like broken glass in his stomach for his entire life.

But Joe also remembered the hurts he'd inflicted on other people. And if he felt he'd done wrong, given time he would try to right the situation.

There's now a fourth glove hanging on the wall of my kitchen. It bears the inscription:

> Tom, to my man
> Right on
> Joe Frazier